MW01089981

INTIMACY IN EMPTINESS

"*Intimacy in Emptiness* is a jewel adding significantly to the treasury of contemplative wisdom. Cultivating the practice of witnessing the human essence reveals the depth and mystery of embodiment."

JEFF GENUNG, COFOUNDER OF CONTEMPLATIVE LIFE
AND MANAGING DIRECTOR OF PROSOCIAL WORLD

"This book is a celebration of and a call for both humanity and divinity, crystallized through the deep healing power of the Discipline of Authentic Movement. In this turbulent and polarized world, Janet Adler's focus on compassion, clear seeing, and embodied consciousness is a necessary and precious gift to our global community."

TONY YU ZHOU, FOUNDER
AND CEO OF INSPIREES INSTITUTE, CHINA

"A must-read for contemplatives, regarding the enfleshed communion of the physical and the metaphysical. Janet Adler's half-century of work and writing calls us to develop our inner witness toward presence, toward coming to know our humanity as consciously embodied, deeply interconnected, and an ever-evolving experience. I will be thinking, being, moving with and through these writings for a long time to come."

DAVID ROBINSON-MORRIS, EXECUTIVE DIRECTOR OF
THE CENTER FOR CONTEMPLATIVE MIND IN SOCIETY

"An important tribute to an invaluable life's work. Janet Adler's Discipline of Authentic Movement unites body and psyche, individual and collective, psychotherapy and spirituality in a profound experiential exploration of the relationship of mover and witness. A unique portrayal of the potential of embodied consciousness."

GAY WATSON, AUTHOR OF *A PHILOSOPHY OF EMPTINESS*

"Janet Adler's life and work are a powerful, creative, and generous manifestation of a process of embodied and relational awakening, so necessary for the healing and transformation of humanity in these critical times."

DONALD ROTHBERG, AUTHOR OF *THE ENGAGED SPIRITUAL LIFE*

"Authenticity is a practice. Although it can arise spontaneously, it also requires discipline. Each of these chapters with their introductions and images are companions, perseverant guides helping us endure with hope and celebrate with imagination."

ANDREA OLSEN, AUTHOR OF *THE PLACE OF DANCE*

July

INTIMACY IN EMPTINESS

AN EVOLUTION OF EMBODIED CONSCIOUSNESS

Collected Writings of

JANET ADLER

Edited by BONNIE MORRISSEY & PAULA SAGER

Inner Traditions
Rochester, Vermont

Inner Traditions
One Park Street
Rochester, Vermont 05767
www.InnerTraditions.com

Text stock is SFI certified

Cataloging-in-Publication Data for this title is available from the Library of Congress

ISBN 978-1-64411-360-8 (print)
ISBN 978-1-64411-361-5 (ebook)

Printed and bound in the United States by Lake Book Manufacturing, Inc.
The text stock is SFI certified. The Sustainable Forestry Initiative® program
promotes sustainable forest management.

10 9 8 7 6 5 4 3 2 1

Text design and layout by Virginia Scott Bowman
This book was typeset in Garamond Premier Pro with Century Expanded,
Futura Std, Gill Sans MT Pro, Hypatia Sans Pro, ITC Legacy Sans, and
Optima LT Std used as display typefaces
Drawings by Rosalyn Driscoll

To send correspondence to the author of this book, mail a first-class letter to the
author c/o Inner Traditions • Bear & Company, One Park Street, Rochester, VT
05767, and we will forward the communication.

*To the humanity and
the divinity within every person*

CONTENTS

*indicates previously unpublished writing

CHAPTER SEVEN

WITNESS CONSCIOUSNESS INTO THE WORLD   299

ADDENDUM

EARLY ESSAYS AND RESOURCES   323

JANET ADLER AND THE DISCIPLINE
OF AUTHENTIC MOVEMENT:
ADDITIONAL RESOURCES   343

---

*indicates previously unpublished writing

Dizang asked Fayan "Where are you going?"
Fayan said, "Around on pilgrimage."
Dizang said, "What is the purpose of pilgrimage?"
Fayan said, "I don't know."
Dizang said, "Not knowing is most intimate."

BOOK OF SERENITY,
CASE 20, *DIZANG*

PREFACE

Curving along the arc of the spiral, somehow all the way around now into the wholeness of a mandala, I know a way of work emerging through time, shaped by a longing for clear seeing. This way for me—the Discipline of Authentic Movement—is a path not chosen but gratefully followed, cultivated in reverence.

In the discipline, a voyage inward always begins inside relationship, always begins with moving in the presence of an outer witness. This sacred gift invites the utterly mysterious and lifesaving experience of growing a loving enough inner witness. An inner witness maturing becomes one way of understanding a core vibration of the evolution of embodied consciousness.

Compassionate witnessing of oneself and another—our luminosity, our wounds—is a loving act, healing, often redemptive. Sustained focus on a body moving, a body not moving, that very place within which we humans dwell, grounds a process of self-emptying as density dissolves. Refined through committed practice, such concentration becomes devotion. As both the rigor and the elegance of ritual practice deepen, the intimate and direct experience of clear seeing can manifest as an indwelling god, still silent awareness, a knowing of unitive consciousness.

This book of collected essays, reflections of my experience in studio practice for the past fifty years, marks thresholds appearing in response to emerging questions. It is being offered because of Bonnie Morrissey and Paula Sager. With ineffable gratitude to each of them, I recognize their gift of presence, their trust in not knowing, and their remarkable capacity for joy. Each woman, a uniquely gifted elder of this way of work, brings great sensitivity and insight in connecting the essays, generously lifting up shapes made of moments, making more visible the web, its strength and its delicacy, now resonating within this contemporary mystical practice.

The Discipline of Authentic Movement continues to teach me that individual consciousness is not enough. But such consciousness is a requisite for individuals who are ready to participate in embodied collective consciousness. Each person, one by one, risking in the presence of an inner and outer witness, turns when they are ready toward what is true, making whole our collective journey within the mystery of an inherent order.

JANET ADLER,
WINTER 2022

But compassion!

—that transparent bloom
poised, apparent
in the white
fire
of the soul—

How will it find us?

without the devastation
of suffering
boldly carving
the pathway

JANET ADLER,
SUFFERING: A PERSONAL INQUIRY

INTRODUCTION
by Bonnie Morrissey

In 1980, while Janet Adler was founding her teaching practice in Northampton, Massachusetts, prior to the impending throes of her experience of initiation, I was in graduate school nearby at Antioch University in New Hampshire studying dance/movement therapy. Janet and her colleague Joan Chodorow* came to Antioch to offer a daylong retreat in a developing approach to embodiment called *authentic movement*.[1] We met for the first time, and I was literally at Janet's feet, on the welcoming warmth of the studio floor with my eyes closed, while she and Joan sat with eyes open, holding the space with a quality I experienced as meditative care for our group moving. My first taste of this way of work was vivid, startling, and ultimately life changing. Then and there I recognized the promise of a way of coming to know myself, so directly centered in the authority of what the body holds and knows, so clearly honoring of kinesthetic, emotional, and intuitive phenomena. Right away I felt met: what I could see and know with my eyes closed was regarded with as much respect and dignity as what I could see and know with my eyes open. I felt acutely *seen,* both inwardly by an awakening sense of self, and outwardly by these two fascinating teachers.

Janet was at that moment (1980) on the cusp of developing a new

---

*Joan Chodorow, Ph.D., is a Jungian analyst. Both Joan and Janet studied, separately, with Mary Whitehouse. Joan's experience with Mary integrated with her studies in Jungian psychology, leading to her research and writings on dance/movement therapy as a form of active imagination. Her publications include *Dance Therapy and Depth Psychology: The Moving Imagination* (author), and *Jung on Active Imagination* (editor).

1

practice, based on her own desire to study "not only the experience of the mover but of the witness and of the developing relationship between the mover and the witness" (see "Who Is the Witness?," page 86). She named this relational inquiry *Authentic Movement,* capitalizing the already existent phrase describing a *process*—an approach to movement she learned from Mary Whitehouse*—in order to honor the formalizing of a dynamic *practice.* Over the next four decades, through Janet's inquiry—her teaching and study—this new practice continued to develop, evolving into what, in the 1990s, she began to call the *discipline of Authentic Movement* (deepening practice including transpersonal experience), and eventually (in the 2000s) the *Discipline of Authentic Movement,* or simply *the discipline,* a full-fledged contemporary mystical practice.

This evolving practice became a home for my personal and professional development. Over the course of the next four decades I studied with Janet alongside her other students, learning to be present with and articulate all that arises through the body. As we practiced the art of listening internally, we received the gifts of a silence that is the antithesis of being silenced and a stillness that is the antithesis of being bound: a silence and a stillness that equate with freedom. Many of us acquired a profound trust in this practice that asserts an honoring of that which is experienced as true within each individual body, every step of the way. Our shared trust in the discipline has become a light-filled prism; it accurately reflects the integrity with which Janet taught and the quality of her presence.

The Discipline of Authentic Movement is Janet's unique contribution to the field of consciousness studies. Her work helps to return the fullness of form that is *body* to its rightful place within both secular and sacred realms of human inquiry. Her offerings allow us to reunite body and

---

*Mary Starks Whitehouse, (1911–1979), a student of Martha Graham and Mary Wigman, was a professional dancer and then a teacher of dance with a developing interest in the inner life, and subsequently in Jungian thought. She developed and taught an approach she called "Movement in depth."

soul, psyche and soma, without merging them. Her inquiry serves to bring a new dimension of human potential into view, which is a result of a radically deep and intricate investigation of spirit as consciousness manifesting through flesh.

Janet's study of embodied consciousness is radical primarily because it dives beneath the narrative content of human experience into the pre-symbolic world of *direct experience*. The immediate reception through the body of the touch of energetic phenomena, such as vibration and light, may be known unmediated as direct experience, before meaning is made and before language is formed. Perhaps Janet would not have charted this territory if not for her unanticipated experience of initiation, wherein these experiences were received with such intensity directly in and through her body. Her inquiry might not have occurred without her prior immersion in the study of movement, preparing her to track her embodied experience of initiation with such rigor. And her life's inquiry might not have offered a mystical practice that others can enter had it not been for the qualities of precision, impeccability, and devotion that she brought to her teaching and her creative work, leading to the discovery of a developmental arc of embodied consciousness, revealing itself within the crucible of intimate relationship.

Janet's investigation brings a new dimension of human potential into view because it concerns not just the development of the individual but also the development of embodied consciousness within groups. Her passionate insistence on the sovereignty of the individual voice—and her equally passionate insistence that the individual voice alone does not suffice—led to innovative explorations of emergent qualities that may manifest when enough individual consciousness is brought to and integrated within collective bodies. The importance of this study to our times is enormous, as our continued survival as a *humane* species, interconnected with all other species, is dependent upon the evolution of conscious collaboration.

One of the great puzzles of human consciousness is the discernment of one's place in community. Each student who chooses to commit to the Discipline of Authentic Movement is invited, through their ongoing awareness practice, toward full recognition of their own inherent worth, potential, and relationship to the whole. I remember the exact day, within a large group of students in Western Massachusetts, when I first realized viscerally, all in one moment, the full impact of my individual presence within the group. *Your voice, your presence is necessary,* Janet might say. Flabbergasted in such moments of embodied realization, through this practice we may comprehend something essential about the interdependence of individual gestures and voices within the wholeness of the larger body of the group.

The recognition of the true but not inflated significance of the individual in relation to the whole has yet to become generally conscious in human evolution, though perhaps we are on the verge of greater understanding. One by one, as students mature toward the unique expression of their own embodiment, their voices weave toward conscious participation, cooperation, and cohesion. I sometimes experience this phenomenon as a *murmuration,* the intricately coordinated pattern of a flock of birds, or a school of fish, a herd of elk, as they move in flawless synchrony, with a seemingly united mind. Conscious-enough collective bodies may cohere and evolve, as we realize on a cellular level that the voice of the individual, though it may at times seem inaudible, or bring discomfort, must be welcomed and honored within and by the whole. Room must be made, gestures received, a diversity of voices heard, or any group becomes vulnerable to tyranny. We are utterly dependent on one another to know our way forward.

As a clinical psychologist, I have had the privilege of accompanying hundreds of individuals as they bring their questions and their suffering to the open space of intimacy between us. My intention always is the practice of the *I,* the witness who is consciously holding the role of therapist, so that my client may surrender to the experience of *thou,* to all that can transpire through concentrated and compassionate attention on their experience.[2] A sacred and invisible relational vessel shines bright and central between us. Within this vessel, the intuitive guidance of the client may be found if it is lost and cultivated if it requires nourishment. Whether within the therapist-client relationship or within the teacher-student relationship when I teach students of the discipline, the emanation of this inner voice is the thread we follow.

As a writer of poems, I treasure the possibility of an evolution of language that can arise directly from embodied experience. Poetry that includes mystical experience is an attempt at expression of that which is ineffable. Within the Discipline of Authentic Movement, as students of a contemporary mystical practice, we are poets of the invisible searching for words on the doorstep of the unknown. In an eternally imperfect effort to articulate experience that is made up of light, sound—vibrations experienced directly in and through the body—we find ourselves stringing words together, giving voice to that which is ultimately nameless. Sometimes an invitation to awareness is offered simply through eye contact, through silence. The silence between our words, like the space between our cells, may create a charged space of potency, a generative space that encourages the appearance of something new. Can our words eventually arise more directly from the well of silence from which all language is born? Can our words and our consciously contained silence be of service to others and to the world? A practice of consciously embodied speech is one more significant contribution of the Discipline of Authentic Movement, a practice we may strive to carry from the protected space of our studios to the commonwealth of the world.

Cultural understandings of gender are rapidly evolving. Given the levels of suppression and oppression that have for so long caused suffering for so many, this burst of consciousness is needed in our world. In our introductions to each chapter, as editors, Paula Sager and I use the ungendered pronouns *they/their,* as this best reflects our wish to be inclusive. Written over the course of fifty years, Janet's choice of pronouns reflects her own wish to be inclusive. She attempts this by frequently using the pronouns *she/her* for actual individuals there in the studios with her, who were primarily—though not exclusively—women. After centuries of patriarchy, we may marvel at the cracks where light finally shines through, where women may be honored for leading all of us, whatever our gender identity, into creative ways of seeing and knowing.

Throughout her writings, Janet changes the names of her students in order to respect their confidentiality. What Paula and I find to be most inspiring in her writings, as in her teaching, is her steadfast commitment to honoring the unique and inner truth of each individual who finds their way to her, each one welcomed and ultimately recognized as "the you in me."

Life is a slipstream of uncertainty. This book was compiled during a global pandemic, during which it has become abundantly evident how reliant we are on one another for continued sustenance. Our humanity is an intimate web of shared destiny, whether through the contagion of a virus or the communion of kindness, compassion, and collaboration. Perhaps our individual and collective crises, devastating as they are, may also help awaken us to our responsibility to care for each other and this planet, our home, without delay. Walking on many paths of change, we can create antidotes to despair that help soothe and alleviate suffering. The Discipline of Authentic Movement is one such transformative path, grounded and reliable, welcoming those of any ability—or difference—who are drawn to the alchemy of healing and wholeness through a practice of conscious embodiment.

May each reader receive this book as a gift. For those who worked with Janet during the early phases of her teaching practice, may you find joy in comprehending the further evolution of the Discipline of Authentic Movement, including the appearance of the *mandorla* with its developmental roles etched across the arc.* For those entering the practice more recently, may you be nourished by an enhanced understanding of the depth of lineage that has come before and by the scope of evolution of the form. And for those elders who have been near the practice from

---

*See "The Mandorla and the Discipline of Authentic Movement" in chapter 5.

early on and have stayed near throughout the evolution of Janet's work, may you receive this book as an expression of a wholeness you recognize.

For all who have participated or are participating in Authentic Movement in any way, and for all who come to this book from other disciplines, may you experience through Janet's collected writings the mystery and wonder of a new form, the Discipline of Authentic Movement, continuing to manifest as an evolution of embodied consciousness.

Paula Sager, our carrying together of this manuscript across the threshold into the light of day feels ceremonial. From the first time we moved together on the honeyed wooden floor at Stump Sprouts studio*—witnessing each other, sharing words and worlds—enormous support has been given and received. My gratitude is immense.

Janet Adler, my words of gratitude to you over the years—for who you are and for what you have offered, to me individually and to so many others and to the world—have brought me full circle to a place of speechlessness. In this place I am silent and still, resonating with a quality we call love.

---

*Stump Sprouts, a retreat center in Hawley, MA, was the East Coast home for Janet's teaching from 1991–1996.

INTRODUCTION
by Paula Sager

A pilgrimage of not knowing, in Janet Adler's words, is one way of describing her five decades of studying embodied consciousness, evolving as the practice of the Discipline of Authentic Movement. Bonnie Morrissey and I met in this work in the early 1990s and found ourselves frequently traveling together to study with Janet, to teach with her, and now to collaborate with her in creating this book. We shared the vision and the task of compiling Janet's essays from a variety of publications and previously unpublished writing into one volume. To support the legacy of her work and its potential resonance for future generations, we chose to focus on how the Discipline of Authentic Movement has evolved through time. How is this practice unique? Why is it a discipline? What does Janet mean when she calls it a contemporary mystical practice?

Many of Janet's essays were initially presented as keynote talks, each shaped for the occasion as she synthesized the most pressing questions in her current phase of studio work with students. For the most part, the writings in this book appear in chronological sequence, in much the same way Janet experienced what she writes about. She frequently describes feeling compelled to follow what was emerging in her teaching practice, not knowing exactly where she was being led.

Our introductions to each chapter are intended to help guide the way for readers, and serve as a form of connective tissue weaving through the book. Often we zoom in close to details of how Janet is tracking what is developing, other times we pull back for an overview, and occasionally we look toward the future, anticipating how some aspect of the practice will clarify or develop later. Simultaneously, we are tracking the meaning of words over time, through changes and refinements that arise organically within the studio practice. Words, images, and phenomena central to Janet's inquiry that appear in her early writings reappear in subsequent essays in more developed form. When core terms, essential words that live at the heart of the discipline, appear in our introductions for the first time, we italicize them. A vocabulary comes to life as Janet's writing voice echoes the discipline's evolution. Language itself transforms as the process of speaking and listening becomes more rooted in embodied experience and words are freed from abstraction.

In September of 2019, Bonnie and I joined Janet in Northampton, Massachusetts, as she arrived from British Columbia, returning to where her teaching practice began. The occasion was the Somatics Festival,* a celebration honoring Janet along with Bonnie Bainbridge Cohen,† founder of Body-Mind Centering, and Nancy Stark Smith,‡ a foremost teacher of Contact Improvisation. In the 1970s, each of these three women chose to settle in the Pioneer Valley of Western Massachusetts. Affordable neighborhoods and abundant, empty loft spaces in downtown Northampton attracted artists, writers, musicians, and a profusion of dancers who were exploring the intersection of performance, creative process, and somatic practices. From within this milieu, Janet's devotion to her own emerging inquiry was both singular and collaborative, informed by her work with students.

---

*The Somatics Festival 2019 was a celebration of the work of Janet Adler, Bonnie Bainbridge Cohen, and Nancy Stark Smith and the 45-year heritage of Contact Quarterly. It was organized by festival curator Andrea Olsen.
†Bonnie Bainbridge Cohen is a movement artist, researcher, educator, therapist, and developer of Body-Mind Centering™. Bonnie founded the School for Body-Mind Centering in 1973. Visit the school's website for more information.
‡Nancy Stark Smith (1952–2020) was a dancer and teacher of Contact Improvisation and the Underscore. More about her can be found on her website of the same name. With Lisa Nelson, Nancy coedited and produced *Contact Quarterly: A Vehicle for Moving Ideas,* a journal of dance and improvisation.

After days of festival performances, interviews, film showings, and panel discussions, Janet hosted a gathering in the Crew House, a beloved dance studio perched over a pond on the Smith College campus. Even with fifty people, the spacious setting felt intimate as Janet prepared to speak of how the work has evolved since her early years of teaching. Autumnal light cast a soft glow through the westward-facing windows of the converted boathouse, as Janet's students, some of whom she hadn't seen for decades, found their seats in a large circle. Inviting each of us to locate ourselves in time, she asks: "When did we first meet in this work?"

A woman begins,
I met you and we began working together in 1971, right here in the Crew House.
A man says,
I studied with you at Hampshire College in the early 1970s. We moved, you witnessed, in the library . . .
Another woman said,
I worked with you in 1982, a few blocks away on Henshaw Avenue.

Other voices follow, each one naming when and where they began working with Janet—through the '70s, the '80s, the '90s, and into the 2000s, until another woman speaks, saying:
I am meeting you today for the first time. I am meeting you now.
In this simple way, Janet welcomes the voice of every person in the room as they participate in recreating the full time-span of her teaching life. This gesture of inviting each one to find their place in the whole perfectly embodies Janet's conviction that each individual's presence matters in the shaping of a group form, which Janet refers to as a *collective body.*

Throughout Janet's writing, the word *discipline* is a recurring presence, a needle leading the thread. It first appears in a 1968 paper, "Study of an Autistic Child," which summarizes her research at the University of Pittsburgh focused on dance/movement therapy for children with severe autism (this paper is included in the Addendum). Janet intuitively understood that for such children, "the body, the common denominator, is the basis for shared communication."[1] Her commitment to meet a child in their seemingly impenetrable world is documented and stunningly evident in *Looking for Me,* an award-winning 1968 film directed by Janet, and the first film made about dance/movement therapy.*

Drawn to what was unseen and known only as an absence—the child's capacity to be in relationship—Janet carries a question throughout "Study of an Autistic Child," potent from the beginning: "How to know another and how to let another know you." Recognizing the subjectivity of her question and the intuitive nature of her engagement with the children, she alludes to the possibility of a "'laboratory' discipline" involving "a new kind of work." Her question—how to know and be known—reveals the epistemological roots of what Janet is seeking: the rigor of a discipline grounded in embodiment and relationship.

Over an intensive period of nine months from 1968 to 1969, Janet met and studied with two gifted teachers, John Weir[†] and Mary Whitehouse. It was from John Weir that Janet first heard the word *witness*. In the summer of 1968, Janet attended a Personal Growth Lab,

---

Looking for Me, which documents Janet's early work and research, was funded by the Falk Foundation and received awards from CINE Golden Eagle Award, Landers Associates Award of Merit, and Rio De Janeiro Film Festival/First Prize and Fritz Feigl Trophy. It also received honoree awards from American Psychological Association, American Psychiatric Association, Council for Exceptional Children, American Speech-Language-Hearing Association, and National Coalition of Arts Therapy Associations.

†John Weir (1913–2006) was a professor of psychology at Caltech, a faculty member at National Training Laboratory Institute, a clinician, and a leader in the Human Potential Movement. In 1964, John and Joyce Weir led the first Personal Growth Lab in Bethel, ME, incorporating non-verbal techniques in the lab process. In 2006 his work was acknowledged in *The Journal of Applied Behavioral Science:* "No human development theorist-practitioner from the 1960s to the present has created as radical and powerful an instrument of personal authenticity, accountability, and self-empowerment . . . no theorist-practitioner has placed personal responsibility for one's own development so firmly at the core of their personal growth work." (Philip J. Mix, "A Monumental Legacy: The Unique and Unheralded Contributions of John and Joyce Weir to the Human Development Field," *Journal of Applied Behavioral Science* 42, no. 3 (September 2006): 276–99.

facilitated by John, and in his presence experienced feeling deeply *seen* by another person while she was moving. His teaching of "percept language," an approach to verbal processing within a group context, was centered in the practice of autonomy, self-ownership, and conscious speech.[2] "My own development of this way of speaking and listening," writes Janet, "became the practiced response to all moving and witnessing within my teaching of the discipline for the following fifty years."[3] From John, Janet received an experience of what she would later understand as *witness consciousness*.

In the two previous summers of the "lab," Mary Whitehouse was a guest teacher introducing participants to a process-oriented approach to movement that Mary referred to as "Movement in depth."[4] In the year that Janet participated, one of Mary's senior students, Josie Taylor, took Mary's place in leading the movement sessions. Janet describes her experience in Bethel, Maine, as a "profound unraveling." Decades later, she can still recall seeing "the sheen on the pale yellow kitchen cabinet" as John hands her the telephone at the end of the retreat, and she speaks for the first time with Mary.[5]

Compelled to follow her felt connection with Mary, Janet soon relocated to California. During the next five months, in Mary's presence, Janet immersed in a process of yielding to a depth of inner experience through the body. This receptive way of opening to spontaneously emerging movement invited a more conscious relationship to her body. From Mary, Janet received what she would later call *mover consciousness*.

These two important teachers, Mary and John, prepared the fertile ground for Janet's gradual integration of their distinctive offerings, which led to a far-reaching exploration of two essential aspects of human nature. The first is what arises as bodily experience, and the second is the awareness of that experience, the perception of what is occurring. Often these two—experience and perception—are merged, blended in a manner of which we tend to be unaware. With elegant simplicity, Janet sees that within an active dynamic of relationship the two can be teased apart, one person embodying the role of mover and another person embodying the role of witness.

In 1979, during her years in New England, Janet began a collaboration with a trusted friend, an artist, who had been looking for a model willing to move while she drew. The two women met regularly in the Crew House, one following her own impulse to move or to be still, the other sitting on the periphery of the space with sketchbook and pencil in hand, a silent witness. The drawings are an invaluable record of that time which was, unbeknownst to either of the two women, a preamble to what ignites within Janet's body as initiatory experience in 1981. With tremendous gratitude to Rosalyn Driscoll* for sharing her work, we include a selection of these drawings between each chapter of this book.

Gazing at one of these drawings, I see a mover sitting, her back to me. Her head drops forward, her upper back curves, her face is hidden. Her knees open to either side. I feel myself opening to something I cannot see. This place of a mover within her embodied experience is so familiar to me. Sensing the support of the ground beneath me, I notice a relinquishing of effort. If I were to become a mover, I would close my eyes; vision veiled brings other modes of awareness to the fore. I recognize instead that I become a witness, the felt sense of my body awake in my seeing.

In the drawing, I see a form shaped by the dark draping of the mover's hair, the firm line of hips meeting floor below, and the shaded weight of arms defining either side of torso. Spare pencil markings gently contain and reveal an expanse of light—the mover's back—an experience in me both empty and full. Warmth stirs at the base of my spine, the back of my ribcage fills with breath. Just where the mover's lower back begins to curve forward, I see a faint wavy line rising upward. Something is beginning.

The seed from which a new living form emerges may be visible, but we cannot know, by eye alone, the inner germ awakening. Out of seeming nothingness, out of emptiness, something invisible stirs. An impulse. By the time we notice, something unseen is already happening. This

*Rosalyn Driscoll is a visual artist whose sculptures, installations, collages, photographs, and drawings explore the senses, perceptions, and body. More on her work can be found on her website: www.rosalyndriscoll.com.

book chronicles just such a process unfolding as a contemporary mystical practice.

In reviewing the full sweep of Janet's writing and her development as a teacher, Bonnie and I realized that her initiation belongs front and center. The phenomenon of energy directly known in the body, as Janet experienced it, is acknowledged by many cultures with names such as *ch'i* or *qi, kundalini, n/um, quaumaneq,* but at that time, living in New England in 1981, Janet had little context for what she was undergoing.[6] Navigating profoundly unknown territory, the presence of her own inner witness served to ground and sustain her. Over time, as she withstood and integrated the fierce and concentrated infusion of energy, the discipline of her inquiry was indelibly shaped, and became a vehicle for transformative and healing energies.

From this vantage of seeing all that *led up to* the initiation and everything that developed *because of* the initiation, we decided to place two of Janet's early writings, "Study of an Autistic Child" and "Integrity of Body and Psyche," in an addendum. Both papers, written from her perspective as a practicing dance/movement therapist, express many of her core themes and values. "Integrity of Body and Psyche" also reveals Janet's skill in tracking layers of emergent process as she encourages a client to stay with her movement experience a little longer each time, not always knowing why it arises, what it means, or how to come into relationship with accompanying emotional content.

The potential of a new discipline lives within the seedpod of Janet's early work. Over many years, she witnesses and articulates the unfurling of this nascent form. In retrospect, we can trace Janet's path of inquiry beginning with her love of the intimacy of one mover and one witness meeting in the dyadic form, continuing with her need to study and understand the larger collective body, and then returning to the intimacy of small groups, where individuals can deepen their practice. In time, the separate roles of mover and witness integrate to become known within each individual, more often, as an embodied and undivided experience of presence.

In working with Janet's writings, we began to see their progression as curvilinear, offering a more holistic, circular form in which fruition is present from the beginning. It is therefore possible to enter at any point; any one of Janet's writings can be a doorway into learning about embodied consciousness. For this book, we have chosen to begin with "Presence: From Autism to the Discipline of Authentic Movement," an offering from 2003, midway on Janet's journey. In this essay, Janet directly draws the correspondences between her profound discoveries in relation to the young children, and the mystical practice that clarified and grew from these early encounters. From here we follow, chapter by chapter, the thread of the discipline developing through individual and collective processes of evolving consciousness.

A million gestures, maybe more, if they could be counted, have brought this book into existence. To trace the arc of embodied consciousness evolving over fifty years is to acknowledge these gestures and each person who brought them forth. As one who came to this work as a dancer, I celebrate each bending knee, tilting head, turning wrist, each hand forming a fist, each hand gently opening, each gesture not counted but seen. And for every impulse freely followed into movement, I celebrate each choice made to *not* follow an impulse. Freedom of choice and fidelity to detail are hallmarks of this way of work.

Janet calls the developing inner witness, whether within a mover or a witness, "the heart, the innermost gem of this discipline" (see "The Mandorla," page 213), an inner presence becoming known as guide and companion. Presence arriving, presence deepening, is impossible to *make* happen, impossible to analyze. Presence is an experience to be awake in, an offering that is alive, benevolent, healing, and nourishing.

In welcoming readers to Janet's writing and to the Discipline of Authentic Movement, I feel myself at the edge of the empty circle, much as I do when joined by others. Each of us, arriving with our own personal history, remembered and unremembered, known and unknown, belongs here. In the circle, turning toward emptiness, we are invited to step into the intimate and infinite mystery of who we, each and together, are becoming.

CHAPTER ONE

PRESENCE

Introduction

By Bonnie Morrissey & Paula Sager

At this time in the Western world, in response to our deepening need for authentic spiritual experience, all we can do is to return to our physical selves.

JANET ADLER, "BODY AND SOUL"

This book is about the mysterious journey of that which is invisible becoming conscious through a process of embodiment. The journey within the Discipline of Authentic Movement is remarkably subtle, nuanced in immeasurable moments of detail that deserve compassionate witnessing. Something unseen becomes apparent, something unknowable shapes a way of being. At the heart of the discipline, Janet Adler's lifework, is the development of the *inner witness,* individual consciousness evolving within the fertile sanctuary of compassionate relationship.

In "Presence: From Autism to the Discipline of Authentic Movement,"* Janet elucidates a central task of the inner witness: *tracking* embodied experience, a focus since her early work with children diagnosed with autism in the late 1960s. Her initial development of this

---

*"From Autism to the Discipline of Authentic Movement" was first presented when Janet was the keynote presenter at the American Dance Therapy Association's 37th Annual Conference in Burlington, VT, in 2002 and was later published in *American Journal of Dance Therapy* 25 (2003): 5–16; *A Moving Journal* 10, no. 1 (2003): 10–15; *Contact Quarterly* 31, no. 2 (Summer/Fall 2006): 11–17; and *Authentic Movement: Moving the Body, Moving the Self, Being Moved—A Collection of Essays Vol. 2* edited by Patrizia Pallaro (Philadelphia: Jessica Kingsley Publishers, 2007), 24–31.

capacity occurs as she moves with the children, empathically reflecting their idiosyncratic body language back to them. A mutual dialogue through movement becomes more synchronous as trust develops. In "moments of grace," Janet witnesses sparks of *presence,* flickers of an awakened recognition of self and other within the child. This early seed-form of the discipline is already germinating through Janet's experience of an inner witness developing through relational awareness.

Janet's work with two of the young children was filmed as part of her master's research (1968). Using the Natural History approach* to the microanalysis of movement on film, she studied her interactions with each child frame by frame. In describing this process, Janet has said, "I continue to center all of my inquiry in what I learned from the Natural History approach. You wait for what is truly happening to arise. You project nothing on to it, not even questions."[1] The laboratory practice of tracking physical and relational details of bodies in motion revealed to Janet the value of emptying oneself of projections in service of *clear seeing,* as unclouded as possible by one's own interpretations, desires, and biases.

In "Presence," the discoveries and substance of Janet's early inquiry with children expand into the gradual unfolding of an embodied awareness practice, through the study of an inner witness within each individual evolving toward the fullness of presence. While locating the discipline within a "web of lineage" in all three root systems of dance, healing, and mysticism, Janet expresses her enduring gratitude for the foundational work of early twentieth-century dancers. In their words of embodiment, she discovers an intersection with the language of mystics. Like these dance innovators before her, Janet is a pioneer, forging her own way of learning through a process of inquiry, teaching, and inviting others to join her in a collaborative space of practice where she and they bring their most vital questions.

This essay draws upon insights garnered in the writing of her sec-

---

*The Natural History approach to phenomenological research was introduced to Janet in 1967 by Dr. William Condon and Dr. William Ogston at the Psychiatric Institute and Clinic at the University of Pittsburgh Medical School.

ond book, *Offering from the Conscious Body: The Discipline of Authentic Movement* (2002). In this previous book, Janet's process of tracking embodied experience extends also to tracking the developing form of the discipline itself. An arc of developmental progression becomes evident within the work: from mover consciousness to witness consciousness, from individual to collective consciousness, and from duality to directly experienced states of unitive consciousness.

In her earlier work with clients in the 1970s, Janet becomes increasingly interested in the relationship of the separate yet intertwined roles of the one who moves with eyes closed and the one who sits to the side and attends with open eyes. Her essays articulating this investigation, and the development of the *inner witness* within each role, begin in chapter 3 with "Who Is the Witness?" During this period, Janet creates her second film, *Still Looking* (1988), which vividly brings the warmth and intimacy of the practice of moving and witnessing to life within an aesthetically supportive environment.* In "Presence," we see glimmers of the conscious reintegration of these two roles, mover and witness, beginning to evolve toward what she eventually refers to as *ceremony*. Particularly in the work with her Mystical Dance retreat groups in the late 1990s, the boundary between mover and witness that was consciously cultivated in order to distinguish, clarify, and learn from these two roles begins to loosen.

A Note on Capitalization and Use of Terms

This essay was written in 2003, before Janet began capitalizing the *d* in "Discipline of Authentic Movement." In this book, we choose to stay faithful to the sequential development of the naming of the discipline, which echoes its fifty-year evolutionary arc. Janet initially capitalized the phrase "Authentic Movement" to name and honor a *practice* originating from an *approach to movement* ("Movement in depth") that she learned from Mary Whitehouse, who described this way of moving as

---

Still Looking received the International Film and TV Festival of New York Finalist Award and the Dance on Camera Festival Honorable Mention.

genuine or "authentic."[2] As this dyadic, relational practice deepens to become more purposefully inclusive of transpersonal phenomena, Janet adds the term *discipline* ("discipline of Authentic Movement"), honoring the ritual elements that develop to support the presence of a wider range of experience. As these elements of ritual practice refine toward an embrace of the full arc of embodied consciousness, in 2013 Janet begins capitalizing the *D* ("Discipline of Authentic Movement"), honoring what she recognizes as wholeness within the evolution of this contemporary mystical practice.

Regarding our use of the phrases "embodied awareness" and "embodied consciousness," we attempt throughout this book to stay close to Janet's use of the terms. The words "awareness" and "consciousness" are used in various ways by various writers and thinkers. Janet typically refers to awareness as an infinite energetic field, the ground from which consciousness can emerge.* She notes that "awareness is always here, though not always accessible."[3] As an embodied awareness practice, the discipline is a way of work that accesses this infinite field of awareness directly through the body, thus offering the development of embodied consciousness.

Janet uses the term "emptiness" to refer to a direct or non-dual experience of the larger field of awareness, "transcending and embracing both emptiness and fullness."[4] Janet also refers to "stepping into the emptiness" as an embodied act of entering this infinite field of potentiality, a mystery, a field encompassing that which is not yet known.

---

*In "From Seeing to Knowing," in chapter five, Janet follows Arthur Deikman's understanding (*The Observing Self*) that "awareness is the ground of conscious life, the background or field in which all elements exist, different from thoughts, sensations, or images."

Presence

From Autism to the
Discipline of Authentic Movement

In this time of great privilege, there are many forms through which we can awaken. There are many disciplines, practices, teachers from which we can choose. We discern, we distinguish, we clarify, we choose this, we do not choose that. We sort, we categorize, we separate, and, before we know it, we glimpse our path unfolding. Each one of these precious details profoundly contributes to the manifestation of who we are. I have been asked to weave some threads about the evolution of my own path, about the relationship between my experience with autistic children and my experience of the discipline of Authentic Movement.

I don't know what I am doing. I am searching hospitals and clinics for the child who cannot be found, for the child who cannot be touched. I am searching for the child who I need to find, the child who I need to touch. I am twenty-one years old. I see a boy in a big, dark room. The ceiling is so high, the chains on the furniture so shiny. I watch him from a distance as he spins. He is spinning with his arms spread wide and high, with his first fingers touching his thumbs. He is spinning and spinning in the back ward of a state hospital in New England. I remember how he brings his body into stillness. I see his eyes. He sees my eyes. In my heart I call to him. I imagine that he is calling to me. I need to come nearer to this mysterious being, this unknown presence. Yet why do I feel that I recognize him? Is it the indwelling God within this child that I need to touch, that I need to be touched by?

Is it his suffering or my own that I need to open toward?

Forty years ago, autistic children were described as those beings who never had an experience of relationship with another human being. In such a child there is no hint of an internalized other, a mother, an inner witness. There is no internalized presence. For a decade I worked in big and empty rooms where autistic children, one by one, filled the space with their absence, until, because of a momentary presence, we experienced a connection. Such moments of grace created resonance within our relationship, revealing a glimpse of light.

Children with autism represented the unknown to me. Now, so many years later, my desire to experience the unknown persists. I continue to be very drawn to that which I cannot see, that which I cannot touch, that which I cannot know. And this is very much what the discipline of Authentic Movement is about. I have had the privilege, for the past thirty-some years, of inviting movers to step into the emptiness of the studio with their eyes closed, to step into not knowing and to open toward becoming more and more of who they are. Now I no longer move with the other as I did with the children, moving with my eyes open as I witnessed them. In my current teaching practice, I sit still, with my eyes open, to the side of the movement space. I have shifted from being a moving witness to a seated witness. My wish is the same: I want to accompany the other; I want to participate in these moments of discovery of a presence embodied, of a developing inner witness.

The development of an inner witness is an excellent way of describing the development of consciousness. With the children and within the discipline of Authentic Movement, there is much learning about distinguishing between when we are here and when we are not here. In times of grace there is a shared presence and in these moments, with the children and in the studio, ritual occurs—an immediate sense of inherent order becomes apparent within a felt sense of sacred space.

I cannot trace the history of my own work without tracing the work that preceded it. In the beginning of humankind, being and dancing were inseparable within sacred space. I see one circle. In this one circle, individuals, in the presence of each other, are dancing in relationship to their gods. Dancing, they are healed. I see one circle, whole. Within this one circle, the embodiment of spirit heals. Within this one circle, I see the creative force entering from the earth through the feet of the one who dances, moving through the body of the one who calls to God, bringing God down into her body, down into the earth through her feet and back again, now circling up through her body, his body, their bodies until the world is whole, until the world is whole.

Our ancestors—dancers, healers, mystics—knew much about this longing to be present, to enter the unknown. I believe that our ancestors trusted the body. I believe that they embraced suffering and that they undoubtedly desired clear manifestation of spirit. Their work tells me that surrender, in conscious relationship to will, was necessary. Their work tells me that direct experience of union with the Divine occurred. Their practices describe ritual space and from that space, their offerings were known.

I cannot look into the history of modern dancers without discovering spirit in the bones of their dances. I cannot address the history of healers and mystics without acknowledging the depth of spirit that called them toward the suffering of others. The work of dancers, healers, and mystics forms the ground of the discipline of Authentic Movement in which we practice compassionate witnessing of movement becoming conscious.

Looking for my roots, I read words of my teachers and my teachers' teachers, each one absorbing from his or her teachers what is needed, just as I did from mine. Looking for the web of lineage of this work, I find many dancers (Mary Wigman, *The Language of Dance*; Martha Graham, *Blood Memory*; Isadora Duncan, *My Life*) as well as teachers of body-based disciplines (Don Hanlon Johnson, *Bone, Breath & Gesture*), writing of a specific sense that they must descend into their trust of intuitive knowing without yet feeling the form of it. As if they have no choice. Many write of the pain of their descents, wondering why then they continue to pursue their course. Some speak of their experience of sacrifice, but within the sacred meaning of that word. And through such an intense process of learning, often they are teaching others and, in doing so, acknowledge their choice to teach from their present, most current, experiences and questions.

What follows are words from specific modern dancers who I believe are a strong part of the ground of our work and who speak to me especially about spirit.

Rudolf Laban writes about an inner witness, about body dancing soul:

> [There is] an inner attitude out of which true dance arises like a flame . . . There is an energy behind all occurrences and material things for which it is almost impossible to find a name. A hidden, forgotten landscape lies there, the land of silence, the realm of the soul, and in the centre of this land stands the swinging temple . . . in which all sorrows and joys, all sufferings and dangers, all struggles and deliverances meet and move together. The ever-changing swinging temple, which is built of dances, of dances which are prayers, is the temple of the future . . . We are all one, and what is at stake is the universal soul out of which and for which we have to create.[1]

Mary Wigman writes about presence as if she is speaking the mover's prayer:

> Dance wants to and has to be seen . . . I have always been a fanatic of the present, in love with the moment . . . the dynamic force . . . moving and being moved . . . is the pulse beat of the life of dance. . . . Not turning oneself, but being turned. Time and again I gave myself up to the intoxication of this experience . . . a process in which, for seconds, I almost felt a oneness with the cosmos . . . I became the caller and the called all in one.[2]

Isadora Duncan writes about the longing for union with the Divine:

> I spent long days and nights in the studio seeking that dance which might be the divine expression of the human spirit through the

medium of the body's movement . . . Listen to the music within your soul. Now while listening, do you not feel an inner self awakening deep within you—that it is by its strength that your head is lifted, that your arms are raised, that you are walking slowly toward the light? . . . This awakening is the first step in the dance . . . I had come to Europe to bring about a great renaissance of religion through the Dance.[3]

And Martha Graham also writes about the present moment, movement patterns, risk, death, fire:

> Movement never lies . . . I fear the venture into the unknown . . . In order to work, in order to be excited, in order to simply be, you have to be reborn to the instant . . . anything that quickens you to the instant . . . each moment is a new one and terrifying and threatening and bursting with hope . . . You risk. Everything is a risk . . . When you have to do the same movement over and over, do not get bored with yourself, just think of yourself as dancing toward your own death . . . The ordeal of isolation, the ordeal of loneliness, the ordeal of vulnerability. . . . One begins to realize that all human beings are the same. . . . At least I think I know what it does mean to burn slowly from within . . . to feel so possessed by flame as to be infinitely hot and about to disintegrate into ash at any instant.[4]

Finally, she says: "I would like to feel that I had in some way given my students the gift of themselves."[5]

I want the autistic children to have the gift of themselves. I want every being to receive, to discover the gift of themselves, the gift of their own authenticity. Mary Whitehouse gave permission to the dancers who came into her studio to discover the gift of themselves. They were encouraged to explore their unique, personal experience of the archetypes, the same archetypes that the Graham and Wigman dancers embodied on stage. Within the intimacy of relationship, Mary's presence made it possible for each dancer to return toward the one circle where being and dancing were the same.

And it was Marian Chace, whom I knew before I met the autistic children, who taught me about spirit manifest in the body moving. I had the great privilege of breathlessly running behind her, pushing a record player on a cart on wheels.* I can vividly see her now working with psychotic adults in her flowered cotton skirt, her hair on top of her head, extending her arms wide toward the patients, and a room full of collapsed and broken spirits, perhaps remembering themselves, rise and dance.

The connection between my experience of autistic children and of the discipline of Authentic Movement not only concerns the blessing, within relationship, of arrival into the unknown but also the discovery of form, conscious embodiment, within such emptiness. What happens once we commit and stand, listening, opening into the vastness?

Our ancestors also knew about this. They knew about the practice of discernment. They knew about the impeccability of tracking movement and inner experience. They knew about the art of concentration. As many of us know, autistic children have a tremendous capacity to concentrate. They can do one movement indefinitely. What is the force in these children that draws them, continues to sustain them, into repeating certain movements over and over?

Needing to find the children, to find myself in their presence, I chose to concentrate into the very stuff of each gesture by actually entering the precious detail of their bodies moving, trying to move exactly as they did. In doing so I had the privilege of learning their silent language. I found them in a merged state with their own movement—because of an absence of an inner witness—fervently focused on their idiosyncratic movement patterns. These children taught me about movement patterns. Could their prayer have been: "See me and then I can see myself"? And so, slowly, accompanied by an outer, moving, open-eyed witness, they began, just began, to see themselves. In such moments of grace, an inner witness was born, barely born—tiny beginnings, enormous moments in my life. It was here that

---

*Marian Chace (1896–1970) was the first recognized dance therapist and the first president of the American Dance Therapy Association. Janet was Marian's intern (1963–1964) at St. Elizabeth's Hospital in Washington, DC, a federal psychiatric hospital.

an opportunity for a dialogic relationship between us emerged.

Meeting the children in such an intimate way was a direct source of my experience with the phenomenon of the inner witness, with the phenomenon of the development of consciousness. Meeting the children in this way also was the direct source of my future experience of the development of my own mover and witness consciousness, within my continuing commitment to the discipline of Authentic Movement.

In looking for more of the consciousness that I had glimpsed while working with the children, my questions brought me to brief but profound encounters with John Weir and Mary Whitehouse. I became a mover with eyes closed. The mover's prayer could be the same as the prayer of the autistic child: "See me and then I can see myself." Because the mover in the discipline of Authentic Movement studies the art of concentration, she is attending to her longing to stay present. "Where am I now? What is my inner experience?" *Hineni*—meaning "Here I am" in the Hebrew language—*hineni*. "I am here now with my wrists snapping together, my palms opening, my fingers extending, cupping. My shoulders are dropping, my arms are lifting. Here I am."

When the mover comes back after moving, she is intending to remember what she has been doing so she can speak her experience of embodiment in the presence of the outer witness. Because language is the bridge between the body and consciousness, as the mover speaks her experience, she begins to see herself, hold herself, take herself seriously, attending to the detail, every precious detail of each physical movement and the concomitant inner experience.

The witness practices the same thing. The witness asks, while sitting to the side of the space with her eyes open, "Where am I? What am I doing? Oh, here I am, sitting on this chair. My hands are in my lap; my head is tilted slightly to the right. *Hineni, hineni*. Here I am. I see the mover's wrists suddenly snap together, her palms opening, her fingers extending, cupping. Her shoulders are dropping, her arms are lifting. I see the light pouring through the window into her hands. Here I am. I am seeing her, tracking the sequence of her gestures, their idiosyncratic qualities, and my experience in response. I am remembering her, holding her within my energy field, taking her seriously. I want to remember all of this and speak these experiences in her presence after she speaks of hers."

It is within such dialogue that the mover and witness begin to name an awareness of movement patterns. When the little boy repeatedly spins, he has no conscious understanding of what he is doing. When a mover in the discipline of Authentic Movement becomes aware of a movement pattern, she has no understanding of what it is about. The inner witness is not yet in conscious relationship to it. Both with the child and with the mover, following the pattern becomes possible because of the relationship—with the moving witness for the child, and with the outer witness, sitting in stillness, for the mover.

The center of the work in the discipline of Authentic Movement is about relationship: between a mover and an outer witness, between the moving self and an inner witness, between the self and the collective, between the self and the Divine. Relationship, relationship, relationship. This gift, this work, this challenge of being a person, is about relationship.

In my book, *Offering from the Conscious Body: The Discipline of Authentic Movement,* I explore three aspects of the discipline of Authentic Movement. In all three realms, I am studying the phenomena of being merged with experience, being in a dialogic relationship with it, and being in a unitive state with it.

In the Individual Body section, the development of the ground form is traced, revealing the phenomena of mover and witness consciousness. Beginning with a mover in dyads and then triads, the evolution of the work continues as the mover becomes a moving witness, the moving witness becomes a silent witness, and the silent witness becomes a speaking witness.

In the next portion of the book, beginning with small groups, the Collective Body is explored. It is here in the development of the practice that individual movers and witnesses have the opportunity to experience themselves as part of a circle of witnesses and a body of movers within it. How do we consciously distinguish between being merged with the collective body and being in a dialogic relationship with it? The dangers of being merged are terribly evident in history as well as at this time in our own culture.

In working with the Conscious Body—the third section of the book—mystical text, dance, and energetic phenomena are studied. "Direct experience" is at the core of energetic phenomena. Within the discipline of Authentic Movement, direct experience is known as a unitive phenomenon, occurring when the felt separation between the moving self and the more familiar experience of the inner witness dissolves. There is an awareness of and immersion in the ineffable experience of nonduality. This definition is similar to the descriptions of direct experience in the mystical traditions derived from monotheistic religions and of *samadhi* in Buddhism.

Direct experience within the practice of the discipline of Authentic Movement is related to the phenomenon of presence. It is not necessarily true that we are more present as our practice matures, but we are more aware of when we are present and when we are not. When we are present, more than the details of our personal history engraved in our body matter become evident. The details of our personal history never change, but our relationship to them can change. This changing relationship in the studio happens because of the experience of being seen, seeing, participating, and belonging. Such experiences bring each mover and each witness toward the blessing of clear, silent awareness.

As the work deepens, "Where am I?" is less frequently asked. "Here I am"—*hineni*—is more frequently known. As individuals cultivate an inner witness with developing clarity and compassion, there is a felt distinction between personality and presence. Practice toward presence evolves into moments in which the body as vessel is experienced as empty. Longing to offer emerges from such emptiness. The form itself becomes transparent. Out of silence comes a word. Out of stillness comes a gesture. Out of presence comes direct experience of the numinous.

What follows is a short excerpt from the chapter on mystical dance.

We begin in an offering circle, standing, witnessing the emptiness:

> *I see one woman step in, her gaze*
> *downward, her eyes open.*
> *She begins to turn and*
> *turn and turn in one place.*
> *She spins, her hands lifting*
> *her shawl up behind her: She spins*
> *and I hear one witness*
> *singing a wordless, joyful song, a song full of*
> *light. She spins and I see the gaze*
> *of every witness riveted on her dance.*
>
> *Now I see two other witnesses*
> *lift their shawls up behind themselves,*
> *as if joining her but from their stationary places.*
> *Another witness becomes a mover*
> *and begins spinning and another*
> *and another: Now we are all spinning.*[6]

It is no longer necessary for some to remain outer witnesses because the presence of the inner witness is clear enough within each person. We spin and spin until the song and the dance complete themselves. We return to our places and witness the emptiness.

It is here that my first teachers, the autistic children, again appear. I see the little boy in the big and dark room, the ceilings so high, the chains on the furniture so shiny. This child spins, and I hear him calling and calling. Responding, I spin with him, offering my presence, inviting the awakening of his inner witness. This woman in the dance circle spins, calling and calling. Responding, one witness sings, others enter her gesture, spinning, each one offering presence. Within this circle, in these moments, each one knows wholeness because of the presence of his or her inner witness in conscious relationship to the presence of all others.

The stone bowl in the corner of my studio silently receives the spinning, the singing—all that occurs here. It holds emptiness and now water, emptiness now stones, emptiness and apples, now a candle glowing at the bottom in the center—emptiness emptiness, all that begins, all that ends, again and again and again.

I conclude with these words from the epilogue of *Offering from the Conscious Body*:[7]

Dusk arrives once again. The studio is empty. I light a candle and sit at the stone bowl, tracing the rim of this empty circle with my hand, slowly, very slowly so that I can feel the tool marks with my fingertips. Now I see others sitting with me around the bowl. Each one is vivid, present.

Now my fingers stumble into a place where a tiny chip has fallen away, marking an indentation. Putting my finger in this hollow, I trace a dark and delicate line, a fissure that moves away from the wounded place. I must enter this crevice, this sacred imperfection. My heart follows the fault line into the density of the stone, into the density of this vessel, within this studio, this home, this nation, our world. How will this crack in the container, this woundedness that is inherent in wholeness, call toward and receive the light of unbounded, conscious forces, strengthening our vessel? How will this same crack release the uncontained darkness of unconscious forces, threatening to shatter the whole of our fragile humanity?

May the quality of consciousness
that is emerging collectively
within our world
outweigh the quantity of unconsciousness
that suffers on our planet
May all suffering become compassion
May we be ready, may we be able.

CHAPTER TWO

INITIATION

Origin of a Contemporary Mystical Practice

Introduction
By Bonnie Morrissey & Paula Sager

I experience a knowing beneath the not knowing, beneath the dying of my old form, that I am a participant in transition from one world to another, embodying a new passageway toward new life.

JANET ADLER, *ARCHING BACKWARD*

The Discipline of Authentic Movement, a contemporary mystical practice sourced in *direct experience,* invites and supports the unmediated reception and immediate knowing of the numinous directly through the body. Because the practice includes a foundational focus on individual healing within personality development, a crucial base is formed from which authentic experiences of the numinous can safely emerge, be witnessed, and become integrated into the fullness of the whole person.

Mystical experience is a realm of subjective communion with that which is invisible, the infinite unknown. Within the lineage of the Discipline of Authentic Movement, the mystical tradition intermingles with the traditions of dance and healing. Whether alone in a hut in the woods or with their practices and knowledge held quietly in small circles of community, mystics, dancers, and healers are our ancestors within sacred traditions throughout time. The gifts of their offerings sustain our bodies and souls.

In the autumn of 1981, preceded by two years of increasingly vibrant imagery, Janet's body unexpectedly became the ground and the vessel for a spontaneous flood of powerful energies and visions. Over the next five years, an organic and humbling process of inner development ensued, irrevocably changing her life and setting in motion the unfolding evolution of the Discipline of Authentic Movement. While continuing to teach and care for her two young sons, Janet was bearing these new occurrences in the only way she knew, through an intensely demanding process of tracking each detail of her embodied experience. She describes this process, recorded in journal entries, as phenomenological. "The methodology," she writes, "is that of the inner witness."[1]

> The inner witness is the aspect of the self that functions as a companion, the one who sees the phenomenon being experienced by the acting self. The intention of the inner witness, within any discipline concerned with the development of the self, is to see as clearly as possible without judging, interpreting, or merging with the experience.[2]

Guided by an inner imperative to stay in conscious relationship to the physical and visionary manifestations of this energy rather than merge with them, Janet's *inner witness* necessarily expanded to include this deluge of experiences from the transpersonal realm, beyond ordinary perceptions of time and space, and beyond the usual limits of ego and personality. At the time of this spontaneous eruption of energy, her focus was not on any spiritual pursuit, she writes, but "relentlessly on a movement discipline," which she had been "studying and practicing for ten years, propelled by an eagerness to better understand the relationship between body and psyche."[3]

This chapter is comprised of excerpts from Janet's first book, *Arching Backward: The Mystical Initiation of a Contemporary Woman,* in which she offers finely detailed tracking of the metamorphosis she underwent during this remarkable period of her life, from 1979 to 1986.* From her

---

Arching Backward: The Mystical Initiation of a Contemporary Woman was published in 1995 by Inner Traditions (Rochester, Vt.).

maturing work of the 1990s expressed in "Presence: From Autism to the Discipline of Authentic Movement," which provides an overview, we turn back in time to Janet's initiatory experiences. In doing so, we hope to offer a map that highlights her initiation as central to the evolution of the discipline. We follow the excerpts within this chapter with a more sequential arc of the step-by-step development of the Discipline of Authentic Movement through each subsequent chapter and essay.

These excerpts from *Arching Backward* offer a synopsis of Janet's passage through three distinct phases: "Lying Down" (1979–1981), in which portents of the initiatory experience appear within her movement practice; "Initiation" (1981–1985), in which the fullness of her initiatory process unfolds; and "Return" (1985–1995), as the energies gradually integrate within her body and life. In choosing these specific excerpts, our intention is to reflect the integrity of the wholeness of her journey. The excerpts in the "Lying Down" section were written during Janet's collaboration with artist Rosalyn Driscoll (called Rosa within the text), who over the course of a year and a half sits to the side of the space and draws as Janet moves.

In these excerpts, Janet describes the *energetic phenomena* she experiences as a fiery force, utterly overwhelming at times, seeking form through gestures, language, and highly detailed, light-infused visions, the latter being a primary way her nervous system translates the raw energy. Writing becomes indispensable, helping to "bring into form that which originates in formlessness."[4] Language becomes an important ally as she articulates what is occurring in her body. Her writing helps her to survive and contain the experiences; her words are the text of the body.

Janet surrenders to a process that expresses its own rhythm and direction. She begins to recognize an *inherent order,* a seemingly natural intelligence or pattern within the hundreds of visions as they unfold with archetypal images from a variety of spiritual and indigenous traditions and blend with forms and people both familiar and unfamiliar to her. In relation to this mysterious process, Janet writes, "I learn that my teacher is the energy itself . . . the emergence of a subtle, unmistakable clarity."[5]

We follow as Janet navigates between her ordinary life and these extraordinary experiences, crossing and recrossing the liminal thresholds between worlds. During vision retreats, what she experiences in her body instructs a necessary ordering within her environment and directs the precise formation of ritual, creating just enough containment, a nascent vessel, so that Janet's journey may safely continue. In the midst of this new—sometimes frightening and even excruciating—territory, the presence of support from Janet's personal circle of close friends and family is vital. Their aid and comfort interweave throughout the text, as does crucial inner support appearing in the form of guides such as the Old Woman, "cross-eyed and sauntering" through these subtle dimensions.

Only after significant resistance, surrender, and awe in relationship to her inner experiences did Janet find some relief in accepting the energy itself as a process that could be called *kundalini*. It took several years for these energies to integrate enough for Janet to come to terms with her experience as initiatory, a thoroughly transformative process that included the death of who she knew herself to be, and a birth into new ways of perceiving and experiencing her life. In *Arching Backward,* she clarifies her receiving of a teaching: "this particular energetic phenomenon is metaphysical, its potential existing in every person . . . it comes into existence because of the movement of a specific vibrational energy field in the universe, mysteriously touching the vibration of that same energy within a human being."[6]

The challenges of Janet's initiation, though great, were endured and ultimately eclipsed by the gifts of radical transformation. In response, she has devoted her life's work to the study of the inner witness as a way of understanding the development of embodied consciousness. As Janet's experiences imbued her teaching practice with profoundly new energy, the Discipline of Authentic Movement has evolved as a living form born of her body, born through her experience of initiation, which offers accessible guidance to others who are drawn to this way of work.

From the first vision, Janet somehow knows intuitively that what is occurring, this cellular transformation of consciousness, does not belong to her. In preparing to publish *Arching Backward,* she recognizes her body as "a conduit for energy destined for the collective body" and writes that her "experience is inseparable from the offering."[7] Though mystical experiences have been described throughout written history, Janet is a modern woman experiencing and writing of a classic initiatory journey in a nondenominational context, "not bound to any particular root system except that of the universal human psyche."[8] Her initiation is contemporary: the reverberation of something ancient seeking entry right now into the collective body of humanity in preparation for transformed ways of being, seeing, and knowing within the evolutionary journey of consciousness. Janet's writing serves as a map of the meeting of embodied individual consciousness with transpersonal forces, and it contributes directly to the evolution of the Discipline of Authentic Movement as something more than an approach to personal or psychological growth and development. The discipline offers a developmental pathway through both personal and transpersonal realms of embodied consciousness and beyond, toward the fullness of *witness consciousness,* which may be experienced as presence emanating from a unitive source.

Mystical experience is a persistent thread wending its way throughout human history. The Discipline of Authentic Movement sends its taproot deep into the fertile soil of the depth traditions of the mystics, inviting continuity of the evolution of spirit manifesting within humanity. In retrospect, inside Janet's early experiences of being moved, we discover the seeds of opening to energetic phenomena wondrously folded within a conscious surrender to impulse.

LYING DOWN: PREPARATION

November 11, 1979

Longing to move, I have come to the studio above the boats. I see the pond through these windows that roll open, out toward and over the water. In here, the floor, walls, and ceiling are of dark wood placed in long, thin strips. Returning again to Authentic Movement, I return to the only vessel that can hold the complexities of my life. As long as I can move and be witnessed within the form of this discipline, I find a way through to a clearing.

I want a witness while I move here, another person to hold consciousness. . . . Rosa and I have been spending more and more time together. Recently in conversation we discovered that she wants a moving model at this time in her work as a visual artist. Since I need my witness to be silent, we try this collaborative approach for the first time today. Rosa sits to the side of the space, drawing as she witnesses me.

I step in. This space, open and empty, invites me. There are no other people in this space or nearby. There is no need to fill it. Moving through it, slowly, in such awe, it is hard to believe how clear, how free it is. This space is mine. Putting my cheek in my hand, I sink slowly toward the floor.

I lie down on my back, knees bent, feet flat. I feel warm, the grey wet of the morning surrounding me. I sink slowly into my body, receiving my weight, receiving myself. I am opening. An energy field appears between my legs, pushing them apart. The movement is infinitesimal, slow, until my legs fall open wide. With eyes closed, I see images.

February 14, 1980

Rosa and I have been coming here once a week for the past three months. Each time, she sits to the side of the space, drawing while I move. Afterward we do not speak together of our experience. I always begin moving with the deep, slow pull downward and into the floor. Increasingly rich images appear in vivid detail. They are different from fantasies I have experienced in the past, the texture and light more vibrant. Over time, people, animals, places and things begin to reappear in these images. . . As these grey, quiet mornings have evolved, the magnolia tree outside the windows behind Rosa has become winter bare, the light finding more space between branches as it filters into the studio. . . .

Today the studio is surrounded by white snow vibrating on every surface. Rosa begins to draw. I lie down, knees bent, feet flat, clearly a process unfinished. Something new, small, and undulating curves upward, beginning in my lower back, up through my torso, neck, and head. This movement expands as I roll, my arms falling out and down. I feel desperate, reaching for something, knowing fully that I am nowhere near it.

April 28, 1980

It is late afternoon, a low, quiet day. Rosa and I walk here together. In the studio I find myself in the same starting position as always: on my back, knees bent, feet flat. My movement is unusually fluid, free, sensual and from a deep source. Again with eyes closed, I see images.

A river runs fast and downward to my right. Reaching, I grab a duck floating by, bringing her to me. She walks into my mouth, looking down my throat. Discovering a silver ring around the inside of my throat, she pulls it out, placing it around my neck. Now I spin the ring in my lap as it pulls me away into the rushing river.

May 30–June 4, 1981

A year has passed. . . . Rosa and I met in the studio regularly through the year. She witnessed. I moved. I am so grateful for having what I needed—a place, a safe place, the right witness, and the discipline itself.

As the winter melted I saw ahead a bit. By next autumn, with both boys in school, there will be more time to practice, study, and teach Authentic Movement. I began preparations for the opening of a small institute where this could happen. The idea of returning to my questions within the discipline is exciting.

Now there is time for another layer of preparation, my own inner work. I have come to Rosalind's house for a seven-day retreat. . . .

. . . Finally there is time and space to listen . . . moving into another space within me, empty, untouched. How I long for this, how I fear it.

As I lie down, knees bent, feet flat, the sun emerges from the clouds, its light pouring into me. I feel starkly seen. I am the edge of a sharpness in bright light. It is painful. My arms slowly cross and block the light. The darkness, deeply soothing, is correct. Suddenly my arms fly open, straight out, my hands bending back at my wrists. The light shoots into me, hurting me. Back and forth—from being seen to utter darkness. I so prefer the dark, silent, inside place. So it is true. I am ready to go there, a place where no one can see me, shape me by their experience of me, a place where only I can see myself.

Excerpts from *Arching Backward*

Becoming an Initiate

July 30, 1981

. . . I awaken in the middle of the night. I see images, now definitely not fantasies. I have no words to describe this experience of seeing. Still more vivid in light and line, these images brand me, marking me with fire.

October 4, 1981

. . . The new students have finally arrived for a year of work at the Institute. I wanted our first meeting to be elegant. We set a beautiful table in the empty studio downstairs. . . . I wanted Lady Godiva chocolates for dessert. I wanted beauty at every level. I wanted the women to feel welcomed, to somehow recognize each other, to be glad that they have risked committing to this tiny new school that will be finding form in direct relationship to the discipline of Authentic Movement finding form.

October 29, 1981

The house, full of flowers, good food, and generous people, is quiet again. The public opening celebration for The Mary Starks Whitehouse Institute is over. Earlier, as I was talking to the guests about the discipline of Authentic Movement and then introducing the featured speaker, Clara, I felt quite strange and suddenly without an ease or comfort on which I count when I am speaking in front of others. I thought maybe I was becoming ill. Maybe I am ill. I cannot walk up the stairs to bed. Theo helps me. We lie down. There is much pain in my lower back, and I am barely able to move. With eyes closed, I see my students.

> *Eight women*
> *make a circle*
> *around me.*
> *I lie in the center.*
> *My whole body*
> *burns.*
> *The flames*
> *two inches high*
> *sear me*
> *silently.*

> *The pain is unbearable.*

October 30, 1981

. . . There is so much vibration in my body as if another force or energy is filling me. After a deep but short sleep, I feel almost completely immobile and can barely talk or keep my eyes open. Surrendering, I close them.

> *. . . I am burning.*

March 26–29, 1982

I know now that these images are visions. Adele has helped me to understand this, and my own experience makes it clear. This energy, which burns through my bones, my cells, directly and deeply affecting my entire body, also somehow creates pictures. These images are made of light, of an electric vibration. The clarity of line, form, and depth reflects a reality beyond fantasy, dream, or ordinary perception.

I also know that I am in a process. I perceive an order, a direction, even a rhythm, though the impact of each vision on my body, my awareness, is so great that there is no space yet for understanding or even sensing a context for all of this. Each vision expands the universe, changing my perception, changing then my experience of myself. Though my life is becoming extremely complex and difficult, I do feel deep gratitude. I am receiving a gift. I remember the words of John Weir in Bethel: "The only way out is in and through." I do not know what else to do. . . .

In the loft, in bed, I surrender to a kind of exhaustion I have never felt before. The burning and aching, the weeping, and the strange deep sleeping are relentless. How will I be able to continue to teach?

April 1, 1982

It is late into the night. These visions, and many I cannot record, continue to bombard me for hours, all night, tumbling on top of each other. They are brutal. I must sit up. I cannot lie down, even for a second, because I cannot risk surrendering my capacity to witness myself. There is less separation between me-in-the-visions and me. I *know* I must not merge with the images. If I should merge, I would risk losing my relationship to them. It is the relationship that sustains my consciousness and my hope of integrating this material. I know this from my years of work as a therapist. Merging with the material, identifying with it, can surely create psychosis.

April 2, 1982

. . . It is becoming a rigorous discipline, trying to balance the force of the energy and my deep ambivalence in relationship to it with my great desire to mother my boys well and consistently. This ambivalence is tricky. The energy is saving my life in some indescribable way and simultaneously, it is taking my life.

June 22, 1982

> *Running*
> *running terrified*
> *I am smacked*
> *in three places*
> *the inside*

of each ankle
and the nape
of my neck.
Signs
rosy pink
rise into shape.

Marked by the spirits
I am an initiate.

July 4–7, 1982

. . . I am deeply in what we now refer to as my "slows." I move very, very slowly, feeling great weight in my body and feeling at the same time suspended. As the day progresses I move more and more slowly. At the market I feel as though I am a different species from the other people around me. . . . My mind is completely clear. My body will not always move.

I see two black
half-moons
facing each other
trying not to close
the circle.

Words tell me:
Never let the wound
close completely.
It must always
stay open.

October 7–9, 1982

. . . The summer is over and I have decided to try and teach again at the Institute. Adele will offer her weekly seminar, but it continues to be my responsibility to cover the rest of the work, in the studio and in seminars.

The new students have arrived. Like last year, they are either artists or newly trained therapists coming for postgraduate study. As I begin my new teaching schedule again, I realize I must find someone to live with us, someone who can help. I have to be able to teach through the academic year this time. Today I notice that the energy is coming back, but I cannot believe that it might continue. I feel exhausted just at the thought of such disruption, pain, and lack of control. . . .

> *Light pours*
> *through the top*
> *of my head.*
> *Weightless*
> *I am inside*
> *and also outside*
> *my body.*

More and more frequently, I find my fingers making certain shapes while the visions come through me. They are very specific, each finger placed in exact relationship to the other fingers. Sometimes both hands move identically in this regard. Holding these hand positions is calming.

November 4–7, 1982

I have come here to Rosalind's land to be totally alone. . . . At sundown I sweep the hut, bring in the wood, and make the fire. I feel like making an altar, though I have never made one before.

> *. . . A tree grows through me*
> *cracking my pubis*
> *piercing the base*
> *of my spine*
> *and out.*

> *. . . Another tree grows up*
> *into and through*

my heart.
I am dead now
and suddenly quite still.
This tree grows tall
beyond the others.
At the top, in a nest
lies a very large egg.

. . . Suddenly
the big egg
drops
into the earth
down
through the trunk
of the tree, with intent
burrowing
through tunnels
beige in color
a myriad of tunnels
that connect all places
a grand crisscrossing
a pattern complete.
At the center
of the earth
the egg starts spinning
I read the languages
shining
on each facet
spinning, spinning
faster and faster
becoming a diamond. . . .

Since I have come here, the quality, the deep texture of everything that exists in the universe feels the same. I do not wash. I sprinkle sage ash on my pillow. I wrap myself in a blanket covered with leaves and sticks. All food tastes the same. Light and dark, outside, inside, me, the night—we are all one. The world is of one matter and my flesh and blood are no different than the rabbit's or the leaf's.

This morning with no more vibrations, shortness of breath, tiredness, back fire, I know a great resolution. I rise and want to wash, clean the hut, prepare to leave. My time here is complete. When the candle on the altar burns out, I will go.

December 13–19, 1982

. . . Rosalind comes for a visit. We sit in the study. The world outside is white and ever so quiet. In here, we drink tea. Though it is impossible to describe these experiences, I try to tell her about my Old Woman and how much I honor her. Though she cuts, chops, and slices me to bits, which can be horrifying at one level, it is the energy itself that I know can destroy me, not the content of the visions. Somehow, within the context of the Old Woman's clear intention to see me through these trials by fire, even when she is actively involved with the burning, unraveling, and emptying, she repeatedly becomes my devoted guide. . . .

The Old Woman
tucks a pearl
into my third eye
way deep into the center
of the vortex
of the earth.

She cuts me
cuts my hands
cuts my legs
placing all the little pieces
in small leather pouches
left hand pieces

in one bag
right hand pieces
in another bag
leg pieces
in a dark yellow one.
Placing the pouches
in the hollow of her back
she saunters
away.

December 29, 1982

I get into the hot bathtub. I feel drawn to the water time after time as the energy builds and I inwardly prepare to see a vision. The heat, the weight, and the texture of it somehow support the part of me that surrenders to these experiences. The hot water becomes my medium. . . .

My physical health is so depleted, I long for someone who knows how to help me become strong again. I imagine most physicians would make a diagnosis related to psychological disturbance. Fear of the medical establishment's lack of understanding has kept me from seriously seeking help from them. . . .

I consult with two doctors at the department of neuropsychiatry at Columbia University Medical School. It is confirming to hear the director of the program tell me that he believes the source of my physical problems is kundalini energy. Three people have mentioned this word to me since these experiences began. The doctor briefly explains the meaning of the word. He says it is a Hindu term used to describe an initiation process by which an individual awakens into the fullness of nonordinary perception through the experience of an infusion of energy burning through the entire body. He has little else to say other than suggesting that I read Dante's *Inferno*. Apologizing for his lack of time, he writes something in a folder and quite genuinely wishes me luck.

December 31, 1982–January 6, 1983
Increasingly I need to be alone when I embody a vision retreat. . . .

> *I place a circle*
> *of protection*
> *around the house*
> *a black circle on the ground.* . . .
>
> *I see my people*
> *in their places*
> *guarding me*
> *the Old Woman*
> *at the foot of the bed*
> *on the green pillow*
> *to the right.* . . .

I am exhausted and aching all over. It is hard to write all of this, to remember it, but since the first vision two years ago, each time I feel compelled to write. . . . The weight is unbearable as I walk again out into the night hall, into the bathroom, into the hot water. I light the candle as always before getting in. Small rituals such as this one have become mandatory somehow, a call for impeccability in the simple gestures that precede and follow the receiving of visions.

January 30–31, 1983
. . . Hannah makes some soup as she tells me about her trip to Nicaragua, the orphanage there where she worked, and the great fear among the families. When I hear about other people's suffering, I am aware that my sensitivity to others' pain is becoming magnified beyond description. This energy teaches me in such subtle but clear ways that we are all the same. I know this. . . .

After teaching a small group in the studio at home this morning, I take a walk in the woods, ending at dusk at Paradise Pond. Only one person is skating, backward. I go up the many steps and into the Crew House studio. This room is abundant in its emptiness. When I first moved to the area, Rosalind welcomed me and offered me time in this space. It was perfect for my Authentic Movement therapy groups then, for my more private work with Rosa later, and now we meet here weekly for the large group training work at the Institute. Sometimes I bring the boys here, late in the afternoon, after the college dance classes are over, and we run round and round. Today I cannot run. I lie down.

I see me
here
in my corner
witnessing students. . . .

Moving
out and away
I turn
seeing in my place
a creature.
It is the Old Woman . . .

. . . I dive into her chest
coming out
through her yoni
facing forward
locked
in the vice
of her bones
my head
of bird and fish
my mouth open
wide.

I see me
stuck and weeping.
With compassion
I hesitate and reach
stretching, pulling
gathering
receiving me.

A birth.

February 6, 1983

Not knowing, not knowing enough about this process, I am constantly wondering if I can endure the not knowing. I can only know what my direct experiences teach me. In the meantime, the rounds of visions keep coming. Often just as I begin to recover from one round, the signs of the next round appear—pressure behind my eyes, fire in my back, and my movement slowing down. There is no time for rest, recovery, and integration. The experiences themselves deplete me, no matter how ecstatic. . . .

Will the visions ever be about other people's suffering, not always about my disintegration? How much longer will I be able to work? Are the children having a normal enough childhood? Will my body ever be healthy again?

March 2, 1983

I feel that I am dying. The boys are with Nathan for two weeks. I am desperate for help. I sense that people who believe they can help or wish to try can easily misunderstand this energy, mostly because it has not been directly experienced by them. They can, without intention, interfere energetically, emotionally judge, or intellectually interpret what is happening.

March 3, 1983

. . . Today it is unbearably difficult. I cannot keep my eyes open. Theo is working at his drafting table. I try walking in the woods nearby. . . . As I walk I realize I am holding the delicacy of a new form and its breathless fragility. Simultaneously I carry the stiffness, the death of the old form.

March 4, 1983

When I work with my hands, I do best. I draw the tree roots, knit with smooth big wooden needles, and work in clay. I learn I must stay in the present as it is a command. Any thinking that ventures off into past or future is disastrous—I immediately feel pulled out of my body and into the direct experience of seeing visions. . . . I need time. I know I do.

. . . I cannot resist. I see.

> *Four transparent figures*
> *beckon to me.*
> *I move the essence of me*
> *into one of them.*
> *Still alive*
> *I do not have to die*
> *to become*
> *another form.*
>
> *This is good.*

May 22, 1983

I am better. Something has shifted, or sifted inward. I spend as much of the day as I can playing with the boys outside. They are my anchors. I experience my weight differently. I walk and move in wonder at the subtle newness of each gesture, each sensation. Though my voice is still very thin, with no strength or volume, this body, my body, becomes new. The crocuses are up.

September 19, 1983

The summer was renewing. I became stronger—strong enough to not see visions and to stay in the realm of daily reality most of the time. . . .

I learned more about my own ability to ground the energy. . . .

> *My mind*
> *unrolls, revealing*
> *nothing.*
> *Unfolding*
> *into emptiness*
> *the spiral*
> *spins, becoming*
> *fragments*
> *of star light*
> *celestial and fine.*

September 28, 1983

> *. . . Inside I see*
> *empty space.*
>
> *My mind is empty.*

Peace, complete peace, fills me. I feel empty and clear, reborn.

March 13, 1984

It is now two years since the spontaneous eruption of this energy. My life is externally rather limited. I do fine if nothing extra is required. Anything beyond my simple schedule produces extreme exhaustion, fire around my shoulders and neck, and familiar disaffection with myself. I have worked hard at not letting the visions through, at holding back the energy. I am learning that it can be dangerous to allow them through if my body cannot withstand the impact, and yet it can also be dangerous to not allow them through. In a specific way, resistance can lead to paralysis and despair. Timing.

June 15, 1984

Fruits of this process become increasingly apparent. I notice that I have stopped identifying with feeling, thought, sensation in my daily life.

Everything enters me, I experience it, and it leaves. Nothing stays. I am free. This quality of living is more than worth the suffering. I could have never imagined such a way. My gratitude is great. . . .

Vividly, I see
animals talking
to each other
to their young.
Close up I watch
the sea otter
speaking
to its baby.

August 3–6, 1984

I am ready to begin another retreat. My slows increase these last few days. The vision energy is building. I feel too tired, my body aches, the pressure behind my eyes is strong.

. . .

I do not know how to find a teacher. I remember again: The only way out is in and through. This transition time is difficult—I am nowhere yet. I have left here and am not there.

October 24, 1984

I feel an instinctive need to embrace the new energy by embodying a different lifestyle. I do not want to live as I do. I feel a primitive pull, fierce, underlying everything, toward a new way. How can I learn what to choose, where to go? How will I create a life that honors what has happened? . . .

I want to sleep. Instead I see.

I see and feel
an explosion
from the base
of my spine

a white sphere
diffusing
into white light
gently, slowly
a boom, but quiet.
In slow motion
this light fills
my entire back
jarring me.

I become light.

October 26–28, 1984

. . . My torso begins rocking in a circle as I chant. I do not know any chants or how to chant, but I am chanting as if I have been chanting for one hundred years.

October 29–31, 1984

. . . Thoughts of what to do, how to participate in the embodiment of becoming collective, becoming conscious, interfere with a flood of visions, of people moving and witnessing in continuous circles, of people awakening into clear presence.

. . . My heart opens

just at the place
where the diamond
pierced
my skin.
It is red, of blood.

March 8–10, 1985

. . . There continues to be a band of energy through which I have to move before I can receive the visions. In that place, I am filled first with emotion—sadness, fear, confusion, loneliness. Then I weep more fully, feeling such despair about our world. And then somehow I feel as though I am out on the other side of an edge on which I am directly experiencing infinite time and space. The visions exist there. All of this paradoxically occurs within me. Sometimes, coming out of the visionary state, I again pass through these specific spaces of sensation. . . .

Dusk finally arrives. I light the candle, feeling weepy. The light and the quiet are exquisite and foreboding. I go into the water for the changing of the light.

> *I see infinite*
> *numbers of people*
> *coming toward me*
> *each suffering. . . .*
> *There are thousands*
> *I see each one*
> *each one's uniqueness.*
>
> *May I learn*
> *to help. . . .*

I am increasingly distracted. I do not know what to do. May I be able to see what I am ready to see.

> *People sit in pain*
> *in great need*
> *one by one*
> *the circle filling.*
> *My helplessness*
> *mounts. . . .*

. . . A ritual is developing that I like. It feels correct.

Sitting up, I straighten my legs and pull a long imaginary thread from between my knees, hand over hand.

The needle
in my right hand
enters
my third eye
moving out the other side
behind me
and down
back into my heart
out the front of me
and up
to the next person
slightly above me.

Looking down to my left
I see endless people
threaded this way
looking up to my right
endless more
looming larger.

An exquisite and unusually powerful image, born directly out of specific movement in my body. I begin to draw this configuration on the rug because I want it whole. I want these threads to complete a circle and they never do, of course, because there is always a new individual, a new configuration.

March 31–April 2, 1985

. . . My life before these recent years of total immersion in the numinous was replete with expressive movement in response to the texture of my world. My creative energy always found form through dance. And I often discovered form through deeply satisfying work with clay. Now it is obvious to me that words become the form that best reflect my initiation experience, not choreography, not sculpture. Intuition and clear thinking are becoming the same. This union can be voiced in writing or speaking. The way opens directly from body to word. . . .

I get into the hot water, slowly opening my eyes. I see the reflection of the candle flame in the water burning exactly over my yoni, the small gentle flame where it was when all of this began, down at the base of my spine. I see it reflected there in the water and simultaneously I feel it, the white light, no more burning, just white flame throughout my body. I find my hand on my heart. This is what the flame has done. It has opened my heart.

April 7, 1985

I make applesauce. I wash the apples, quarter them, core, peel, and slice them. And I stir. I stir and stir. Mostly I walk. I walk every time I feel pulled away. Slowly I witness the increments of my realignment. I walk and walk and begin to be hungry. I am safe if I can keep my eyes open, stay present. Sometimes I walk two to three hours a day. I still cannot read, really. I take no baths and never light candles.

My last effort has been to let go of even hoping that this experience might have value or meaning in my life or in the lives of others. Yesterday I surrendered to that too, surrendering to absolute nothingness. Since then, I am better. There is no past, no future, no hope. Infinity is now. The simplest activities are miraculous. There is no reality other than the present, and the present is whole. I know it directly.

Return

Reentry into the world was awkward and extremely demanding. My fragility required strict adherence to my tremendous need for protection from most foods and most people, from traffic, from noise, from information about ways in which to build my life. Within the austerity of such carefully measured external stimulation, the internal process of return evolved. . . .

Enactment of private ritual, which I learned and developed within the initiation itself, created a container for the journey back into life. I soon realized that I could again safely choose to see visions, either in response to the familiar signs of the impending energy or if I felt that it was the correct time. The content of the visions was a weave of some of the original themes and rhythms apparent in the initiation, with new symbols and sensations arising from the continuing and extraordinary changes in my perception of reality. . . .

Gradually the passion, the fire, the utter vividness of image and the concomitant impact on my body, faded. I mourned the loss and at the same time felt profound relief as well as wonder in the development of my new life. Vision retreats became less frequent and I engaged in the outer world with more strength and endurance. The sensation of emptiness within my body and my mind became increasingly manifest and I longed for its reflection around me. . . .

Recently, while preparing this text for publication [of *Arching Backward*], the fire has reappeared quite differently. The flame is no longer yellow-orange, no longer white, but now clear, transparent. The energy repeatedly moves in the rhythm of labor, not contracting, but instead moving as a snake moves, undulating through my neck and out the top of my head.

This undulating curve exquisitely becomes the rushing, narrow river, the one into which I was pulled by the silver ring fifteen years ago. The river now runs between the edge of my initiatory journey and the edge of my culture. In a vision, I see that I must cross a delicately formed bridge that reaches over this river. With all of me, every cell concentrating, focusing on specific tasks, I move the energy from my body across the bridge to the collective body. The tasks completed, I become the bridge, arching backward over the ever-changing, dynamic force.

> *Now I see*
> *the silver ring*
> *closer to the front*
> *of my mouth*
> *radiating light*
> *glowing.*
> *Transparent forms*
> *roll*
> *out through the top*
> *of the ring.*
> *My voice?*

Discovering my new voice, contained by the silver ring, invites consciousness concerning an ancient fear, enabling me to better understand my original need to publish this text under a pseudonym. Fear . . . lives within me, within the history of my woman's body, within the history of my Western psyche. . . .

Sand is the ground.
Out of the sand
emerging up and
toward me
I see three
great fossils, men
clearly the patriarchy
of the synagogue
of the church
of the ashram.

These men look
exactly alike, crumbling
full of holes
fragile, indeed
fossils. Bearded
and with thin voices
they speak to me
but I cannot understand
their words. I see them
reaching slowly
a hand toward
my mouth.

They intend to silence
my voice. My words
my embodied experience
challenge, interrupt
confuse the order
of ancestral
theological structures.

Seeing these men and thus embodying them reduces their power instantly. It no longer matters what name I use. I am free.

~

Now comes the dusk. I have been waiting all day. Feeling gratitude for the hot water, for the light shifting, for the gift of my journey, I step in. As I sit down, I am my clear self, no longer separate from my personality. . . .

I bend my arms, holding my hands up, open. I hear so clearly the sounds of the universe—all creatures, all beings, one sound, strong and delicate. I notice how my elbows are banging the sides of the tub, sounding like big bells, ringing in celebration. I lie back down into the water.

> *I see* Arching Backward
> *floating along*
> *the narrow river*
> *rushing*
> *toward the left.*
> *The silver ring*
> *loops*
> *through the pages*
> *of the book*
> *from top to bottom*
> *protecting*
> *washing down a page*
> *out and then back*
> *down and through*
> *a simple*
> *a clear way of knowing.*

I get out of the tub, looking through the glass doors into the night.

> *I see an arc*
> *the bottom third*
> *of a shallow bowl.*
> *Not reaching very high*

on either side
it lies open
wide, almost flat
on the bottom.

This arc glows
warm, a hope
a new vessel
to receive others
who take their turn
after me
seeing
hearing and knowing
becoming
bringing full-bodied
themselves
because of the fire
into the vast body
of the collective.

May this arc, this vessel, welcome—hold—correctly receive initiates returning.

Now I see my body
not male
not female, curled
arching forward
becoming the soft
stone of alabaster
lying down
so small
in the very center

of the arc
the wide embrace.

My journey
complete
I lay down
this burden.
I lay down
this gift.

CHAPTER THREE

THE GROUND FORM

Moving and Witnessing,
Speaking and Listening

Introduction

By Bonnie Morrissey & Paula Sager

. . . This arc glows
warm, a hope
a new vessel
to receive others
who take their turn
after me . . .

JANET ADLER,
ARCHING BACKWARD

From her earliest work in the 1960s with children diagnosed with autism, Janet is drawn to an invisible, "infinitely mysterious" process of development that is centered in the subjective experience of the one who is moving and the subjective experience of the one who is seeing. In 1969, Janet meets her teacher Mary Whitehouse, from whom she receives a way of accessing the unconscious through the body. Mary, almost sixty years old when twenty-eight-year-old Janet arrives, had studied with choreographers Martha Graham and Mary Wigman. As a dance professional, Mary Whitehouse became increasingly disillusioned with the teaching methods of her day, concerned by what she saw as a widespread lack of awareness, with "the body . . . regarded as an object to be trained, controlled, or manipulated."[1] In response, her teaching changed in radical ways. Mary encouraged students to close their eyes and move in her presence, inviting them into an inner experience of *moving and being moved*.[2] Mary used the word "authentic" to describe movement that was "genuine, belonging to that person . . . truth of a kind unlearned,"[3] but she never codified the term "authentic movement."

Throughout the 1970s, Janet integrates what she learned from Mary into her work as a movement therapist with adult clients, describing this way of moving as authentic movement. By the end of the decade Janet capitalizes the term, beginning to recognize Authentic Movement as more than a way of moving, now also a practice. Within relationship, within the process of *seeing and being seen,* Janet longs to "articulate what actually happened to the two people, before the movement or witnessing carried specific meaning for the psyche, before symbol" (see "Who Is the Witness?," page 83). Her early and distinctive interest in prereflective experience, infused with the profound impact of her initiatory process, lead to the centrality in her work of the nonsymbolic and nonassociative elements of energetic phenomena and direct experience.

In 1981, Janet establishes the Mary Whitehouse Institute, named in honor of her teacher, in Northampton, Massachusetts. This formative time marks a clear transition in her professional life from therapist to teacher. She invites eight students to participate as "interns" collaborating through their practice of Authentic Movement in a depth of relational inquiry. During this time Janet clarifies the role of a *mover,* who moves with eyes closed in the presence of a witness, as distinct from the role of a *witness,* who sits to the side and offers their presence to a mover.

The Institute serves as a laboratory for the study of embodied relationship, and it opens just as Janet's initiatory process is becoming an uncompromising force in her life. The concurrence of her initiation with the work of the Institute grounds the early seeds of what will become the Discipline of Authentic Movement, a practice that can receive and guide individuals through transformative passages, an informed and experienced well of support that Janet does not herself have during her own passage. "Visions of wholeness, in my body and in the universe, and recurrent sensations of union," she writes, "brought balance to the despair and loneliness inherent in receiving visions, intensified by the continued and painful absence of help from a teacher or community with developed knowledge of the meaning of initiation or return."[4]

During her own ongoing experience of energetic phenomena, Janet is gaining tremendous capacity to hold a deep and wide spectrum of experience, revealing entirely new perspectives concerning the source of movement impulse. She is attuning simultaneously to both the fine details of the physical body and the subtle phenomena of the energetic body. She is learning, in collaboration with the interns, to distinguish between movement originating in personality or personal history and movement arising from a transpersonal source, experience she describes as both "not circumscribed by . . . personality" and "not felt in relation to the body ego" (see "Who Is the Witness?," page 88).

A decade prior to her initiation and the opening of the Institute, Janet had explored the parallels between movement therapy and verbal psychotherapy in her essay, "Integrity of Body and Psyche" (see the Addendum), where she noted the distinctive way movement can be the medium for direct inquiry into the relationship between conscious and unconscious dimensions of the individual psyche. In this 1972 essay, she differentiates the surrender required in moving freely without inhibition from the will that can come into relationship with this intentional surrender, honoring their balance. She describes clients "choosing to listen to and speak from their inner lives with care" (see "Integrity of Body and Psyche," page 331), a nascent description of a core quality of what will become known as the "inner witness." Janet also observes, within this depth work, that there may be useful returns to unresolved aspects of development.

Now as a teacher at the Institute, Janet becomes even more devoted to tracking the detail of movement patterns and to the developmental aspects of embodied consciousness, echoing her work as a therapist with children and then adults. In the presence of her students, she holds an abiding awareness of each one's implicit wholeness and capacities for personal development. Janet makes clear throughout her work that the heart of this practice remains the close, caring, and ever-evolving relationship of one person with another, a mover and a witness.

To highlight the centrality of the dyadic form, we begin this chapter with "The Ground Form," an excerpt from Janet's later book, *Offering* *from the Conscious Body,** as she introduces a new student to the discipline. Janet's warm presence and welcoming language offer the mover full permission to be just as they are, helping to form a relational vessel that may come to contain all that transpires between them. From her experience of initiation, Janet carries forth a deep appreciation for ritual as a means of shaping a space where inner experience, emerging spontaneously, can be held safely and intentionally. She introduces elements of ritual through her heightened awareness of physical space, of light and emptiness, and through eye contact, encouraging a commitment of shared connection and responsibility between mover and witness at the thresholds of entering and returning from their practice.

In her essay "Who Is the Witness?"† Janet offers a synthesis of what she and her interns are learning at the Institute. She maps out the basic shape of what will become the Discipline of Authentic Movement, revealing the "ground form" of the practice and how it is inspired by and different from the work of Mary Whitehouse. In this essay, Janet delves into the relationship between a mover and an outer witness, clarifying how their work together may cultivate embodied consciousness for each. She describes the complexities and intricacies of the work and the developmental pathways that open for each individual, because of the presence of the other.

As a result of a consistent felt sense of being seen, the mover develops what Janet then called an "internal witness" or the "guide within." While she has not yet named the inner witness, she is clearly mapping this journey that flows from a longing to be seen toward an internalized capacity to see oneself more clearly, toward the natural emergence of a longing to more clearly see another. In this essay, though not yet clarifying the roles of *moving witness, silent witness,* or *speaking witness,* she names for the first time the practice of silent witnessing as a transition

---

Offering from the Conscious Body: The Discipline of Authentic Movement was published in 2002 by Inner Traditions (Rochester, Vt.).
†"Who Is the Witness?" was first published in *Contact Quarterly* 12, no. 1 (Winter 1987): 20–29 and was later published in *Authentic Movement: Essays by Mary Starks Whitehouse, Janet Adler, and Joan Chodorow,* edited by Patrizia Pallaro (Philadelphia: Jessica Kingsley Publishers, 1999), 141–59.

between the role of a mover and the role of a witness who meets the mover in dialogue after the movement.

In "Who Is the Witness?" Janet describes the way in which language is central to this inquiry, informed by her earlier study with psychologist John Weir and by all that she is learning through her initiation. Within her initiation, Janet's words are forged in the fires of a longing to speak the ineffable. At the Institute, as the discipline "expands to include experiences that occur outside of personality," it becomes necessary to develop a "language system within which to place these experiences." Janet and her interns practice speaking *from* their embodied experience, both personal and transpersonal, staying close to the detail of the physical body as they speak. What she and the interns are learning about language will evolve to become the *ritual practice of speaking and listening,* an essential counterpart to the *ritual practice of moving and witnessing.* These two practices will come to comprise both the fullness and the simplicity of the discipline, as students weave back and forth again and again, from moving and witnessing to speaking and listening, refining their practice and their skills, developing individually and as an embodied collective.

We complete this chapter with "Remarks at the Closing of the Mary Starks Whitehouse Institute,"* in which, due to her fragile health, Janet must formally say goodbye to her interns and draw the work of the Institute to a close. Through her offerings to each student, we are invited once again into the intimacy of her teaching practice. The ethos of the discipline becomes apparent as both a practice and an art, as does the high regard she has for each individual who participates in this way of work. Evident within her remarks is a coalescing of respect for the phenomena of energy. As she burns with kundalini energy and visions sweep through her, Janet honors each student as a witness to the evolution of the discipline.

---

*"Remarks at the Closing of the Mary Starks Whitehouse Institute," previously unpublished, were given by Janet at the closing ceremony in the spring of 1983. All names of interns have been changed. Two of Janet's fellow teachers were also present and acknowledged in her remarks, Edith Sullwold and Rosalind DeMille.

The Ground Form

An Excerpt from
Offering from the Conscious Body

"Hineni." Here I am.

It is time to begin. A mover is sitting on her cushion on the carpet, here near the low table. I am the witness, sitting on my cushion across from her, speaking to her now.

Before us is an empty space, shaped by the walls and the floor, by the open, high ceiling, by the door and window frames and the light spilling through them. All of it, all of this emptiness, is a reflection of our potential experience of emptiness within. I invite you to enter this emptiness as a mover. Here the emptiness can fill and empty because of you. Here you can fill and empty because of it.

As you leave your cushion be aware that you will return to it when your experience as a mover is completed. After you move to the edge of the carpet, either before facing the unknown or once you've stepped in, I invite you to make eye contact with me. When our eyes meet we will be consciously connecting in a shared commitment toward the longing to be seen and to see in the presence of each other. We will be marking a gateway in that moment as we formally begin our relationship within the Discipline of Authentic Movement.

75

As the mover in this practice you will step into the emptiness not knowing, not knowing what you will actually do, how you will move. There is no way that either of us can know what you should be doing. Remember there is no right or wrong way to move. When you are ready, intend toward listening inwardly. Close your eyes to erase the visual world around you, though perhaps you can still sense my presence or where the light is coming in.

It will be here, when you encounter the possibility of making conscious choices, that the practice of discernment begins. You may choose to move or you may wait for an impulse to move. If an impulse arises you may choose to surrender to it, or you may choose to bring your will in relationship to it and say no. What matters more than what you choose is your freedom of conscious choice, creating a developing clarity of your own subjective experience.

Once moving, if you make big movements or you move suddenly or fast you must open your eyes so that you don't hurt yourself. If you find a place in the room that feels correct for you, you can stop there or keep moving. If you stop, you do not have to know why you are stopping or why you are choosing that particular spot. You could be choosing it for rational reasons or because intuitively it welcomes you or calls to you. Or perhaps you are not consciously choosing it, it just happens to be where you are in that moment.

As I am speaking, I see the mover's white shawl draped over her lap, the soft threads of one end just touching the carpet.

Your inner witness might notice many things happening. You might be moving or be still, making a sound or being silent. You might be moving quickly or slowly, with large gestures or small ones. You might notice inner experiences, such as sensations, emotions, or thoughts. Sometimes it is difficult to sort out all of the different kinds of experiences you are having. As a way to begin, I invite you to try to bring your awareness toward what your body is doing. Try to focus primarily on the movement itself. It is here that the practice of concentration begins.

And the practice of discernment continues. At any moment, for any reason, you can choose to open your eyes and either make eye contact with me or not. You can then close them again and keep moving or you can stop and return to your cushion. If you choose, you can keep moving until five minutes have passed. Then I will call your name and ask you to bring your experience to an end.

As I witness you move, I cannot know your experience. I can only know my own experience in your presence. I commit to tracking my experience as best I can. It is my intention, my practice, to notice all that occurs within me as I witness.

When you finish moving and you open your eyes, before you come back to your cushion, I invite you to make eye contact with me again. As we look at each other then, we will be moving back through the gateway of conscious connection that we marked by our eye contact as you were entering the space. We will be acknowledging our commitment toward consciousness in the presence of each other. Then when you are ready, come back to your cushion.

Now the mover stands and turns toward the emptiness. May I be able:

>to see what I am ready to see
>to hear what I am ready to hear
>to know what I am ready to know
>and to be as I am

Wrapping her shawl around her shoulders, she walks away from me toward the carpet's edge. Standing there, I see her toes curled around the softness of the carpet as it meets the hardwood floor. Now she turns back toward me and our eyes meet. She closes her eyes and her movement begins. I am flooded with gratitude for her willingness to trust me enough.

Her inner witness*:

> *I long*
> *to move freely*
> *with no inhibitions*
> *but I don't know how.*
> *I am inhibited*
> *by this body*
> *this body*
> *that I know*
> *and that I don't know.*
>
> *I want you to accept this body*
> *just as it is*
> *but how could you?*
>
> *I am self-conscious*
> *as I walk*
> *wondering if you*
> *think I am*
> *clumsy*
> *wondering what you think of me.*
>
> *Will you like me*
> *if I move*
> *this way or that?*
> *Don't project*

---

*The voice of the inner witness as it appears throughout *Offering from the Conscious Body* is a composite of students' experiences and expressions.

all that is unconscious
in your own life
onto mine. Don't
interpret
my being.

I witness the mover for five minutes. It is time for her to bring her experience to an end. I call her name and ask her to open her eyes when she is ready. We make eye contact and she returns to her cushion.

After moving there are many ways of being. You can choose not to speak and we can sit together in silence. You can choose to speak of your arrival here now, what it is you experience coming out of all that movement. Or you can choose to open now toward finding words that are born, moment to moment, from the movement itself.

If you choose this way, try closing your eyes again as you begin discovering words, choosing some of them, surrendering into others, just as you discover, choose, or surrender into the movement itself when you are working in the space. This continuation of your inner focus as you are sitting here on your cushion also makes speaking in the present tense natural. The present tense reminds us, holds us, encourages us to remain in the embodied moving experience, riding it as it becomes language. Learning to speak experience rather than speaking about it means learning how to speak without abandoning the authenticity of the moving experience.

The shift from moving with eyes closed to talking with eyes open occurs over time. In the beginning, not only speaking in the present tense but speaking with eyes closed helps such a transition to become more seamless. Sometimes a mover, when embarking on the experience of speaking, reenters the gestures in a modified way while sitting here or actually returns to the wooden floor and walks through the movement, talking to me as she goes.

Try now to remember what your body was doing while you were moving, and perhaps the sequence of your movements. Together we will articulate a map that names, places, your body moving in time and space. This map is the essential ground from which all of our experience can become known.

. . . Embodied consciousness requires a study of articulation not only of body but of word. This mover begins speaking with very little consciousness of what she was actually doing. She is mostly merged with her moving self, her inner witness barely aware of her body's movement, at times her inner witness not present at all. Like this woman, many movers remember their movement only as they are reentering the gesture while speaking it into consciousness.

. . . The mover learns to keep asking: "Where am I now?" "What am I doing?" And responding: "Here I am. Here I am in front of the bowl, curled on my side, my hand resting on my cheek." Trying to be present for each moment of gesture invites the mover to take herself seriously. The mover learns about this new way of experiencing herself as she listens to me, her witness, taking each of her movements seriously. Doing this I am remembering her, marking, holding each gesture. When I name each gesture in this way the mover can learn that each one of her movements is worthy of being seen. This profoundly simple act of acknowledgement creates a spaciousness early in the development of the practice, before the mover and the witness share more of their experience.

Who Is the Witness?
A Description of Authentic Movement

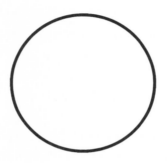

Like the river,
Return to the source.
Tao Te Ching

The Mary Starks Whitehouse Institute

In November of 1969 I closed my life in Pittsburgh and flew to Los Angeles to study with Mary Whitehouse, the first person to describe authentic movement in the presence of another. I went directly to Mary's studio, which was closed. Three doors down the block I found a motel room and settled there. Getting through to Mary by phone was impossible. Though we had not yet met, I knew she had just learned that she had multiple sclerosis and she knew I was coming. So I waited, mostly in the room, in case she returned my call. I ate popcorn and watched television for seven days. At the end of that preparation, we met and began work immediately. I came to her every day for either individual work, group work, theoretical work, breakfast, lunch, or dinner. We met at many levels during those five exceedingly rich months. Among the many things I learned from Mary, most importantly, she taught me about consciousness.

By mid-March of 1970 I had returned to the East Coast. I invited my first client to explore authentic movement in an old and beautiful light blue loft in Amherst, Massachusetts. For the following eleven years I sat in the corner of studios, in the presence of people descending toward themselves as we together learned about seeing and being seen.

In the Fall of 1981, two-and-a-half years after Mary's death, I was ready to try to objectively study the phenomenon of authentic movement in the presence of another without the complicating responsibilities of being a therapist. Because I learned the form, the basic structure of the work, from Mary, I named the center which I then founded "The Mary Starks Whitehouse Institute." Eight postgraduate students were invited to come for a nine-month intensive excursion into an infinitely mysterious process.

The outer form of this work is simple: one person moves in the presence of another. It was at this time at the Whitehouse Institute that I began to use, without realizing it, the term "witness" to describe the person whom Mary called the "observer" or "teacher." I imagine I learned of this word "witness" while working with my teacher, John Weir, a master psychologist, in 1969.

The witness, especially in the beginning, carries a larger responsibility for consciousness as she sits to the side of the movement space. She is not "looking at" the person moving, she is witnessing, listening, bringing a specific quality of attention or presence to the experience of the mover. The mover works with eyes closed in order to expand her experience of listening to the deeper levels of her kinesthetic reality. Her task is to respond to a sensation, to an inner impulse, to energy coming from the personal unconscious, the collective unconscious, or what Wilber calls the "superconscious."[1] Her response to this energy creates movement that can be visible or invisible to the witness. As the work deepens, the movement becomes organized in specific patterns, in specific body parts, within specific rhythmic and spatial forms. In a broader context, it often becomes most readily organized within the dominant function of the personality—that is guided more by emotion than intuition, or sensation rather than thinking.

After the mover moves, the mover and the witness usually speak together about the material that has emerged during the movement time, thus bringing formerly unconscious processes into consciousness. Though the mover's work, especially initially, is the primary focus of both the mover and the witness, the inner reality of the witness appears to be as vast, as complex, and as essential to the process as the inner world of the mover. With the movement of one as catalyst, the witness and the mover work together, over time, each refining her capacity to integrate her experience of formless material into form.

Before the Institute was established, I had some understanding of the relationship between the mover and the witness in the realm of therapy. In the preceding ten years I had been learning about the witness as a therapist and the mover as a client. In the dance world I was intrigued by some of the parallels between the therapist-client relationship and that of audience-dancer. By 1981 I wanted to be able to articulate what actually happened to the two people, before the movement or the witnessing carried specific meaning for the psyche, before symbol. I needed to describe the process.

As a mover, I knew in my bones about the relationship between surrender and will. Mary explained the experience of authentic movement as one of "being moved and moving" at the same time.[2] As this balance becomes manifest, one begins to lose the illusion that one is anything other than one's body. In so doing, what is ultimately affirmed is the body, not the knowledge of the body.

Even though I had been a witness for a decade, because the witness does not move, I did not fully understand the relationship between surrender and will in that experience. There are two major reasons why it is more difficult. First, the witness is responsible for seeing her mover as well as her self. Second, the witness does not enact or engage in her own experience; she witnesses it. Thus the Institute was created to gain a deeper understanding of the experience of the witness and of the relationship between the witness and the mover.

Each week in the Institute, the interns and I met for a theoretical seminar, for a group training experience, and for training experiences in dyads. They also met weekly with my deeply gifted colleague, Edith Sullwold, for a seminar focused on the emergence of creative forms. The first task was to teach the experience of moving authentically. Then, because, by definition, learning to be a mover must precede learning to be a witness, the interns were asked to be silent witnesses for the first three months of training. Finally, when we began to explore and share actively our inner realities as witnesses, those experiences became visibly more complex.

Several months after beginning the Institute, I repeatedly saw the following shape in my mind:

I began to see the dynamics of the two parties as inseparably linked. This is how the process might be described when it is working well. The witness (the light curve) is witnessing the mover (the dark curve) move. Suddenly, the mover becomes immersed in material that engages her totally (marked by the X). In the intensity of her experience, she has seemingly forgotten her witness and lost her self-consciousness. Her movement is more dominant than her mental image of her witness. She might be feeling, repressing, or expressing anger, joy, confusion, sadness. She might be seeing images, hearing sounds, immersed in a memory, or thinking a particular thought. She might be simply experiencing the kinesthetic sensation of the movement. Any or all of this is happening between the X and the O.

Simultaneously, at the moment of the X, something is awakened in the witness by the particular movement quality or form of the mover. Now both people have embarked on their own individual path. The witness is having her own active internal experience: image, sound, feeling, idea, memory, kinesthetic sensation. Because of this awakening, there has been a shift in the quality of the presence of the witness. In some ways, though the empty space between them in the drawing symbolizes how powerfully they are connected, the witness and the mover are separate. When the witness is fully alive to the mover, she is, paradoxically, completely present in relation to her own inner experience. They meet again, in dialogue (at the O), where new consciousness and insight can become apparent, possibly shared and even expanded.

Another, and, perhaps, more authentic, representation of this process would be a shape that reflects not only the passage of time but the fact of sequential places of meeting and not meeting. It might look something like this:

As the work develops and the discipline of the mover becomes refined, she learns to internalize the witness. This seems to happen exactly the way the infant, with no sense of self, gradually develops one, because he internalizes the mother. Thus the mover learns consciously to witness her own unconscious material as it finds form through her movement. As this begins to happen, the same experiential loop or loops in the drawings can represent the process of one person rather than two.

For the mover, the dark curve represents the process of moving and the light curve now represents the process of internal self-witness. Here, too, in the beginning (before the X), there is a self-conscious awareness of witnessing oneself. When the mover and the internal witness meet (at the X), they lose their sense of distinctiveness. She can "see" herself as she is. Insight can follow at the O.

But for the witness, the same drawing appears to be incomplete. Though the dark curve can represent the process of her own internal activity, it also must somehow represent the movement she sees in her mover. Similarly, the light curve must represent not only her internal self-witness but her continuous and dominant process of witnessing the mover. Her loop, one of double vision, then, could look like this:

Authentic Movement and Psychoanalytic Work

By the end of the first year, with the skeletal map described above, I began to understand this developing relationship between moving and witnessing as a discipline. Somehow, I named the discipline "Authentic Movement," based on Mary's phrase, which describes a specific kind of movement. But, without realizing it, I began to use these words to speak of not only the experience of the mover but of the witness and of the developing relationship between the mover and the witness.

We continued to primarily carry our consciousness of the discipline within a psychoanalytic framework. When the witness enters the work within the perspective of psychodynamic process, she is a trained therapist with a strong background in the psychology of movement, developmental psychology, and psychoanalytic theory. Such knowledge rides immediately behind and informs her intuitive capacity to know, to see, and to hear the presence of her own body and the body of her mover.

There are many similarities between psychoanalytic treatment and Authentic Movement. The client in psychoanalysis lies on a couch so that he cannot see the analyst sitting behind him. In Authentic Movement the mover also cannot see the witness because her eyes are closed. This fact seems to be of paramount importance in both traditions. Such a format invites surrender to the process that ensues—that of free association. The client in psychoanalysis is encouraged primarily to develop and use the mode of free association. Similarly, the mover, in developing the discipline of Authentic Movement, is engaged from the beginning in a free associative process, but at a nonverbal level.

Both disciplines require long-term work because regression in the service of the ego is not possible otherwise. Because of the natural wisdom of the body and its capacity to store every memory at a seemingly bone level, Authentic Movement is particularly helpful to people who have experienced early, especially preverbal, trauma. Transference and countertransference are thus inherent and central forces in both ways of work. The clientele for both is also similar. Both disciplines are most helpful to adults who have a strong enough ego structure to choose and to sustain extensive exploration of the unconscious. When a client enters either analysis or Authentic Movement for treatment, there is an assumed end to the work. The major difference between the two ways is that the analytic client usually lies still and the mover actively embodies the material. In so doing, the experience of being "seen" is somehow heightened and elongated.

Within this psychoanalytic framework of Authentic Movement, the mover actually feels bound to her personal body. The qualities of time, space, and weight are specific to, and in direct relationship to, her experience of her body. Her body is her ego. The attitude of the witness toward the mover is nurturing, protective, empathic, and parental at times. The witness honors the mover's dependency on her and understands its value. Talking together after the movement clarifies and slowly organizes the material within the language of psychodynamic theory. This sharing can reduce tension and expand the understanding of both people, and it is almost certain to develop a deep bond between them.

Authentic Movement and Meditative Practice

As the first group of interns—therapists and artists—brought their intensive training to a close, my own experience of reality was undergoing unsolicited and terrific change. Perhaps, because the laws of nature have a tendency toward balance, my extreme concentration on the personality was irrevocably shifted to an awakened awareness of transpersonal energies. These energies imply experiences that are not related to personality or to personal history. Witnessing myself surrendering to this impersonal force brought me toward a new understanding of the relationship between surrender and will as a witness. Related to my work with John Weir, we have made the assumption that the mover can only go as far as her witness has gone. Consciousness of transpersonal energy in the experience of the witness automatically expands the potential experience of the mover.

By the time the second group of interns—again artists and therapists—came the following fall of 1982, this new consciousness created new questions. For example, we began to notice that there were times when the mover did not seem bound to her personal body. Her energy was not contained there and the qualities of time, space, and weight were not specific. Those qualities were not felt in relation to the body ego.

When this transpersonal energy was apparent, we realized that the attitude of the witness toward the mover was quite different. Because in these situations the material with which the mover is working is not about her personality, the witness is seeing from a place not circumscribed by her personality.

It seemed that under these circumstances the dynamics of transference and countertransference, as we have come to understand them in therapeutic work, are less central, less binding and, somehow, expanded. The witness can experience herself beyond the boundaries of her personality as she shares the same energy field with the mover. She is seeing with much less projection, judgment, and involvement in content. Talking afterward is often not helpful. There is not the same need to sort, organize, and understand the material within the language of psychodynamic theory. At these times there is an experience of no edges, no boundaries. There is a sense of clarity, within and without, a feeling literally of no density, no obstruction, no place in the body through which light cannot move. In these situations, the body becomes a vessel through which energy or light can pass unobstructed.

The psychoanalytic framework began to feel limited, as if we needed a larger form within which we might understand the process. It began to be apparent that the roots of the discipline stretched more broadly than originally conceived. Psychodynamic theories of the ego structure were only one root system. Though much less familiar to me, meditative practice and its roots in Eastern philosophy was another. We have just begun to articulate some of the similarities and differences between Authentic Movement and meditation.

In both disciplines there is a primary focus on the relationship between observation and action. However, in meditation both the witness and the activity are internal.* Usually, the meditator is not actively moving his body although his experience of his body is a very active aspect of this process. He learns to be an undistracted observer of his body and of his mind. The activity in meditation is that of the active mind, which automatically includes the sensed body.

The discipline of Authentic Movement, at the basic level, is about the relationship between two people, the witness and the mover. Initially, one takes the role of the one who sees and the other the role of the one who is seen. Yet, as the work develops, a conscious witness emerges within the mind of the mover and, concomitantly, unconscious activity surfaces within the experience of the witness. Increasingly, like the meditator, both mover and witness carry the tension and the union between these polarities within themselves.

*Here Janet is referring to sitting meditation. Mindfulness meditation, which includes all postures and activities, invites further comparisons.

In both the discipline of Authentic Movement and meditation there is a continuous effort to witness the conscious mind as it habitually interferes with the deep listening encouraged in both practices. In both ways of work several years of commitment are necessary for a continuous development of the process, which can bring experiences of balance, clarity, and wholeness. The major difference between these two disciplines is that meditation usually requires specific body posture. In Authentic Movement the "right way" is defined through the movement itself, not specific body shape or form but only the shape that awakens or is awakened by the psyche, the spirit, or the Self.

People who seriously practice meditation or Authentic Movement are similar in that they have an established body ego structure. They are people with a self-awareness, an ability to concentrate, a curiosity about the unknown. The longer both of these disciplines are practiced, the more developed is the witnessing mind. Such development produces a sense of clarity in relation to one's own behavior, enacted or internal. A long-term commitment to either way of work can occasionally generate an intense experience of spiritual rebirth.

Beginning to understand Authentic Movement as a spiritual as well as a therapeutic discipline offered new perspectives on the work. By the end of the second year of the Institute it was clear that through Authentic Movement a broad developmental spectrum of energy can be manifested from preverbal to transverbal, preegoic to transegoic, from subconscious to "superconscious." We have come to believe, as does Wilber,[3] that people need not be prisoners of their history but are impelled to transcend it.

Relationship between Personal and Transpersonal Experience in Authentic Movement

I would like to offer here three examples of Authentic Movement work that concern the relationship between personal and transpersonal experience: one in which the witness, Julia, consciously chose to respond to the mover's personal material from a transpersonal perspective; one in which the witness, Gail, consciously chose to respond to the mover's transpersonal material from a personal position; and one in which the mover, Lila, worked with both personal and transpersonal energy while her witness was synchronous with her throughout the experience.

In Julia's case the mover was talking about her need to be near Julia, to be held by Julia, to be nurtured. In her movement she repeatedly moved close to Julia, touching her and struggling with her need to climb into Julia's lap. Finally, she forcefully rolled into Julia and began crying as she lay face down in front of her. Julia felt a pull to gather her up and rock her. While debating within herself how to respond to the situation, she realized she had shifted to sitting on her knees, had placed her right hand on the mover's back and heard herself saying inside: "Protect this woman. Let her remain in this position, as she is now, as long as she needs to. May she learn to be patient, to allow time to experience her pain and to know when to get up." Julia had moved from a pull to be the woman's "mother" to another pull to be her "spiritual mother." When the mover finally got up, she reported a feeling of great peace. She said that the experience felt "just right," though she did not understand what, if anything, had happened.

In Gail's case the mover was sitting with legs crossed, rocking in a deep but sharp rhythm, with a "beatific" expression on her face. Her hands were crossed over her heart. When she finished moving and began speaking, she talked of white light encircling her heart, opening it and then radiating throughout the room. Gail, in response, spoke of her images and feelings as she watched the movement. She felt as though she was in the presence of a fifteen-month-old baby who was all alone, rocking, maybe to soothe herself, and "looking like" she was detached or not related to what her body was doing. Gail felt deep sadness and wanted to rock her baby. When hearing this, the mover began to cry and talk of early abandonment and her attraction to "religious" experiences as the only way to forget about her loss and pain.

We have found, as Mary did, that a witness must learn the very subtle differences between being quiet and letting the experience stand alone and speaking about it. She must further learn, as the preceding vignettes reveal, discernment regarding the differences between personal and transpersonal experiences in her body as she witnesses, as well as what she chooses to share with her mover.

In the following description, as the witness, I continually responded to the mover's work out of a similar energy source from which she seemed to be moving. In this case, Lila's movement work was both personal and transpersonal in one session. In this particular session there is a clear sequential order, with the movement originating continually from a deep and unconscious impulse. Although she had done extensive work as an intern in the Institute over a period of time preceding this session, the breadth of material within one session is unusual.

What follows is my experience as the witness of Lila's work. She begins lying against a wall as an infant, with deep pleasure in her own sounds, her skin sensation, her nondifferentiated movement. Her fingers look and act like those of a baby as they explore her mouth and her skin. I feel peaceful, soft, and content. Now, with no apparent line of demarcation, the same fingers become those of a young girl, of a preadolescent. They are tentative, not lingering, and are moving under what might be a self-conscious eye. Now Lila shows clear signs of distress as if she is actually in physical pain. Her hands eventually pull herself into a sitting position. I feel anxious, a bit confused and wanting to help.

As this phase of the work progresses, her arms cross. Her left hand is delicate and exposed, her right hand grows large and strong. Now she begins to look like a woman. She seems grounded as she stands up, reflecting a quality of firmness as she leads with her right hand. It is as though the space between her head and her pelvis fills up, fills in, becomes solid and mobile. I feel relief, wonder, and met in the presence of this woman.

Again, with no recognizable transition, Lila changes, this time into a woman with great strength and clarity but, at the same time, with less and less form. The quality of her movement is larger than her physical form. It is as though a figure has arrived from the inside of her form but now extends, in its expression, vastly beyond her form. She stands much taller than her usual self, her head turned to the left as her fingers and face reflect a very ephemeral quality. Her face actually appears radiant as this quality sustains itself. Her "Lady" has appeared, an archetypal guide and teacher familiar to her from earlier work. My body becomes warmer and slowly my awareness of my weight and form diffuses. I experience wholeness, within myself and with Lila.

In this one session Lila traversed and embodied a time span that included moments of resolved and unresolved personality work as well as a moment beyond her ego structure in which the pain and pleasure of her personal history and present reality were transcended.

New Questions

Enlarging the perspective of Authentic Movement work to include the spiritual as well as the psychological not only enriches the work in significant ways but also creates new questions. Using Lila's work as a base, it seems appropriate here to explore some of the questions.

Is it useful to use the spectrum as developmental?

That is, should personal work precede transpersonal work? It is clear that the stronger the body-psyche connection, the more the body can contain, withstand, and ground the spirit. A well-developed ego structure helps an individual not to identify with material from the transpersonal realm. In Lila's case, because there is still work to be done with the shadow at the time of adolescence, encounters with the shadow in the transpersonal realm could be premature.

On the other hand, though the logic of personal work preceding transpersonal work seems convincing, could the opposite also be true? Can transpersonal energy guide and direct personal growth? The answer must have something to do with timing. In Lila's case it seemed as though the Lady was instructing the less developed aspects of the adolescent Lila, helping her to grow up: "By example, by the Lady being in my body, I could know by experience how to be in my body as a woman instead of an adolescent."

In Lila's case transpersonal energy was helpful and, perhaps, no more helpful than a psychological exploration would have been. It seems that there are times when this energy is the only source of help and, ultimately perhaps, an essential source in order to perceive this world as a whole. Continual effort to see all experience within the framework of the ego structure can dramatically limit an individual's capacity to see oneself. On the other hand, as in the case of Gail's mover, transpersonal energy can distract, confuse, seduce, enchant, inflate a mover so that essential developmental work within the ego system is avoided or even betrayed.

Is it necessary for the witness to offer the mover a form, beyond the body itself, within which she can bring her experience to consciousness?

First, is it essential for the mover to talk after moving, make associations or consciously remember personal history? We know that movement followed by talking can expand the experience, especially when the material concerns personal history. Words as symbols are often a natural way to respond to the movement work, a common language for the witness and mover. Sometimes images as symbols are deeply connected to the material. If images are dominant and/or there is little specific emotional content, making a drawing, a piece of sculpture, or creating a dance or story are vivid and rich ways of bringing form to and further enhancing the energy that has been awakened. When strong emotional content or transpersonal energy first infuse the movement, it can often be overwhelming in its newness and power. When this happens, or when significant transitions occur, verbal response from the witness seems helpful.

Are there times when any response, verbal or other, from the witness or mover is unnecessary? Logically, it seems that as long as we live in the human form, at some level our need for form exists. Some movers report that when the experience is transegoic, sometimes there is not a need for form other than the form of the body itself to either contain the energy or release the energy into an experience of no form, no boundaries. Can the body be the container, the form, in relationship to the energy? Is it possible that the movement witnessed over a long period of time can be intrinsically transformative, whether the energy source is personal or transpersonal? Can this process, without the overlay of Western psychological theory, be in itself a cohesive and sufficient way of knowing?

As a witness of Lila's work, I felt as though I had nothing to say in response, though I often spoke in response to work that preceded this session when both personal and transpersonal work were the center. This time it was as though her body was a sufficient container, a form that could completely hold and sustain her energy at any point along the spectrum of work as it developed. The work resolved itself. As witness of this work, it seemed unnecessary to offer anything beyond my presence, which felt synchronous with her experience.

Can one ever do Authentic Movement without a witness?
Certainly, within a therapeutic context, by definition, a witness is essential. As long as the mover is developing a "good enough"* internal witness and as long as the phenomenon of tension, which is a primary seed for growth, is apparent, the presence of an external witness is critical. When the unknown is being explored through the arrival of and encounter with unconscious activity, there is often the element of fear and/or awe. The presence of another in either case can be a response to the human need for safety, containment, or balance.

However, when fear and/or awe are not experienced as overwhelming, it becomes less and less clear why a mover working, especially with transpersonal energy, needs a designated witness. Would Lila have been able to move through the energy layers as she did in the session being discussed if she had been alone? Moving toward the answer to this question first concerns the idiosyncrasies of Lila and this particular session: Lila's familiarity with the personal aspects of the work, her tolerance for and understanding of the pain around the unresolved adolescent

---

*The phrase "good enough mother" was first coined in 1953 by Donald Winnicott, a British pediatrician and psychoanalyst. Winnicott observed thousands of babies and their mothers, and he came to realize that babies and children actually benefit when their mothers fail them in manageable ways. Janet has said: "This phrase had a continuous and important effect on my understanding of wholeness and how it differs from perfection. . . . Wholeness includes all of everything, especially as consciousness invites compassion for our own imperfections." (From a personal communication.)

work, whether or not the Lady had appeared before and the quality of energy radiating from the Lady. But, most important, was her nonattachment to her ego—to the self needing to be seen—so established that the intrinsic power of her internal witness could carry the intensity and clarity of the experience?

Relative to this question, there is a larger context. One of the very first experiences of life is that of being seen. The parent witnesses the infant. The infant, as it grows into childhood and adulthood, moves through endless experiences of being seen and seeing oneself. This could be one way of describing the development of the self. It is interesting to notice in our movement work so far that being seen inevitably precedes seeing oneself: "I can't see myself here. First you see me as I am in this unknown place, then I begin to witness myself anew."

Witnessing oneself in Authentic Movement can thus only be developed through extensive experience, first as a mover being seen by a witness. Because of being witnessed, the mover is automatically developing an internal witness, which is, in turn, preparing her to witness another. (It never, of course, is so neatly developmental in practice.) It is at this point, mastering the witnessing of another—loving another—that the next essential step occurs. For no matter how well and objectively one can witness oneself, that self-witnessing is transformed after truly seeing another as she is. It is as though there is now a reversal. In the same way that being seen by another originally enabled me to see myself as I am, in a further sweep of the spiral, seeing another as she is—loving her— enables me to see myself as I am. This is a different seeing myself as I am because it is no longer birthed by another—the mother, therapist, witness, or lover.

This seeing myself as I am is birthed by myself and is it not then a birth of humility? It somehow miraculously evolves from loving rather than being loved. The deepest longing now has shifted from being seen as I am by another to seeing another as she is, others as they are, my universe anew. And so the cycle continues to recreate itself, each time expanding consciousness. Increasingly, the concern is about seeing and loving. Being seen by another gradually becomes irrelevant and uninteresting. Now who is the witness? A synopsis of this spiral could be:

I long to be seen (narcissism)
I feel seen (trust)
I long to see myself (ego)
I see myself (healthy ego)
I long to see another (love)
I see another (compassion)
I see us both as one (union)

Did Lila's body actually look different when the personal energy was active than when the transpersonal energy was manifest? If so, how?

As mentioned earlier, we have been trying to learn to see how the body itself is different, literally, when moving from a transpersonal source of energy rather than a personal source of energy. The Japanese word *koshi* means "essence of the body." It refers to the pelvic bone. In my opinion, this is the first, and continues to be the most important, place in which there is a difference. As the Lady entered Lila's body, her pelvis held her in a very specific way, a way which I sadly cannot yet articulate. As the interns worked, especially in the first two years, I witnessed some of them, sometimes, "drop" into the essence of the body, the pelvis. As this happened, the work inevitably shifted toward a greater capacity to contain larger amounts of energy.

When the pelvis is free from unresolved developmental issues, when the psyche's energy can ride in the pelvis unblocked, and when the legs and the feet can ground the pelvis, then transpersonal energy can be ignited from the "ground" up, as in the rise of the kundalini, which can begin at the base of the spine. This grounding can sometimes assure a safer and, possibly, more integrated spiritual journey.

Another place in Lila's body in which a distinct difference was obvious was in her wrists, hands, and fingers. When the Lady arrived, the quality of this area of her body became heightened, as if her hands were almost shaping mudras in the most organic and unconscious way. Two associations come immediately to mind. First, there are the autistic, autoerotic children whose wrists, hands, and fingers are so distinctly expressive. Having never bonded, these children live at the beginning of the spiral of human development in a preegoic state. They spin, they rock, they can seem "out of this world." Second, there are the people found in the expanded sweeps of the same spiral, whose wrists, hands, and fingers, in the form of mudras, reflect a transegoic state. Some of these people, as messengers between God and man, spin, rock, and sway. They too can seem "out of this world." The autistic child can be as focused, as passionately engaged in repetitive spinning, as is the whirling dervish. Though one is preegoic and the other transegoic, we cannot help to ask: "What is the relationship between these two kinds of people? How do they know one another? Where do they meet or have they met within the mandala of life?"

To come back toward the center, whether the energy source is personal or transpersonal, whether the experience is one of regression or egression, underneath the differences the basic ground is always the same in Authentic Movement. With an increasing capacity to concentrate, to listen to inner impulse, the mover learns to recognize the channel within which the creative or authentic energy flows. In so doing, each movement, no matter how small, becomes impeccably ordered, placed, or sensed. Her honoring that knowledge holds the transformative power of this work. In both personal and transpersonal work the mover learns to allow and accept the early experience of chaos, of irrational forms embodied or imagined, of not knowing.

In both ways of work the witness must honor her developing awareness in exactly the same way as the mover, but she contains her experience rather than actively expressing it. She learns to begin a session with no expectations, no plans, no directions to her mover. The witness strives to bear, to contain, to embrace her experience of the early chaos within her mover, the irrational and idiosyncratic patterns that emerge, the unknown that is explored in her presence. She is also open to the messages from her own unconscious and is responsible for a growing consciousness of them. She is highly selective in choosing what to share with her mover of her own internal process.

Death, loss, and suffering are integral aspects of both ways. Encounters with the shadow within the frame of transference and countertransference bring death of old patterns, old ways in which the ego developed in its need for survival. In the transpersonal work there is also the possibility of a death, death of the self as it was known prior to a spiritual rebirth:

> In the beginning, dance was the sacred language through which we communicated with the vast unknown. In these earliest times, the dancer was at the same time healer and priest. Then, through the centuries, in the name of progress and civilization, mind and body were split apart.[4]

The collective unconscious was "the beginning." The personal unconscious evolved from it. From that came personal consciousness. Now our task, and our longing, still in an effort to heal a split, is to bring our consciousness as individuals into a conscious collective. Though the collective unconscious informs and instructs us in this task, there is no way back. Transegoic is completely different from preegoic.

It is interesting to note a parallel, admittedly a general one, in the evolution of Authentic Movement. Often, the first format is a group of people moving with a single witness. The first task of the witness is to begin to distinguish elements of the collective unconscious from elements of the individual or personal unconscious. Next, the experience of an individual moving usually deepens when she is witnessed alone, the result often being an opportunity for strengthening the development of her individual consciousness. In this year, the fourth year of the Institute, we have found ourselves working within a form that might reflect a part of the next step. One individual, after many months of being witnessed by one person, moves alone in the middle of a circle of eight witnesses. These eight people, a conscious collective, help to carry, contain, and strengthen the mover as well as themselves. Each witness, then, one by one, creates and strengthens the experience of the mover as well as the other witnesses.

To bring this discussion of the evolutionary process in the Authentic Movement work toward completion, we are finding that after years of sitting still as witnesses, the individuals forming the circle around the mover are beginning to join the mover, to move again themselves, but this time as personally conscious individuals dancing together. At this point, sacred dance is revealed as the true source of the work. Marian Chace, in her original dance therapy groups, from my perspective, offered a way to embody the collective unconscious.[5] Mary Whitehouse offered a way to explore the relationship between the personal unconscious and personal consciousness.[6] Now these two traditions begin to unfold into the manifestation of the conscious collective.

Conclusion

Whether challenged by the unknown within the embodiment of personal or collective consciousness, the evolutionary process that we are each living, as clients, therapists, artists, and seekers, is about the transformative power of suffering. The task of locating, listening to, and then trusting the guide within is always, by definition, hard work. Much of the work in Authentic Movement is difficult, painful, redundant, and frustrating. It involves hiding, risking, premature insight, and paralysis, as well as reward. When it works, as when a piece of art works, the clarity and simplicity—the gift of wholeness—is stunning.

Inherent in being a person in the cultures of the West is the longing for a witness. We want, deeply want, to be seen as we are by another. We want to be witnessed. Ultimately, we want to witness, to love, another. Jung speaks of the phenomenon of the witness:

Thus the underlying idea of the psyche proves it to be a half bodily, half spiritual substance, an *anima media natura,* as the alchemists call it, an hermaphroditic being capable of uniting the opposites, but who is never complete in the individual unless related to another individual. The unrelated human being lacks wholeness, for he can achieve wholeness only through the soul, and the soul cannot exist without its other side, which is always found in a "You."[7]

Traditionally, people expect such a blessing in relationship to a parent, a mate, a child, a friend, or a god. We are given or not given, find or don't find, create or destroy that "other," or the potential for that "other," as we move through our lives. Whether the other is another individual, God, or the god within, our developing relationship with that other is one of our greatest tasks, one of our greatest opportunities. Archetypally, we experience this in images of loving parents, of their union with each other, of their union with us. We live always in relationship to these archetypes, though as we grow they evolve and deepen into the union of Earth and Spirit. Authentic Movement is one more way—Mary Whitehouse called it the "Tao" of the body—a way that can lead to union and wholeness, whatever the source or shape of energy, as it infuses the time and space of our lives.

Remarks at the Closing of the Mary Starks Whitehouse Institute

I wish to tell you a little about what I have been learning because of the Institute: from the work itself, from each of you here, and from the kundalini which is so inextricably and profoundly woven within my experience of our work together.

The Work

+ I created the Institute so that I could understand authentic movement. I learned instead that authentic movement does not get understood, it becomes manifest.
+ I learned that this way of work is a *discipline,* one sourced in witness presence, because:
  - it requires concentration, full commitment in ongoing practice which can ultimately lead to the experience of being moved by something larger than the self.
  - it has ethics, aesthetics, a deep structure, a desire for that which is true.
  - it is riddled with paradox, which means it invites again and again, as we become more fully ourselves, an experience of not knowing.
+ I learned that the work is an art because it concerns:
  - depth revealing darkness, profundity.
  - simplicity, which can appear within a longing to reveal the depth of emptiness in space, stillness, and silence.

- stillness in movement, motion in stillness.
- asymmetry, as assumed perfection must be broken.
- naturalness, which can be an expression of the "nonself" without willfulness.
- external loneliness, which can invite becoming one with the Divine.

+ Thus as our movement becomes conscious, because of the discipline—the work of it, the art of it—we become more our clear selves and thus automatically become a "home ground" for others.

Each of You

Edith—You make an enormous and deep contribution, teaching about ritual, about the collective, about loving. How you love each one of us, one by one. You carried the entire institute single-handedly on several occasions when I was challenged by the energy.

Kendall—Witnessing you watch the egg in the fire. You teach me that I don't have to witness so carefully right now. I learn: someone else, Kendall, can witness.

Barbara—Your arms out, in space, against the window, against the couch, flat on the floor. You teach me about never really knowing what another's experience is, never.

Linde—Seated in front of me, on the white rug, our legs crossed, your gift of the braid, your question about fear. You teach first through your moving and then through your speaking, "The witness is the mover."

Nancy—You and Barbara stand together in the Henshaw studio by the door to the study. You are weeping, to me it seems for all of us, for everything. And often in your movement, I see, I hear you weep about no edges when the self is manifest.

Chris—On your back, this winter, legs and arms up, delicate, receptive, sensual, waiting, exquisitely pulsing. You teach me, when I feel I can only see in the dark and therefore, like a child, no one can see me, that you do see me. This happens when you give me the pearl.

Sidney—Your bare arm going up three times: and the insight you name about the origin of that gesture. And then when you raise that same arm to ask if maybe Authentic Movement is a spiritual discipline.

Libby—Drawing circles on the floor, repetitive, focused, infinite. You teach me about an aspect of loyalty. Within a mysterious crucible that you create, I see a consistently clear smooth green line, in the midst of everything.

Carol—Roaring under the body form, the power, the vibrations, the wholeness of it. You teach me about extreme opposites being the same. I need to learn this from you because the extremes can be so great within me.

Elizabeth—Your hand touching your mother in her grave. In that moment I learn something about the place between "fire and ice," which maybe you know something about.

Jennifer—Spinning in the Hartford studio, your vibrancy and stillness at once. You teach me about receiving love.

Shelley—Walking nowhere, hands in your pockets. You teach me about how sometimes things are how they feel rather than how they appear to be or need to be.

Joanne—Spiraling backward toward the window, conch shell. You teach me about endurance. I need to know this.

Celeste—I see you choosing the long, tapered candle. Turning toward Rosalind with such clear eye contact, you place it in her hands. You teach me about humility.

And Rosalind, spread gently over us all throughout this journey, you are a deep wisdom, an exquisite presence, a spiritual mother, the one who rakes the leaves, and rakes the leaves and rakes the leaves, with no judgment about the leaves.

The Kundalini

In the beginning of my initiation, the visions occurred within a
circle that you women created around me as my experience of my
will and my capacity to surrender deepen.

I am learning to listen a little better, to see a little more clearly, to
love a little more compassionately, to trust the order, the impeccable order of the forces that be.

Rosalind just told me yesterday about the pearl—the one you gave me,
Chris—and how it is created out of the irritation that the oyster feels.
Artists create form the same way. We have created a pearl together the
same way, with commitment, with love. To whom it will be of value, or
how, when, or where, we don't know.

CHAPTER FOUR

THE COLLECTIVE
BODY EMERGING

Longing toward Belonging

Introduction
By Bonnie Morrissey & Paula Sager

This work is a discipline because it is riddled with paradox,
which means it invites again and again, as we become
more fully ourselves, an experience of not knowing.

JANET ADLER, "REMARKS AT THE CLOSING OF
THE MARY STARKS WHITEHOUSE INSTITUTE"

After the closing of the Mary Starks Whitehouse Institute, during the years of recovery and return from her initiation, Janet might have chosen to create a more cloistered and solitary life. Instead, she engages further in her teaching practice, welcoming new students and beginning extensive research into the literature of mystical experience. By 1992, after moving with her family to California, Janet completes a doctorate in mystical studies,* placing her personal experience within the field of cross-cultural experiences of initiation.

The process of integrating the energy and teachings of her initiation direct Janet toward a deepening inquiry concerning the individual's embodied relationship to the collective. Her experience of having been "hurled into an infinite universe"[1] demands that her attention stretch to include these experiences of energetic phenomena as well as questions

---

*Janet received her doctorate in mysticism from The Union Institute in 1992. Her dissertation is "Arching Backward and a Cross-Cultural Study of Mysticism as the Context for a Phenomenological Study." Part One is the basis for her book *Arching Backward* (1995). Part Two provides the foundation of her essay "Body and Soul."

concerning membership in a group. Her teaching practice opens in new directions as she works with larger groups, widening circles often comprising twenty to thirty or more individuals. Increasing numbers of students from Europe and South America travel to North America or commit to annual retreats in Italy and Greece. New questions arise as Janet and her students learn about the impact of culture and language on an inner life.

Within these large retreat groups and in response to some students' desire to move as long as they would like, a form emerges that comes to be called the *long circle,* a structure she hopes will contain and support each group's process as well as the development of each individual within the group. The long circle brings a new fluidity to the roles of mover and witness. Students follow their inclinations from witnessing in the outer circle with open eyes to entering and moving with eyes closed, drawn back and forth intuitively or at will.

Some students who work with Janet during these innovative years of larger groups will go on to teach versions of the long circle from their own developing perspectives, thus spawning multiple iterations of Authentic Movement practice, many still vital today. Janet's own inner need to study witness consciousness will continue to press her forward, and her work with the long circle will subsequently be replaced by the *declaring circle,* in which each student commits to embodying one role, either mover or witness, for the duration of the round of practice. The evolutionary architecture of the Discipline of Authentic Movement means that some former structures and guidelines will inevitably transform or be shed, each one appreciated as once necessary though no longer needed. While the full breadth and comprehensiveness of her contribution to the evolution of the discipline will not manifest until the early decades of the 2000s, each of the essays and the interview included in this chapter reflect Janet's penetrating inquiry and collaborative work with students during the 1990s.

~

Janet draws from her doctoral research in her 1992 work "Body and Soul,"* the first essay in which she clearly introduces what she is teaching as both a discipline *and* a mystical practice, now sometimes referring to it as the "discipline of Authentic Movement," though not yet capitalizing the word "discipline." The most academic of Janet's essays, "Body and Soul" illuminates the ways in which this practice is similar to and different from other mystical practices, especially those rooted in ancient religious or world traditions.

Direct experience of the numinous through the physical body is a common thread within and among mystical traditions. Observing her own inner changes, Janet describes the presence of energetic phenomena as it refines, changing form within her body:

> In practicing my movement discipline, my intention shifted from moving to stillness. It is there, in the emptiness and silence, that the longing to listen magnifies and I encounter an increasing awareness of vibrational inner sound, the infinite and subtle nuances of highly specific frequency variations.[2]

While they may or may not go through their own initiatory process, committed students of the discipline recognize energetic phenomena as an important aspect of a depth study of embodied consciousness, and they recognize direct experience as an occurrence that may become possible for anyone. The placing of the discipline within the lineage of mystical traditions helps Janet's students have the courage to speak these experiences, to find words to name and to honor direct experience of energetic phenomena, as she herself has learned to do. Both words and silence are held and valued more consciously as students discern what can or must be spoken from what is not yet ready or cannot be spoken.

---

*"Body and Soul" was first published in *American Journal of Dance Therapy* 14 (1992): 73–94 and was later published in *Authentic Movement: Essays by Mary Starks Whitehouse, Janet Adler, and Joan Chodorow*, edited by Patrizia Pallaro (Philadelphia: Jessica Kingsley Publishers, 1999), 160–89.

Experience of the numinous, a human birthright, may be reclaimed as we bring to consciousness, through language, our awareness of that which is beyond language.[3]

Within such humbling and empowering inquiry, continuing attention to psychological patterns creates a foundation for distinguishing elements of unresolved personal history from experiences that are sourced from outside of personality. As students of the discipline encounter and seek to integrate embodied experiences of energetic phenomena, they may face challenges similar to those described within the literature of mystical experience. Ongoing commitment to psychological development helps to reduce unconscious projections and to prevent such dangers as the conflation of personality with experiences of the divine, an intrinsic hazard along any path that includes direct experience. Remaining diligent in working with both the gifts and hindrances of personality cultivates qualities of presence and humility. This serves as an antidote to both inflation and deflation, grounding our experiences of the numinous within the context of everyday life. Over time, because of Janet's insistence on an ongoing process of discernment, the relationship of energetic phenomena to suffering and to healing becomes apparent.

As the inner work of this practice unfolds, deeply embedded psychological patterns may continue to heal, essentially "emptying" the personality of content that obstructs the development of a quality of presence. Patterns of trauma held within the cellular structures of the body may soften, release, and integrate, allowing new spaciousness, resilience, and resourcefulness. Our willingness to stand with attentive, radical, even devotional openness at the edge of what is known invites us toward a more intimate relationship with the infinite, the eternal, the mysteries of the universe—not somewhere else but right here within the lived experience of our individual bodies.

In concluding "Body and Soul," Janet writes, "Now our task . . . is to bring our consciousness as individuals into a conscious collective," anticipating the central theme of her next major essay, "The Collective

Body,"* which follows in this chapter. Originally presented as a keynote address at the first International Dance/Movement Therapy Conference in Berlin, this essay reaveals the vast scope of Janet's inquiry, spanning from cell to universe, as well as her widening developmental perspective on the evolution of human consciousness. "The Collective Body" opens with a simple avowal of humility, a declaration of forgetting and long-ing, as she lays bare the far-reaching conundrum of the question "Who am I?" She reminds us that the privilege of individual development and self-knowledge is neither sufficient nor sustainable if it "excludes an integrated relationship to the whole."

Janet's concerns are critically relevant to our current world-wide suffering, her writing infused with a poignant sense of urgency. "Overemphasis on individual development encouraged outside of a sacred circle," she writes, "has contributed significantly to the creation of unbearable rage, isolation, and despair." An ecological consciousness emerges from her own embodied knowing, through unitive experiences of her body as one with the body of Earth. "It is in our bodies where the phenomenon of life energy, a physical reality, is directly experienced," writes Janet. She invokes the human being's shared structure with all of nature and the way in which, at a cellular level, each body shares mem-bership with each other living being.

In the studio practice, Janet and her students are "mucking about," as she would often say, slowly discovering a felt sense of belonging to a group, grounded in the embodied and distinct truth of each person. The longing to know oneself as an individual interweaves with the long-ing to know oneself as part of a whole, and the phrase "I am the one who . . ." emerges as a link, a storied bridge from individual conscious-ness to consciousness within the collective body. Janet and her students

---

*"The Collective Body" was first published in *Proceedings of the First International Dance/Movement Therapy Conference "Language of Movement"* (Berlin, Germany: Nervenklinkjk Spandau, 1994) and was later published in *American Journal of Dance Therapy* 18 (1996): 81–94 and *Authentic Movement: Essays by Mary Starks Whitehouse, Janet Adler, and Joan Chodorow,* edited by Patrizia Pallaro (Philadelphia: Jessica Kingsley Publishers, 1999), 190–204.

notice as spontaneous order arises, finding form in story and archetype. These symbolic forms serve at this time as a way of articulating individual experience in relation to the mythology of the group. In one example of unconscious content becoming active within the group, she tracks a series of synchronistic encounters and events arising over the course of a weeklong retreat. A challenging collective process begins, leading to and enabling each participant to discover their own personal and embodied relationship to an emerging collective theme around the fear of death. Narrative form helps to contain both the intricacy and the immensity of that which was then appearing as the work of the collective body evolved.

In "Toward the Unknown," Janet's dialogue with Annie Geissinger,* we sit in on a conversation between fellow travelers, two women who happen also to be teacher and student during the years when Janet's questions are propelling her into the wild frontier of engaging directly with the phenomenon of the collective body. The title of this dialogue is apropos. As her language continues to evolve to more clearly reflect her experience of energetic phenomena in the collective body, she less frequently uses the psychological term *unconscious,* instead more consistently writing and speaking of the *unknown.* In previous writings Janet has described the development of the "internal witness"; she now consistently uses the phrase "inner witness," which first appears in her Ph.D. dissertation (1992). She recognizes that her experience of the inner witness is connected to descriptions of a more universal phenomenon within other mystical and meditative traditions. The discipline is unique in that the actual practice includes the embodied and relational elements of the developing inner witness.

Janet discusses with Annie her love for offering individual witnessing, core to her teaching practice for so long. Alongside her continuing

---

*"Toward the Unknown" was first published in *A Moving Journal* 5, no. 3 (Fall/Winter 1998): 4–10. Annie Geissinger cofounded *A Moving Journal* with Paula Sager and Joan Webb in Providence, Rhode Island, publishing and coediting the journal from 1994 to 2006.

need to see each person clearly, she chooses now to witness more directly the collective body as a whole. Her "readiness to study containment," her growing interest in the importance of boundaries as supportive guidance, and her unwavering commitment to safety, all support the strengthening of consciousness within each individual as the inner witness comes into relationship with the collective body. As unconscious material becomes conscious through embodiment, and personal or psychological work integrates within each individual, students proceed on their own unique paths of development, no longer separate from but within the collective body. Beyond a sense of belonging, this work becomes preparation for and the precursor to what later will emerge within the participatory mystery of ceremony.

Janet honors her indebtedness to the roots of Western psychology, while observing that her approach to studying intuitive knowing, emptiness, and a nonsymbolic, nondualistic way of perception is increasingly aligned with a more Eastern perspective. A Zen priest, a colleague of Janet's, wonders if "the discipline of Authentic Movement is the feminine form of Zen?"* The question rings, koanlike. It reminds us that the term "feminine" has become associated with relational experience and the honoring of the body. Beyond such a distinction we look toward the evolution of sacred circles where geography, culture, ethnicity, race, and gender are differentiated and yet fully inclusive.

*This question was posed to Janet in 1998 by Abbess Furyu Nancy Schroeder, who is the Abiding Abbess at Green Gulch Farm Zen Center. Janet and Fu continued a public exploration of this topic in an online seminar in June 2021.

Body and Soul

There is no body without soul, no body that
is not itself a form of soul.

SRI AUROBINDO

The human heart can go to the lengths of God.
Dark and cold we may be, but this
Is no winter now. The frozen misery
Of centuries breaks, cracks, begins to move,
The thunder is the thunder of the foes,
The thaw, the flood, the upstart Spring.
Thank God our time is now when wrong
Comes up to face us everywhere,
Never to leave us till we take
The longest stride of soul man ever took
Affairs are now soul size
The enterprise
Is exploration into God.
Where are you making for? It takes
So many thousand years to wake,
But will you wake for pity's sake?

CHRISTOPHER FRY, *A SLEEP OF PRISONERS*
(IN FRY, *SELECTED PLAYS,* 253)

Introduction

Once long ago, when there was a great and terrible problem demanding resolution, a rabbi went to a certain place in the forest, lit a fire and

115

prayed, and the problem was solved. Generations later, when another rabbi was faced with a very difficult task, he went to the same place in the forest and prayed, but he no longer could light the fire. Regardless, his wish was granted. Again, after hundreds of years, a rabbi went to the specific place in the forest because he and his people encountered a great problem. While there, he said: "We can no longer light a fire, nor do we know the secret meditations belonging to the prayer, but we do know the place in the woods to which it all belongs and that must be sufficient"; and sufficient it was. But when another rabbi many generations later was confronted with a great and difficult task, he simply sat down and said: "We cannot light the fire, we cannot speak the prayers, we do not know the place, but we can tell the story of how it was done." And that was sufficient, so the story goes.[1]

The only thing that is left of the great mysteries is the "tale." Is this sufficient? Our current search for the mysteries, the depth of our longing, suggests that the story is not enough. Because of ego-consciousness, maybe we can't go back to that place in the forest, light that fire, and say those prayers. How can we rediscover spirit if we don't know where to go, how to kindle the light, or what to say?

A recent spiritual leader in India, The Mother, speaks of the pioneering necessary to proceed: "You don't know whether this or that experience is part of the way or not, you don't even know if you are progressing or not, because if you knew you were progressing, it would mean that you know the way—but there is no way! No one has ever been there!"[2]

A contemporary mystic, Satprem explains:

It was probably necessary to preach heaven to us, to draw us out of our initial evolutionary sclerosis—but this is only a first stage of evolution, which we have turned into an ultimate and rigid end. And now this end is turning against us. We have denied the Divinity in Matter, to confine it instead in our holy places, and now Matter is taking its revenge. . . As long as we tolerate this Imbalance, there is no hope for the earth. . . We need both the vigor of Matter and the fresh waters of the Spirit. . . . We have lost the Password, such is the bottom line of our era. We have replaced true power with devices, and true wisdom with dogmas.[3]

In search of the password, we gather repeatedly in our particular collectives, among our colleagues, in an effort to listen and to speak together about the evolution of our work, our efforts to better understand the evolution of our own consciousness within the different language systems of our study of human development.

In pursuit of this study, the development of each collective is a microcosm of the development of the human psyche, of the history of religions, of civilizations. We tenaciously adhere to the unfolding of the unconscious into consciousness. Satprem writes that "Becoming conscious is the very meaning of evolution,"[4] and that "This physical life in this physical body therefore assumes special prominence among all our modes of existence, because it is here that we can become conscious—this is where the work takes place."[5] The Mother insists: "Salvation is physical."[6] Satprem explains: "The whole story of the ascent of consciousness is the story of an opening of the aperture, the passage from a linear and contradictory consciousness to a global consciousness."[7]

Another story comes to mind, also from the richness of the Hasidic tradition: Once there was a great force called the universe and it became too big and much too hot. When it exploded, the trillions of moments of light fell everywhere, each becoming the source for new life . . . a salmon, a violet, a baby dove or person, a stone, an alligator. So all of us, including the tomatoes and the giraffes, have within us at our cores, a little light, a divine spark, a piece of the great light energy that is called life.[8]

Satprem writes: "the world and every atom in the world are divine"[9] and "the external veneer of a person usually has nothing in common with that tiny vibrating reality."[10] A Buddhist scholar in Tokyo, Nukariya, speaks of our source similarly: "when our inmost pure and godly wisdom . . . is fully awakened, we are able to understand that each one of us is identical in spirit, in being and in nature with universal life."[11]

At the very center of our differences, this light which we could call spirit or soul, radiating within each tiny newborn, reflects our sameness. The Buddhist most responsible for bringing Zen to the Western world, D. T. Suzuki, speaks of this phenomenon: "Each individual reality, besides being itself, reflects in it something of the universal, and at the same time it is itself because of other individuals."[12] Within a lifetime, or within generations of lifetimes, this oneness of spirit among us is usually threatened as it comes into relationship with power and economics represented by the structures of religion. Satprem tells us that the psychic being "is appropriated by churches, countless churches, which put it into articles of faith and dogma."[13]

How did this happen? Gershom Scholem writes lucidly about the history of religion. Originally, nature was the scene of the individual's relationship to God. There was no abyss between men and women and their God. Then the "break-through" of religion occurred and created an abyss. God's voice directed people with his laws and demands across the vast chasm. People's voices responded in prayer, in longing, in fear, in love. The infinite distance was created.[14] But, as Satprem explains, "Through this separation we have become conscious. We are still incompletely conscious: and we suffer, we suffer, we suffer from being separated—separated from others, separated from ourselves, separated from things and from everything because we are outside the one point where everything joins together."[15]

The individual is lost from a direct connection with his or her God. Scholem (1961) describes the effort then "to transform the God whom it encounters in the peculiar religious consciousness of its own social environment from an object of dogmatic knowledge into a novel and living experience and intuition"[16] The human psyche inevitably demands to experience direct relationship with spirit, to know the sacred.

Grof calls it transpersonal,[17] Wilber calls it the superconscious,[18] Otto calls it the numinous,[19] the Huichols call it Tatawari.[20] The rebirth of spirituality within the New Age culture suggests the growing hunger for direct experience of god. It reflects the longing for a new container for the soul, for a new god. The urgency of this longing is also apparent in the search, signaled by some as a lack of connectedness, an escape, confusion, and illusion. Unquestionably, the desire is to return to the old unity, but on a new plane. It has been the mystic, within religious traditions, who has lived most closely in relationship to this quest.

Is There a Relationship between Mystical Practice and the Practice of Authentic Movement?

Authentic Movement

Exploration of mystical practices reveals some similarities to the practice of Authentic Movement. Useful therapeutically, meditatively, or within any creative process, the discipline of Authentic Movement is defined by the relationship between a person moving and a person witnessing that movement. Inherent in being a person in the cultures of the West is the deep longing to be seen as we are by another. We want to be witnessed, without judgment, projection, or interpretation. Ultimately, we want to witness, to see another.[21]

In this discipline movers work with eyes closed, slowly bringing their attention inward as their movement becomes highly specific to their own nature and history. Witnesses are invited to focus not only on what the mover is doing but on their own inner experience in the presence of the mover. As the witness owns projections, judgments, and interpretations, the mover is increasingly free to risk honoring the deepening need to follow movement impulses which are born out of the unconscious. As the body finds form for the expression of what is at first formless material, personal consciousness evolves.

As movers hone their awareness of their developing internal witness and witnesses become aware of their internal mover, movers work within a circle of witnesses, which creates a deepening possibility for collective consciousness. The experience of the mover, the witness, and the relationship between the two occurs on many levels, creating a complexity that spans the realms of the unconscious, consciousness, and what Wilber calls the "superconscious."[22]

My need now is for a different way of describing what increasingly happens in the practice of Authentic Movement. We are learning that immersion in this practice means immersion in a developmental process in which personal history, as most clearly understood within psychological theory, slowly becomes integrated into the evolution of the psyche, taking its place within a larger self. There is more to us than, at best, highly developed, healthy ego structures. As we bring this developing ego consciousness toward the reawakening of the spirit, the discipline of Authentic Movement expands to include experiences that occur outside of personality and to include a language system within which to place these experiences.

Mystical Practices

Because of the vast number of mystical practices, it is important to limit this discussion of mysticism to traditions that appear to be most germane to our lives at this time: Judaism, Christianity, Buddhism, Shamanism, and a few voices from Hinduism because of the particular way in which certain individuals in that ancient tradition speak to the great spiritual questions of this time.

There are four specific aspects of mystical practice that will be discussed: direct experience of one's god, the impossibility of describing it, its profound effect on the body and the emotions, and the evolution of such experience developmentally. The primary focus in this essay, which is concerned with the relationship between Authentic Movement and mystical practice, will be on the mover because the mover initiates the process of Authentic Movement and is always at its center. The witness, as much as the mover, can find herself experiencing the numinous, but we must take one step at a time.

Direct Experience

In the texts of most religions, mysticism can be described as one's experience of God and religion can be described as one's relationship to, or one's belief in, God. These two perspectives are not necessarily mutually exclusive. Gershom Scholem says that mysticism is a definite stage in the historical development of religion, a certain stage of religious consciousness that has always been incompatible with the other stages. The Christian mystic Rufus Jones writes that mysticism is "religion in its most acute, intense, and living stage."[23]

A foremost authority on the phenomenon of shamanism, Mircea Eliade, explains: "it would be more correct to class shamanism among the mysticisms than with what is commonly called a religion."[24] A contemporary anthropologist who has made significant contribution to her field through her study of shamanism, Joan Halifax (1982), says that "the shaman acquires direct knowledge from direct experience."[25] Richard Katz writes: "The !Kung speak of the gods directly, not of their beliefs about the gods."[26]

The author of a classic text in Christian mysticism, Evelyn Underhill (1911), suggests that mystics are people who "not merely have reasoned about the mystical experiences of others"[27] but instead are doers, not thinkers, and each person ventures for himself. It is said of St. Teresa: "What others believed, she experienced in herself."[28]

A priest and Trappist monk who was an ardent student of Zen Buddhism, Thomas Merton, writes: "Personal experience thus seems to be the foundation of Buddhist philosophy. . . the chief characteristic of Zen is that it rejects . . . systematic elaborations in order to get back, as far as possible, to the pure unarticulated and unexplained ground of direct experience."[29] Zen is direct experience. Merton continues: "The whole aim of Zen is not to make foolproof statements about experience, but to come to direct grips with reality without the mediation of logical verbalizing."[30] D. T. Suzuki insists: "Personal experience . . . is everything in Zen."[31]

A distinguished philosopher of religion, William James (1982), suggests that direct experience is "something more like a sensation than an intellectual operation."[32] Sensation is what the body perceives. It can be experienced as perception of an image, of light, a touch, a sound, or a kinesthetic sensation. In mystical experience sensation is perception through any or all of the five senses plus another sense that is nameless.

Direct experience can be of form or of no form. It can be the experience of nothingness. In mystical experience the power and richness of symbol often expands into the realm of emptiness. An ancient Jewish scholar, Rabbi Akiva, insists: "Man must therefore dispense with the mental ideas, or image of God and by transforming himself, experience

Him."[33] The great and heretical Christian mystic Eckhart discusses the mystical experience as nonsymbolic, urging the destruction of the symbols of nature's nakedness.[34]

For many mystics, stepping aside from the archetype of God, or moving through it, leads them into what they describe as direct experience of an energy field in which no form or boundary exists. Description of such a space can be found within many mystical practices.

Direct Experience Is Indescribable

Like the mystic, the individual who practices Authentic Movement is often challenged by what can be a very disturbing conflict. There is a knowing that says to contain the experience until it is complete—concomitant with a longing to share it. The longing is inextricably linked to the knowledge ahead of time that it is impossible to describe.

For some, this longing seems to be in relationship to completing the experience, as if the verbal or visual description would bring it more clearly into consciousness. For others, describing it brings hope of being seen, understood, or reducing the loneliness that such experiences inherently create. But, often, once this is attempted, the mystic reports a sense of self-betrayal or an excruciating sense that what was once so vivid and profound has been reduced, limited, and incorrectly described. "He does not want it misunderstood or altered in any way in the act of revelation."[35]

In relation to this question, James Hillman writes in his commentary on Gopi Krishna's story of his kundalini experience: "There is something in the nature of mystical experience that demands secrecy, as if the archetype behind the events which are in process needs a certain tension in order for it to be fulfilled. The alchemists envisioned this secrecy in their image of the closed vessel. In many fairy tales the hero or heroine is ordered not to say anything until the ordeal is over."[36]

A distinguished shaman, Black Elk tells us: "I saw more than I can tell and I understood more than I saw"[37] and "When the part of me that talks would try to make words for the meaning, it would be like fog and get away from me."[38] The Bible says: "To attain to this spiritual wisdom, one must first be liberated from servile dependence on the wisdom of speech."[39] Scholem writes: "How is it possible to give lingual expression to mystical knowledge, which by its very nature is related to a sphere where speech and expression are excluded?"[40]

A woman who has made a remarkable contribution to the understanding of medieval women's visionary literature, Elizabeth Petroff, speaks of the illnesses of these women as a manifestation of a conflict related to writing about their experiences: "They are fearful about what they expect to be negative responses to their writing."[41] Fear of response can drastically alter a description. Margery Kempe, a mystic of the fourteenth century discussed by Petroff, said: "I began to consider within myself how difficult and even impossible it would be to find thoughts and words capable of explaining these things to the human intellect without scandal."[42]

Merton says that Zen "resists any temptation to be easily communicable."[43] He insists that one wishes "to grasp the naked reality of experience" but "grasps a form of words instead."[44] A contemporary Buddhist scholar, Bancroft, discusses this challenge: "Words are essential but . . . when we rely too much on words we begin to substitute a world of indirect knowledge—knowledge about—for the immediate intense impact of what is actually there before thoughts and words arise."[45]

An ancient Zen teacher and scholar, Ch'an Master Hui Hai (1972), writes: "To comprehend (real) meanings, we should go beyond unsteady words: to awaken to the fundamental law, we should leap beyond writings."[46] Suzuki (1949) explains: "the human tongue is not an adequate organ for expressing the deepest truths of Zen. . . They are to be experienced in the inmost soul."[47]

The great poets know much about this dilemma. Ryokan, a late-eighteenth-century Japanese poet, writes:

> *Looking at this scene, limitless emotions,*
> *But not one word.*[48]

And the extraordinary Persian mystical poet, Rumi, expresses the impossibility of this task:

In these pages many mysteries are hinted at.
What if you come to understand one of them?[49]

If I could wake completely, I would say without speaking
Why I'm ashamed of using words.[50]

Why can't we hear thought?[51]

Mystical Experience and the Body

A universal and completely central part of mystical experience is its direct effect on the body, which is visibly altered. Transformation of consciousness means transformation of the body. The Mother writes vividly about this: "To transform, you need to go down into the body, and that's terrible . . . Otherwise nothing will ever change, it will remain the same." She continues: "I seek my way downward—that's what I can't find. The way I am seeking is always descending, descending—it's never going up, it's always descending, descending. Oh! I have no idea when it will be over."[52]

The Mother's contributions to this area of inquiry are dramatic as she worked entirely phenomenologically: "One never really understands unless one understands with one's body."[53] "I have had a unique experience. The supramental light entered my body directly without going through the inner or higher planes of consciousness. It was the first time. It entered through the feet. . ."[54]

R. H. Blyth tells us that "Zen means thinking with the body."[55] A great Jewish mystic, Abulafia, who was not unlike a Zen master, assigned each letter of the Hebrew alphabet to a corresponding body part. Focusing on a body part as an expression of a holy letter increased the aspirant's possibility of reaching God. What follows is a description of what can happen:

After much movement and concentration on the letters, the hair on your head will stand on end . . . your blood will begin to vibrate . . . and all your body will begin to tremble, and a shuddering will fall on all your limbs, and . . . you will feel an additional spirit within

yourself . . . strengthening you, passing through your entire body . . .
[like] fragrant oil, anointing you from head to foot.[56]

Stephen Katz writes:

> The concrete meetings of mystic and beloved in Christian tradition,
> moreover, are almost always with the Christ whose physical body and
> wounds . . . are seen and felt by the Christian initiate. Indeed, this
> feeling of sharing in Christ's wounds is a striking feature of many
> Christian mystical occasions . . . Yearning to share in her Lord's
> Passion, [Lukardis of Oberweinar] prayed that [Christ's] experience
> of pain might always be present to her own experience. [The Lord
> said to her in response:] "Place thy hands against My hands, and thy
> feet against My feet, and thy breast against My breast, and in such
> wise shall be so much helped by thee that My pain will be less." And
> when the servant of God had done this she felt interiorly the most
> bitter pain of the wounds both in her hands and in her feet and in
> her breast. . . [57]

A traditional healer in the !Kung tribe of the Kalahari Desert, Kinachau
describes his dancing, in which a longing to unite with his god is
actualized: "I felt num [the kundalini energy] in my stomach. I felt it
rising, I felt it shiver and shiver . . .You breathe hard and fast, your heart
is pounding. You run around because the num is shaking and agitating
you violently."[58] "Num grabs you and throws you up in the air."[59]

A witness to Kinachau's experience, Richard Katz, describes what
he saw:

> Kinachau sits up . . . His look is glazed, and his body trembles
> spasmodically. He returns to dancing and, after three full turns
> around the circle, goes over to one of the peripheral "talking" fires
> and begins to heal. As he pulls the sickness from each person,
> Kinachau's whole body shakes roughly and his legs tremble violently,
> the tendons sticking out. His jerking hands quiver rapidly over each

person's chest . . . He shrieks out the characteristic deep howling sounds which express the pain involved in pulling out sickness.[60]

Often, the bodily experience for the mystic includes much physical pain. The medieval saints left vivid accounts of their pain. Hildegard of Bingen writes of her aching "in the marrow of her bones and the veins of her flesh."[61] Hadewich similarly suffered: "all my separate limbs threatened to break. . . all my separate veins were in travail."[62] St. Elizabeth of Schonau attempted to describe her experience of her body: "after this vision, I remained exhausted with illness"[63]; "I remained in that state of violent bodily agitation"[64]; "with great physical suffering I came into ecstasy."[65] !Kung healers speak of the pain. Richard Katz describes it this way: "Healers speak again and again of the searing pain . . . in the pit of the stomach. One healer said: "Num got into my stomach. It was hot and painful . . . like fire. I was surprised and I cried.""[66]

Underhill explains that psychophysical disturbances are often the result of mystical experiences: "The nervous and vascular systems rebel against a way of life, they don't adjust."[67] St. Teresa said that the power of her movement was lost and her breathing and circulation were diminished. For some, it is impossible to speak or to open their eyes.[68] Another medieval saint, Blessed Angela of Foligno, writes: "I didn't remember to eat. And I wished that it were not necessary to eat."[69] In his autobiography, Gopi Krishna writes:

Aversion from food is a common feature when the rising of the kundalini is sudden.[70]

I had not to eat for pleasure or the mechanical satisfaction of hunger, but to regulate the intake of food with such precision as not to cause the least strain on my oversensitive and over-stimulated nervous system.[71]

The Buddhist nun, Seng-Kuo, from Ceylon, "would go into Samadhi for whole nights on end, her spirit remaining continuously in Buddha-lands. At such times her body was like a withered tree, and people of shallow comprehension suspected that she was dead."[72] James Hillman writes in his commentary on Gopi Krishna's initiation: "Again and again we shall come to passages in the text which emphasize the enormous physical cost of the experience. It is important to realize . . . that transformation . . . is exhausting."[73]

There are times, in the mystic's journey, when physical death becomes a real possibility. Epstein explains in her insightful book about the great text of Jewish mysticism, the Kabbalah: "For this was the moment when the soul so longed to escape the body that it could inadvertently result in the disciple's death."[74] Krishna (1971) writes: "I felt instinctively that a life and death struggle was going on inside me in which I, the owner of the body, was entirely powerless to take part, forced to lie quietly and watch as a spectator the weird drama unfold in my own flesh."[75] A !Kung healer has this to say about death: "As we enter kia, we fear death. We fear we may die and not come back."[76]

It is interesting to note what the Buddhists say about the challenge of death. Suzuki writes: "Eternity, for Zen, is not a posthumous state of affairs. To live in eternity is to tap the infinity of the moment . . . No one is prepared to take that last step until he has first exhausted all his other resources, and finally stands emptied of all contrivances for meeting life. Only then will the need for reality drive him to the final abandoning of his self. The practice and discipline of Zen is to bring one to this point . . . The Great Death is also the Great Awakening."[77]

At this time in the Western world, in response to our deepening need for authentic spiritual experience, all we can do is to return to our physical selves. Individuals practicing Authentic Movement can have experiences in their bodies that are not unlike those just described by mystics. What follows are examples of movers' attempts to write about direct experiences of the numinous in the practice of Authentic Movement. These experiences all occurred for individuals after many years of personal therapy followed by several years of Authentic Movement practice.

A man named Allan periodically encounters a specific energy field that moves from inside his body up and out. He says:

I feel the pushing up from my torso and diaphragm. It's as if a strong life force is pushing up from within me and my body has to follow . . . Once out, a large golden ball emerges from my body—I carry it around the room in both hands, arms outstretched . . . I am very large . . .

For a period of a year I repeatedly witnessed Elena, who was watching her own hands being cut off. After unsuccessfully searching for an explanation within her personal history and personality, she finally accepted this experience, surrendering to its fullness, its lack of emotionality, its specific kinesthetic demands. We subsequently learned that in the earliest form of Jewish mysticism, called Throne Mysticism, the mystic began his descent to the Merkabah, "the visionary journey of the soul to heaven [by having to stand upright] without hands and feet."[78]

Michelle wrote this in her journal after moving in the studio:

I was being pulled to a standing position. I felt as though every cell in my body was being mobilized into an upward motion. My face was lifted up toward the sky light; my arms began to move in an upward fully extended gesture which I held for a very long time . . . perfectly still, perfectly light. Then my body began to shake and tremble as I released or was released from the experience. I felt as though I was being moved by something more than the "little" me or "ego" me.

Another woman, Lauren, wrote in her journal after moving:

I lie still and become more still. In fact, I am so still the word doesn't work anymore, because I come to an experience where there is much activity, but only on a deep kinesthetic level. I am empty, with no density inside, and no density around me, surrounded by nothing, yet incredibly awake and sort of becoming like sound with no form.

Satprem writes about this: "Beyond a certain level of consciousness, it is no longer ideas that one sees and tries to translate—one hears . . . When the consciousness of the seeker is clear, he can hear the sound distinctive and it is a seeing sound."[79]

Jody describes the experience of light after pulling her limbs slowly in toward her torso: "I see and feel an explosion from the base of my spine—a white ball diffusing into white light. It is gentle and slow. A 'boom,' but quiet, in slow motion. It fills my entire back and literally jars me, giving me a jolt."

Mystical texts are replete with reference to light. Hildegard of Bingen writes: "that a fiery light of the greatest brilliance coming from the opened heavens, poured into all my brain and kindled in my heart and my breast a flame."[80]

The following example is of an experience of image within a transcendent state—which is different from fantasy or active imagination. A vision occurs within a mystical state and, therefore, is made of light, or what has been described as electrical energy. In a transcendent state, as Underhill explains, the self embodies the image or vision.[81]

Anna wrote this vision in her journal after lying unusually still for a long period of time, feeling very tired and weighted:

> Feminine white hands caress the stones in a circle. I come down from the sky onto the pole in the middle. I spin. Roots grow from my feet. Branches reach from my arms from my mouth. My third eye grows a branch which is holding a rabbit who sits on top of the full green tree.

For a period of six months, Julie spoke simply and shyly after moving about a kinesthetic experience, the sensation of falling into nowhere. She wrote in her journal:

> This is not an easy task, this surrender to such a life-threatening situation, but it brings a release . . . when I just endlessly fall THROUGH DARK AND EMPTY NOTHING . . . If I surrender and fall more deeply into the material, I must let go of meaning, of attachment to any semblance of things, which once anchored my life, even my physical being.

Mystical Experience and the Emotions

As the body transforms, so does the self. The experience of the self, internally, in relationship to others and to the natural world, is altered. The personalities of some mystics are much more visible in their writing about this than others. For example, the lives of medieval Christian visionaries are more available, more explicitly portrayed in biography and autobiography, than the lives of Jewish mystics, who seemed to experience more "personal reticence."[82] In this context it is also interesting to note that there is strikingly little recorded biographical material concerning Jewish women who were mystics. Scholem tells us that Kabbalism is historically and metaphysically masculine.[83] It was made for and by men.

The phenomenon of resistance and its relationship to surrender regarding mystical experience is repeatedly discussed in many traditions. Underhill (1911) tells us that the mystic "goes because he [or she] must . . . without hope or reward" surrendering "self and all things"—into "the annihilation of selfhood."[84] Eliade describes "the resistance to 'divine election' as mankind's ambivalent attitude toward the sacred."[85] He tells us that "a shaman struggles for a long time with unknown forces before he finally cries: 'Now the way is open.'"[86] It is unusual for the human psyche to do just this without struggle, conflict, terror, despair, and a feeling of helplessness. Richard Katz describes resistance to kia among the !Kung:

> The aspiring healers try to regulate their condition. When they feel kia coming on, they involuntarily draw back from and at times actively resist this transition to an altered state. Others help them to overcome this resistance and to strike a dynamic balance between the oncoming intensity of kia and their fear of it . . .The num must be hot enough to evoke kia but not so hot that it provokes debilitating fear . . . the correct amount is critical.[87]

Scholem describes the Jewish men who were mystics: "They glory in objective description and are deeply averse to letting their own personalities intrude into the picture . . . It is as though they were hampered by a sense of shame."[88] Petroff writes of the Christian medieval visionaries: "Descriptions of physical pain and weakness associated with ecstatic states, accompanied by statements of shame or embarrassment are frequent."[89]

Petroff (1986) discusses Hildegard of Bingen's writing as:

> typical of most women visionaries in its mingling of self-confidence and humility. . . . For in the marrow of her bones and in the veins of her flesh she was aching, having her mind and judgment bound, so that no security dwelt in her and she judged herself culpable in all things. . . .She has been protected from pride and vainglory by these feelings of fear and grief.[90]

Underhill describes the fear as not only of the inner experiences themselves but of deceiving themselves and others in their struggle to believe that what is happening to them is real.[91] This is not at all an unrealistic fear. Epstein mentions that "the Jewish sages have always therefore warned that it is impossible for the average person to have a real prophetic dream without a considerable admixture of worthless information."[92] Petroff also discusses the great difficulty for the Christian mystics to "distinguish between one's own mind and the true information."[93] She explains how the initiate can't yet see her own new forming self and instead sees herself as less significant than others see her. Guyon, a Christian mystic, writes of his feelings of doubt: "I could not perceive of any good thing I had done in my whole life."[94]

Petroff describes the great effort made by the Beguine visionaries "to be in the world but not of it."[95] This conflict caused tremendous pain for mystics in many traditions. Underhill describes St. Teresa's awesome struggle with this split: "At times she persuaded herself that she could enjoy both [worlds] which ended mostly in complete enjoyment of neither."[96]

Underhill writes of other excruciating emotional conflicts which mystics suffer. She discusses their feelings of deprivation and inadequacy.

Visitors are often experienced as torture. They see a tiny detail of imperfection in themselves and inflate it. They have a "wild desire to see god, to die. They can't touch earth and they can't get to heaven."[97]

Eliade discusses the ascetic practice for shamans as an annihilation of secular personality.[98] He writes of the silence and depression that often follow ecstatic states. Hillman discusses this in his commentary on Gopi Krishna's experiences:

> The alternation of his states of consciousness throughout the years, especially the loss of heavenly joy time and again, is also described by the alchemists. They said the stone must be coagulated and dissolved again and again. The more it alternated between these opposites the more valuable it became. This lesson is hard to learn, for after every peak experience one wants to "hold it," and after each valley experience one feels guilty, lost, and humiliated.[99]

The impact of such dramatic change in the body and the emotions challenges the mental health of an individual. Eliade discusses this: "'Possessed' by the Gods or spirits, the novice is in danger of completely losing his psychomental balance."[100]

The Kabbalists were not unaware of the danger of insanity, especially when the mystic was compelled to confront the demonic beings.[101] Participatory visions, for the medieval Christian mystics, were the most dangerous in terms of their sanity. Sometimes, "the visionary so fully identifies with the archetypal experience of grief that she is incapable of observing her vision or reflecting on what she has seen until the vision is over."[102] When the conscious mind fuses with the image, psychosis is possible.

Because of the great stress on the body and psyche, some initiates become psychotic, some die. A crucial factor in this regard is the clarity of ego consciousness and the strength of the boundary between such consciousness and the experience of the numinous. There is, of course, little written about those who, for whatever reason, do not find themselves able to survive this complex journey. We most often read about those who manage to return to tell the story. Those initiates somehow learn a way to balance surrender and will, form and formlessness, body and spirit. In such a process they manage to stay in touch with the daily life just enough. It is said of St. Catherine: "When she was needed, she always came to herself."[103]

In the practice of Authentic Movement, when individuals are experiencing various aspects of a mystical journey, the emotional effect is evident. So much of what has just been discussed is familiar in the speaking and the writing of movers and witnesses: shyness, shame, fear, insecurity, a sense of deprivation, confusion, fear of psychosis, fear of death, as well as bliss, rapture, ecstasy.

Many struggle with physical symptoms that do not fit tidily into Western medical phenomena and fall haphazardly into what is broadly referred to as New Age diseases. Many doubt the experiences of the numinous, working hard to find explanation within personality theory. Others resist the intensity of the energy for excellent reasons. Feeling a great inability to describe these experiences, they suffer from frustration, fear of being misunderstood and fear of being judged as inflated, and, finally, deflate the experiences in order to remain safe.

In the practice of Authentic Movement we are learning how to distinguish mystical experiences from unresolved personal history, how to safely help regulate their intensity, how to receive and integrate such material into developing consciousness. In doing so we are learning how to witness the organic evolution of these energies into new form.

Mystical Experience and Developmental Theory

Mystical experience, like the unfolding of personality, can occur developmentally. In many mystical traditions there are stages through which the initiate evolves. These stages provide an understanding, an order, a way of containing the whole. However, many experiences of the superconscious do not occur within a tidy developmental framework. These isolated occurrences can be related to any of the specific stages, can occur from the same energy source, can be exactly like those experiences that happen sequentially, but simply are not recognizably experienced within a developmental spectrum.

Halifax describes the stages in the shamanic tradition, from death to rebirth to return:

> The deepest structures within the psyche are found in the themes of descent to the Realm of Death, confrontations with demonic forces, dismemberment, trial by fire, communion with the world of spirits and creatures, assimilation of the elemental forces, ascension via the World Tree and/or the Cosmic Bird, realization of a solar identity, and return to the Middle World, the world of human affairs.[104]

Underhill lists the five stages that the Christian mystic experiences: awakening, purgation, illumination, mystic death, and union.[105] As mentioned earlier, in Throne Mysticism the early Jewish mystics passed through "heavenly halls or palaces" in a journey called "descent to the Merkabah." There are seven gates of entry, which finally lead to the "perception of His appearance on the throne."[106] It can be different for many Zen Buddhists because the appearance of symbols does not necessarily contribute to their journey. Yet there is a path clearly described by the ancient Zen masters that aspirants follow.

Within these basic and developmental stages of transformative experience, there is meaning and complexity in each stage that, again, is similar among the different traditions. What follows is a brief discussion of three of these stages: descent, union, and return.

Descent: A distinguished Buddhist priest and philosopher, Yoshinori, writes: "In the mystical traditions of all times and places, conversion is said to begin with self-purification, with a catharsis of soul."[107] Eliade writes of the descent that the shamanic initiate is required to make in which he or she inevitably "encounters" monsters.[108]

Petroff (1979) explains that the first step for Christian visionaries is almost always a direct encounter with evil.[109] Teresa of Avila writes of her experience: "I saw in his hand a long spear of gold and at the iron's

point there seemed to be a little fire. He appeared to me to be thrusting
it at times into my heart and to pierce my very entrails."[110]

In each tradition these early stages, with or without visions depict-
ing such experience, describe the initiate's experience of loss of his or
her physical body through fire, torture, or being devoured or dismem-
bered. Death of the self as one has known it inevitably precedes rebirth.

Union: The arrival in the Upper Realm often includes a meeting with
God. Enoch writes of his encounter in the Old Testament: "And there I
saw One, who had a head of days, and His head was white like wool."[111]
Union with God is experienced in a myriad of ways. Scholem explains
that in the ecstatic state, the mystic is his own Messiah. For many
Kabbalists, union includes letters and words: "every spoken word consists
of sacred letters, and the combination, separation, and reunion of letters
reveal profound mysteries . . . and unravel . . . the secret of the relation of
all languages to the holy tongue . . . In this supreme state, man and Torah
become one."[112] The great Christian mystic, Eckhart, writes about union:

> In my breaking-through . . . I transcend all creatures and am neither
> God nor creature: I am that I was and I shall remain now and for-
> ever. Then I receive an impulse which carries me above all angels.
> In this impulse I conceive such passing riches that I am not content
> with God as being God, as being all his godly works, for in this
> breaking-through I find that God and I are both the same.[113]

A renowned Buddhist scholar, Blofeld, describes it this way: "Reality
will flash upon us, the whole universe of phenomena will be seen
as it really is."[114] The great and recent spiritual leader in India, Sri
Aurobindo, writes: "Thou art He . . . Such is the Truth that the
ancient Mysteries taught and the later religions forgot."[115] In the
Taittiriya Upanishad it is found: "The Spirit who is here in man
and the spirit who is there in the sun, lo, it is One Spirit and there
is no other."[116] Regardless of the framework within which this union
occurs, in each tradition it is undeniably positive, more than worth

the great suffering that precedes it. The initiate becomes whole, one with the universe.

In the practice of Authentic Movement the unitive stage is reflected on three different levels. First, with a very practiced mover, union can occur between the moving self and the internal witness. One no longer sees oneself lifting one's arm, it simply lifts. This can look like preegoic experience, to use Ken Wilber's framework, but, in fact, it is transegoic.[117] Experience in the unconscious state can look like experience in the superconscious state. The difference is that in the unconscious state the presence of ego is not yet established and, in the superconscious state, the fully formed ego has been transcended.

Second, union can occur between the witness and the mover when both are simultaneously without self-consciousness and without the experienced density of personality. They are each completely clear and separate beings, and yet united. This can look like merging but, instead, it is union. Gopi Krishna writes of this when speaking of man's relationship to his god, though it is interesting to wonder about its application here: "The seer and the seen, reduced to an inexpressible sizeless void which no mind can conceive . . . or any language describe."[118]

In Zen this unity is discussed in relationship to the subject and the object becoming one. A contemporary Buddhist scholar, Maseo Abe, discusses this phenomenon. Perhaps mover and witness could be substituted for subject and object: "So long as the field of self-consciousness, i.e., the field of separation between subject and object, is not broken-through, and so long as a transference from that standpoint does not occur, a real self-presentation of reality cannot come about."[119]

Third, a mover can experience union with his god. Any, or all, of these experiences can look like work in the unconscious, rather than superconscious, but the difference is that ego-consciousness has been expanded toward the numinous. These experiences can only occur safely after healthy ego structures are developed.

Return: After the exhausting and impeccably demanding journey of the initiate, after the torment and the terror, the light and the ecstasy, the bone-aching and the emptiness, inevitably, the one who has traveled returns home again. Campbell explains the task of return:

> The hero may have to be brought back from his supernatural adventure by assistance from without. That is to say, the world may have to come and get him . . . After such utter bliss, why would the human psyche choose to leave it and return to the embodied state of humanity? A choice is necessarily made, sometimes consciously, sometimes unconsciously.[120]

Perhaps the return has become even more difficult in the Western world because there is rarely a container or community that believes in, honors, and correctly receives the initiate. Campbell continues:

> How render back into light-world language the speech-defying pronouncements of the dark? . . . How communicate to people who insist on the exclusive evidence of their senses the message of the all-generating void? . . . The first problem of the returning hero is to accept as real, after an experience of the soul-satisfying vision of fulfillment, the passing joys and sorrow, banalities and noisy obscenities of life. Why re-enter such a world? Why attempt to make plausible, or even interesting, to men and women consumed with passion, the experience of transcendental bliss?[121]

The process of return just described essentially has two aspects: the internal experience of the one who has been transformed—the impeccable struggle toward clarity, balance, and integration of the new energy now active within the person—and the equally impeccable task of bringing that embodied energy into clear and correct relationship with the collective. Coming back is not enough. Coming back brings an unwritten, unstated, often unwanted responsibility in relationship to the community.

What follows is an example of work in an Authentic Movement experience, which illustrates an aspect of the phenomenon of return.

Hillary writes:

> I witnessed for hours without moving until I felt I would explode. I
> had to walk out of doors, up the hill to a clearing. Once there I felt
> I was witnessed by God. I was completely contained by everything
> around me. When I returned to the studio I looked at my witness
> and knew that I had been seen. I sat down and felt the presence of
> God come inside through my womb. It felt like a divine child.

She then began to move inconspicuously with other movers, dancing, crying, laughing, engaging completely in the fullness of the movement that
was occurring among them. This experience was reminiscent to me, as
a witness of the tenth of the series of the ox-herding pictures. Bancroft
discusses these pictures, which depict the development of Zen life: "In the
tenth and last picture, he returns to the world, a free man, doing whatever
he does with the whole of himself because there is nothing to gain."[122]

In the practice of Authentic Movement, some movers encounter
mystical experiences that either happen outside of a developmental
framework or do not appear to be sequentially related. Others have
mystical experiences that seem to evolve developmentally. We are now
witnessing several movers who have spontaneously begun a descent in
which there seems to be an inherent order. Their experiences reflect
work at various places on the spiral toward wholeness. What follows is
material from the journal of one mover, Rebecca, in which she describes
different stages in the development of her mystical journey:

> I come to the killing fields. The sea of endless white where I come to
> die away the features of my reality. I tremble; I do not come willingly. I
> know the stakes are high. It is really a matter of one death or another . . .
> I trick myself in murderous ways. I let the ripe time rot in inertia or
> procrastination . . . This is another letting go. Hanging on to illusion
> is a different and I believe more terrible death than letting go; but this
> letting go is a descent into unknown pain, perhaps memory. I can only
> guess how painful by the measure of my own resistance to this action.

~

I begin by sitting, feeling too much, feeling sick and aching. Rest. Empty. By Maria I am comforted. I want the drum . . . I go to Audrey's drum and sit for a long time: I lay my head on the drum; I scratch the drum. I listen. Carefully. Many sounds in the collective. I must go back to the burning fire. I go. I sit. I extend my spine. I fall into the direct heat. I burn and burn. There is a shift from red to white. I am white in the fire. Pure hot in the burning. Time is called.

She ends the weekend with this entry in her journal:

> *Search hard to find the gift, until*
> *your fingertips are shred to bone and*
> *your eyes are water-hollowed stone.*
>
> *Suffer, until breath itself no longer*
> *visits freely, but hardly fills the*
> *spongy billows, sucked in narrowly*
> *in service of pain's hard thrust.*
>
> *Beat, the empty, bloodless chambers*
> *of your heart. Burn, until faith*
> *and surrender are the last dim*
> *embers on earth.*

A year later, after repeated experience of death, she wrote the following poem in her journal about new life:

> *Moving to this new place, now so white*
> *with stillness and emptiness*
> *alive in every molecule. Inside*
> *I am the beating wings of*
> *one hundred birds with*
> *winter*
> *coming on.*

I begin to suspect that I am in an initiation process that has little to do with psychology . . . getting these contents into the psychological realm is, in fact, dangerous to me. When I clear away the dross of my psychology, not deny it, but let it run its own inevitable course, then there is this particular circle in which I am being and becoming conscious. I'm in an ancient and external place. Nature teaches me. I dwell with such immense energy that is ordered in mystery. It is all so vibrant, tender, and fierce.

The Practice of Authentic Movement

It is important at this point to look more closely at the form of Authentic Movement itself and some of the other aspects of it that are similar to mystical practice. The constant external container in Authentic Movement is the relationship between the mover and the witness.[123] We begin with dyads that allow movers and witnesses an intimate and safe container out of which trust and clarity can develop. A contemplative awareness of the other is reflected in the writing of Shantideva, an eighth-century poet and mystic, when he describes the "practice of contemplative identification with other beings." This he calls either meditation on the "sameness of self and others" or the "transference of self and others." "Whoever wishes to quickly rescue himself and another, should practice the supreme mystery: the exchanging of Self and other."[124] The Tibetan Buddhist scholar Gampopa writes:

> Spiritual friends are like a guide when we travel in unknown territory, an escort when we pass through dangerous regions and a ferry-man when we cross a great river. . . When we go there without an escort, there is the danger of losing our body, life, or property; but when we have a strong escort we reach the desired place without loss.[125]

The mover, in the presence of her witness, works with her eyes closed. The Bal Shem Tov told his disciples "when you wish to yoke yourself to the higher world, it is best to worship with your eyes closed."[126] St. John of the Cross said: "If a man wishes to be sure of the road he treads on, he must close his eyes and walk in the dark."[127] In Authentic Movement practice, eyes are closed for similar reasons, to enhance connection with one's inner life.

With eyes closed, the mover's task is to wait and to listen, to trust in the possibility of "being moved," instead of moving, as Mary Whitehouse so beautifully explained.[128] Listening means concentrating. Concentration is the central force of all mystical practices. Satprem tells us that "any concentration releases a subtle heat"[129] and that in concentrating the expanding consciousness "may silently and quietly focus on the desired object and become this object."[130]

There is constant talk in the studio about seeing. The mover strives to see herself more and more clearly via her internal witness. The witness struggles with the developing capacity to see herself as she learns how to see her mover. And seeing her mover means owning her own projections, judgments, and interpretations so that she can bring a clear presence to her mover. Clear presence means seeing what is actually there. Satprem (1984) says: "If we are powerless, it is because we do not see. Seeing, seeing wholly, necessarily means having power"[131]; "In inner silence, consciousness sees."[132]

Castaneda insists that we "learn to see"[133] and Satprem reminds us:

> If our mirror is not clean, we can never see the true reality of things and people, because we find everywhere the reflection of our own desires or fears, the echo of our own turmoil . . . In order to see, it is obvious that we have to stop being in the middle of the picture. Therefore, the seeker will discriminate between the things that tend to blur his vision and those that clarify it; such essentially will be his "morality."[134]

Suzuki writes: "There must be actual seeing on the physical plane, and over and through this seeing there must be another sort of seeing . . . It is not that something different is seen but that one sees differently."[135] Merton describes Zen in an uncannily similar way in which we are trying to describe moving and witnessing:

The monk is "trying to understand" when in fact he ought to try to *look*. The apparently mysterious and cryptic sayings of Zen became much simpler when we see them in the whole context of Buddhist "mindfulness" or awareness, which in its most elementary form consists in that "bare attention," which simply *sees* what is right there and does not add any comment, any interpretation, any judgment, any conclusion. It just *sees*.[136]

The trouble is that as long as you are given to distinguishing, judging, categorizing and classifying—or even contemplating—you are superimposing something else on the pure mirror. You are filtering the light through a system as if convinced that this will improve the light.[137]

In the practice of Authentic Movement the mover's internal witness has developed in relationship to a gradual internalization of her external witness. Originally, the external witness held consciousness so that she, the mover, could open to the unconscious. Now her internal witness holds consciousness for her as she finds more space to open to other sources of energy.

In the Rig Veda there is a striking statement about the internal witness: "Two birds beautiful of wing, friends and comrades, cling to a common tree, and one eats the sweet fruit, the other regards him and eats not."[138] Sri Aurobindo describes it this way: "All developed mental men . . . at certain times and for certain purpose . . . separate the two parts of the mind, the active part, which is a factory of thoughts and the quiet, masterful part which is at once a Witness and a Will."[139]

Perhaps the internal witness progressively evolves into the clear self as unconditional loving presence becomes manifest. As mentioned before, many mystics believe that God is the clear self. In the Tao Te Ching there is an exquisite description of what the expanding and developing internal witness might be:

> *The Tao flows everywhere,*
> *Creating,*
> *Inspecting, remaining silent and unknown,*

It rejects nothing,
Possesses nothing,
Encourages but does not dominate.
Being quiet,
Uncritical,
Nonpossessive,
It does not sign its name,
It is hardly recognized by anyone,
It is too small to see.[140]

After several years of dyad and triad work, the mover enters the witness circle with an increased ability to concentrate, less density from unresolved personality issues, and an increasingly clear internal witness. Because of the strengthening of internal witnessing by the movers, the collective of external witnesses gradually shifts from a more personal responsibility of holding consciousness for an individual mover toward the freedom to see from a broader perspective. The circle of witnesses begins to participate in a collective consciousness that can include what Wilber calls "super-consciousness."[141] In this format witnesses often see a collective myth, a ritual, or simply feel in the presence of an energy larger than one individual can hold.

Also within the witness circle, there appears to be a gradual and subtle shift for movers. Often, the movement is less emotional, with less interference from the negative aspects of internalized parents, unresolved trauma, and current conflict. Sometimes, a specific gateway into the numinous is experienced within the exact same movement pattern that held the most significant childhood trauma. For example, I witnessed a woman, over a period of two years, explore and finally fully relive trauma that occurred specifically in a crib in her infancy. After such work had been integrated "enough," the exact movement pattern that once had elicited infant trauma suddenly elicited what she called transpersonal experience when she moved within a witness circle.

The circle is an ancient, archetypal form that appears in rituals, celebrations, and ceremonies in which the sacred is honored or expressed.

The shamans bring their visions back to the circle of their people, where they are enacted and/or danced by the community. The Hasids dance their dances of joy and praise in circles. The !Kung surround their dancers, who invite the num energy to rise for healing purposes, with a circle of people who sing in support of the process. Satprem agrees with the bodhisattvas that "no individual transformation is possible without some degree of collective transformation."[142]

Ritual often spontaneously occurs in Authentic Movement circles, within an individual's work and within the collective. Spontaneous ritual occurs frequently for Alice. As her witness, I experience myself in the presence of high order and ancient form. She describes it this way:

> I have often found myself embodying, enacting very particular, specific movement gestures, specifically directed by some unknown certainty within me. Often I don't understand why I feel compelled, beckoned to do what I do. Many times when I have completed the movement sequences I return to my place in the circle, open my eyes, and realize I have been in another place/realm, another zone of awareness.

In any ritual, impeccability becomes a critical element. Any movement of an individual or a group becomes increasingly specific, precise, as the inherent order reveals itself. Precision is an essential element in transformative experience. Hillman writes: "The psyche has an affinity for precision; witness the details in children's stories, primitive rituals and primitive languages, and the exactitude with which we go about anything that is important."[143] Impeccability within the occurrence of any mystical experience appears to be essential for the well-being of the individual, for the well-being of the collective, for the completion of the process.

Eliade writes of "man's profound need for initiation, for regeneration, for participation in the life of the spirit."[144] In our longing to rediscover the mysteries, to participate in ritual, it is extremely important not to impose acts that do not organically evolve out of the experience itself. Because of the gift and the burden of ego consciousness, we can be informed and even nourished by rituals from other cultures, but we must patiently continue to listen for our own embodied expression of collective consciousness. How will we begin again to find the place, light the fire, say the words, or dance the dance? As Satprem says: "all we want is our own little river flowing into the Infinite."[145]

Conclusion

After the above discussion of some of the similarities between mystical practice and the practice of Authentic Movement, it is necessary before closing to briefly discuss some of the differences. The major difference is that unlike most mystical practice, Authentic Movement is a practice that has not evolved out of or in relationship to a religious belief system. Instead, it evolved originally out of the art of dance. Mary Whitehouse, Joan Chodorow, myself, and many individuals who participate in the development of this form came to it originally as dancers. People come to the form to learn how to listen to their bodies and, in the process, some are guided from within toward experiences beyond ego consciousness.

In the practice of Authentic Movement there is no church, synagogue, dojo, or temple representing a holy place where participants meet. There is no priest, rabbi, or lama. There is no god whom individuals endeavor to find. There is no teacher who guides the individuals in relationship to religious texts or belief systems. Without a master, without a bible, often without any former direct experience of a god, the mover projects her clear self onto the witness until she is ready to own it. As this ownership is integrated, the individual moves toward wholeness until, at times, she becomes one with what Underhill calls her "indwelling Deity."[146]

Unlike the mystic whose experiences have, in the past, tended to evolve out of specific religious symbols, teachings, and collectives, in Authentic Movement practice we are evolving into a collective in which the conscious individual is a full member. In doing so we find our only external guide to be the form itself, which is free of any symbols, doctrines, or promises.

The discipline of Authentic Movement offers a safe container in which individual and collective experience can become transformed, perhaps because of the evolution of the clear self. Again, Satprem offers guidance:

> We do not seek to "pass" on to a better existence but to transform this one.[147]

> Everything seems to be happening up above, but what is happening here? . . . We need a truth that involves also the body and the earth.[148]

> First, we must work in our individual body, without seeking any escape, since this body is the very place where consciousness connects with Matter; and secondly, we must strive to discover the principle of consciousness that will have the power to transform Matter.[149]

> We are here imprisoned in Matter . . . There are not a hundred ways of getting out of it, in fact there are only two; one is to fall asleep . . . and the other is to die. Sri Aurobindo's experience provides a third possibility, which allows us to get out without actually getting out, and which reverses the course of man's spiritual evolution, since the goal is no longer only above or outside, but right inside.[150]

> We need a way to be opened that is still blocked, not a religion to be founded.[151]

To transform, we must descend into the body: "The more we descend, the higher the consciousness we need, the stronger the light."[152] Sri Aurobindo, the Mother, and Satprem write voluminously about this process of light descending into matter, thereby transforming it, resulting in "enstasy," which is ecstasy in the body.[153] They speak of "luminous vibrations."[154] "The day we learn to apply this Vibration . . . to our own matter, we will have the practical secret."[155] Satprem reminds us of what we all must know but somehow forget: "One discovers only oneself, there is nothing else to discover."[156]

The Collective Body

Things are one; things are many.
The intellect cannot grasp these two simultaneously,
but experience can, if it will.
BLYTH, *ZEN AND ZEN CLASSICS*

Embodiment of the Collective: Belonging

I forget. I am a Western woman and I forget. I am a Western woman and I forget that a source of my longing is related to my great desire to belong. I am a Western woman and have learned that embodied personal consciousness is my goal. The physicist Peter Russell beautifully articulates my concern about this goal when he asks:

> Is each of us simply an isolated consciousness, bound by space and time to the body we inhabit? One among five billion other self-conscious individuals who have been given a brief window of experience onto this world? . . . Can we be sure that our individual self is not part of some eternal consciousness temporarily peeking out through the senses of this body into the physical world around? . . . Could my sense of separateness be just an illusion?[1]

Illusion or not, separate is how we feel. We forget that the human psyche cannot endure without belonging. Within the last century, change away from tribal living has accelerated dramatically. For countless centuries preceding this change, we belonged before we asked "who am I?" We were born belonging, not only to a tribalbody but we belonged to the earthbody. We were held by a sacred vessel. As the Western world has developed, we have increasingly been urged first toward the question "Who am I?"—forgetting about the essential relationship between the individual and the interconnectedness among all beings, and finding ourselves encouraged to leave the sacred circle.

I am grateful for the insistence of the question "Who am I?" for the privilege of personal consciousness. I am grateful for the opportunity to heal original wounds and thus change my experience of myself and my experience of others. Individual development is a remarkable aspect of freedom. Because of this freedom, I have learned to look at many parts of myself, to see how these parts create myself, to see the impact of these parts on my body and, finally, to see that I am my body. This sorting through the parts, a very Western way of understanding, has offered a particular kind of learning, which results in a particular kind of self-knowledge. This knowledge can feel life-saving. And yet, at the same time, it becomes life-threatening if we dare to assume it is enough. Individuals consistently reach for this deserved and blessed freedom, and the unraveling of our world becomes more and more visible. It is not enough when the development of the self excludes an integrated relationship to the whole.

In Daniel Quinn's novel *Ishmael,* a gorilla—who is the teacher—says:

> You [humans] know how to split atoms, how to send explorers to the moon, how to splice genes, but you don't know how people ought to live.[2] . . . . I have amazing news for you. Man is not alone on this planet. He is part of a community, upon which he depends absolutely.[3]

The problem: too many of us don't feel part of anything, really, except the system we create in our schedule books.

In the best of all possible Western worlds, our sons and daughters are becoming conscious as they leave home and move into the larger experience of the collective world. These days they hear about global problems and are asked to help save their world. But these young adults are just barely learning about the presence of their internalized mother and father! And, of course, they feel they must understand these aspects of themselves so their own children, now in the wings, don't suffer as they have.

But they are told that the world's children—people, animals, forests—are suffering and on the brink of annihilation. This consciousness of the possibility of the end of the planet is peculiarly new for the human psyche. Television, literature, even the corporate world, talk about environmental and global questions with a new sense of urgency. Now, instead of just discovering work and a mate, instead of just creating a home and babies, our children must somehow remember that they are part of a larger whole and that the whole is suffering in a particular way.

This is an idea, not a knowing. Most have not grown up as members of a circle—their parents are not members of a circle. Their experience of the extended family, perhaps the nuclear family, is splintered, segmented, not held by or felt to be in relationship with a visible, constant collective. Their recent heritage has taught them the supreme importance of their individual future: getting ahead, gaining power, moving up the ladder.

Overemphasis on individual development encouraged outside of a sacred circle has contributed significantly to the creation of unbearable rage, isolation, and despair. In response, the desire to return to one's unquestioned place in the circle can be awakened. But we can easily romanticize possible membership in the collective without fully understanding the shadow aspects of belonging; why the circle has become absent. Our work in the Western world has been fiercely concerned with freeing the individual from the bonds of religious, political, and familial rule. Accepting one's place in the circle could threaten this process of the development of the self. If membership is unconscious, the loss of freedom results. Unconscious commitment to a group ideology, participating in a mass psychology, means loss of freedom for all people involved.

Individualism, independence, even ego development, can threaten conscious membership in a collective when such processes are not in correct relationship to the whole. However, individuation, which is described by Jung as "coming to selfhood" or "self-realization,"[4] can enable us to richly and responsibly enter our place in the collective. Now our unprecedented task, perhaps unknown to our ancestors, is to bring the gifts of individuation into conscious membership in the whole, to find a way to be uniquely ourselves inside a sacred, conscious circle.

How we discover this is a great mystery. Willing membership just with our minds cannot create the shift in consciousness for which we long. The shift must be an embodied shift. It is in our bodies where the phenomenon of life energy, a physical reality, is directly experienced. One by one, knowing (and knowing implies consciousness), knowing in our bodies that we belong, creates a collective body in which life energy is shared. I imagine the collective body as the energetic consciousness of the earthbody, which includes all living beings. It is the body-felt connectedness among people, profoundly related to the source of our humanity.

Becoming conscious of our part in the whole through direct experience of membership allows exploration of the relationship between the personal body and the collective body. When our individual bodies have been wounded because of our suffering, we often are opened toward embodied personal consciousness. Our earthbody is wounded. Can we, because of personal consciousness, become opened toward consciousness of the collective body? Can we create a sacred, conscious circle that evolves organically from the knowing body of each member?

Embodiment of the Collective Spirit

If we are longing for direct experience of this unitive state with the whole, we are longing, by definition, for access to our souls. One cannot have a mystical experience or access to soul without getting a glimpse of the interconnectedness of all things. Mystics from the beginning of time have known this, but in the history of Western civilization mystics have been at the fringes of society, their absence supporting our forgetting. We have forgotten how mystical experience comes about, that it occurs in our bodies because we are a microcosm of the whole.

Can we remember that our bodies are more similar than different? Can we remember that the basic structures of our planet are repeated in the basic structures of our bodies? Mandelbrot, a contemporary scientist, discovered the phenomenon of scaling or fractal geometry.[5] John Briggs, a contemporary teacher and writer, tells us that fractals are a new pattern, and they could provide a powerful incentive for turning our attention away from the activity of the "parts" of nature toward the activity of the whole.[6] This geometry describes the astounding similarity of form in the patterns of nature. For example, blood vessels, tree roots, and riverbeds have the same basic structure. We, as human beings, have the same basic structure! Embodying collective consciousness means extending such knowledge in our minds toward finding a way to directly experience this membership. I believe we are starving for access to such experience because we cannot endure the pain, the isolation, the despair of the separateness, from our own spirit and from each other. I believe these two are inseparable.

Embodying spirit frees me to remember that I am you and you are me, an ancient practice of many mystical traditions. If you are me, you know how afraid I am, how hopeful, how doubting, how strong, how vulnerable I am. You know that I'm doing the very best I can and how deeply I need to be seen, embraced. If I am you, I know of your fear, your hope, your doubt, your strength and vulnerability. I know you are doing the very best you can and that you desire to be loved as you are. Remembering that "I am because we are," words from the wisdom tradition of Ubuntu, can encourage a freedom from fear and doubt. Such freedom enables hope and strength.

Authentic Movement and the Collective Body

The practice of Authentic Movement provides one way for us to learn about this freedom. In this form we can begin to trace the evolution of the development of collective consciousness through the experience of each body, as unconscious material in mover or witness becomes conscious in the presence of others. Thankfully, there are endless ways in the world for individuals to become conscious of membership. I need to begin to mark some within my practice as my need to know—not think about—the web of interconnectedness is urgent.

The ground of the discipline of Authentic Movement is the relationship between the moving self and the witnessing self. The heart of the practice is about the longing, as well as the fear, to see ourselves clearly. We repeatedly discover that such an experience of clarity is deeply and inextricably related to the gift of being seen clearly by another and, just as importantly, related to the gift of seeing another clearly.[7]

The mover, who is the expert on his own experience,[8] works with eyes closed in the presence of the witness, who sits to the side of the movement space. The mover listens inwardly for the occurrence of impulse toward movement. This movement, visible or invisible to the witness, shapes the mover's body as it becomes a vessel through which unconscious material awakens into consciousness. As he internalizes his witness's desire to accept him, to accept his suffering as well as his beauty, embodiment of the density of his personal history empties, enabling him at times to feel seen by the witness and, more importantly, to see himself clearly. Sometimes . . . it is grace . . . the mover embodies a clear presence.

The witness practices the art of seeing. Seeing clearly is not about knowing what the mover needs or must do. The witness does not "look at" the mover but, instead, as she internalizes the mover, she attends to her own experiences of judgment, interpretation, and projection in response to the mover as catalyst. As she acknowledges ownership of her experiences, the density of her personal history empties, enabling the witness at times to feel that she can see the mover clearly and, more importantly, that she can see herself clearly. Sometimes . . . it is grace . . . the witness embodies a clear presence.

A central aspect of the theoretical structure of the form is that each person, without hurting oneself or another, is free to choose to do what he or she must do, constantly balancing surrender and will in the process. In the midst of such concentration on owning one's own experience as mover or witness it matters that others are attempting the same practice, thus trusting some inherent order in the collective. Trying to be a good group member, putting the imagined needs of the group before individual needs, is not what is intended. When each individual does what he or she must do, regardless of content, we notice that the group as a whole "seems" to be in synchrony.

This synchrony could be related to the presence of each individual's internal witness, which develops in relationship to the clarity and compassion of the external witness. The internal witness becomes awareness itself, silent and clear. It can evolve out of a developing and discerning ego that accepts, rejects, debates, protects, exposes, tracks, and guides our experience of reality. It is the process of the development of the internal witness that creates the possibility of consciously choosing membership in a collective.

Wishing to better understand this organic interconnectedness between individuals and the group, my intention has shifted in the last several years in my teaching practice from focus on the intimacy of interpersonal work within the structure described above to focus on the whole. With the dyadic work between the mover and the witness as ground, movers now always move within a circle of witnesses. Within this newer format, whether moving or witnessing, people are invited to remember that they are not participating alone. Like most individual bodies, the collective body is in the process of becoming conscious.

The only way I know how to become conscious of my relationship to the collective body as a whole system is into and through my own body. My body is my teacher. Joan Halifax quotes the Zen monk Dogen: "You should know that the entire earth is not our temporary appearance, but our genuine human body."[9] I can think about my body as a collective: millions of one-cell units; thousands of two separate cells in relationship; multitude of clusters of cells that create organs, bones, muscles; many clusters in many configurations that make my whole self; and, finally, the energy inside and around me, which could be called spirit.

How does the human body, as a collective in itself, mirror the collective body? In the collective body we can see the intrapersonal work of each person, like each cell doing its job. We can see combinations of two people in a relationship, interpersonal connection, like two cells working together. Now, like a cluster of cells creating an organ, such as the heart, we can see clusters of people, some small like the family and others including more people, like a village. Just as many clusters of cells create a whole person, many villages create counties, states, nations, the whole world. And like the spirit within and around the individual person, there is energy in the universe within and around the earth.

Stories: The Collective Body Becoming Conscious

There are stories from my practice of Authentic Movement about movers and witnesses that mark, for me, the evolution of the conscious development of the collective body. I have selected, among a plethora of potent stories, a few to discuss here. It is important to remember that stories are not what actually happened. Stories are about what the storyteller perceived as happening. As I tell you these stories about people's experiences I am including in the first two stories the feelings they experienced while moving, which they shared with us later when they were speaking about their movement. Participants in my workshops are professional adults—including for example, therapists, artists, nurses, lawyers, and social workers. I am grateful to each participant for making possible my questions, my learning.

One Person/One Cell

I begin with one person in the whole world, whom I have named Marie. This woman closes her eyes and enters the movement space, focused totally on her own work. As usual, she has a small blanket with her. She lies down on the floor and barely moves for twenty to sixty minutes at a time. She feels like a baby. She feels completely alone. Now she remembers: her mother was seriously ill and taken away for many years to a hospital. She and her siblings were cared for by their grandmother, a sixty-five-year-old arthritic woman. She hears her grandmother's voice saying what a good baby she was, never crying. Now, again, she remembers nothing. She simply is still and alone. Like one cell in one body, Marie is one human being on the earth. Her isolated experience occurs

in the Authentic Movement studio, in the midst of nineteen other possibly isolated experiences, individuals bringing unconscious material
into consciousness through embodiment.

Two People/Two Cells

After a year's work in which lying still was her primary experience as a
mover, another mover, whom I shall name Andrea, accidentally encounters Marie. Andrea is crawling around with her eyes closed, as if she
is searching. She finds many different movers doing different things,
but she keeps searching. She does not know for what she is searching.
Now she touches Marie, who seems to be barely breathing she is so still.
Andrea stops. She strokes the side of Marie's face with the back of her
hand and begins to weep. As she cries over this body, she slowly remembers her last days with her dying little child, four years ago. She experiences a depth of pain that had been forgotten, too terrible to remember,
reenter, relive.

Now Marie starts to move in new ways, opening toward remembering, reentering, reliving her last memories of touch from her mother,
perhaps before she left or during brief visits. Her mother stroked her
face with the back of her hand exactly the way someone is now touching her.

This is a synchronistic, unrehearsed encounter between two adult
women, both graced by an opportunity to bring unconscious material
into consciousness through embodiment, this time because of each
other. For both women, energy that has been physically locked within
the cells is now being expressed, released and thus available for new
growth in the future. This mutual exchange, this direct experience, is
not unlike the meeting of two cells in a body—where they must be,
when they must be there, doing what they must do.

A Village/A Cluster of Cells

Another year passes. Ten witnesses are in a circle around ten movers.
Today Marie, as a mover, walks slowly around the room, encountering
people and then moving on. Now she is lying down on this side of the

circle, moving slightly. Bert is pacing outside the witness circle. Now he enters the circle crawling and begins to make angry noises. As his movements intensify and his sounds become roars, he crawls across the circle and out the other side into a corner of the room. He is thrashing from side to side, hitting the walls, roaring loudly. Now Marie gets up, leaves the room, comes back with her blanket, wraps herself in it, curls up on the floor and quietly begins to cry. Jake goes to the corner where Bert is roaring and sits quietly nearby.

Andrea, who is also a mover, stands at the edge of the circle, feet widely planted, and conducts, as if an orchestra leader. Bert thrashes more and more audibly in the corner. A witness, whose gaze is riveted on Bert, begins to cry silently as her hands go to her neck. Dianna, a mover, is lying on her back, tapping her hands lightly on the floor as she sings nursery rhymes. Joanna, another mover, crawls very slowly toward Marie, whose crying intensifies as she rhythmically throws her torso over her knees.

Suddenly, Bert bolts from his corner and heads toward Marie on his hands and knees. Joanna, hearing his approach, races him there, crawling. Arriving first because she was closer, she scoops Marie into her arms. Now Marie, safe in the arms of a woman, screams and sobs, her body fiercely contracting and releasing. Bert continues to make sounds and tries to touch Marie with his face. Lila, another mover, wraps her arms and legs around Joanna and Marie, creating a barrier between them and Bert. Ingrid, also a mover, tries to directly engage Bert in battle. He tolerates this interruption only briefly and goes back to Marie, but with reduced ferocity. Now Lila tentatively strokes his hair and, as he quiets, he gently touches Marie, who is no longer crying but is still safely held by Joanna.

After the movement time, movers and witnesses speak of their experience, not only bringing consciousness to what had been unconscious within their idiosyncratic personal history but finding their part in the whole as the story unfolds. Bert talks of his rage and his memory of the terrible physical presence of the man who repeatedly abused him when he was a young boy. Marie tells how Bert's angry noises awakened her feeling, encouraging her to express her own pain.

Jake is now realizing that when he sat near Bert in the corner he was reentering his childhood experiences, his need to stay near his deaf brother, as if to protect him from his parents' confused and erratic responses. As Andrea heard the raging, she found herself conducting, reentering, reliving her efforts to control her father's rage at her when she could not save her dying child. Dianna tells us that nursery rhymes were a familiar cadence—her mother trying to soothe her when her father lost his temper. The witness with her hands on her neck tells us how she experienced Bert as a caged lion and how her experience of him being trapped awakened her claustrophobic terror of being caught in the unconscious web of her family.

Joanna speaks of her experience as an abandoned baby in a hospital and how she felt when she heard a baby cry in an unsafe room. She had to protect the baby. Marie tells us that when Joanna scooped her into her arms it was then that she could fully and safely surrender to her pain, her rage at the neglect of being left alone and unattended for long periods of time when she was a baby. Bert responds by speaking of his great need to get to the unprotected child in himself, somehow connecting his innocence with the power of his abuser. One witness said: "I saw a caged lion whose cub had escaped. He was only trying to get to his cub. He wasn't going to hurt it." Lila, the woman who wrapped her long limbs around Joanna and Marie, suddenly speaks. Just now she is remembering how often she tried to mediate between her father and her mother, quietly, hoping no one would notice. Ingrid hesitantly speaks of her anger toward her husband and how it was ignited as she heard Bert roaring. She tells us of her relief as she embodied her anger.

This unrehearsed, synchronous unfolding of events creates a village story. Movers and witnesses participate within the complexity of their individual personalities, doing what they each must do. It is the story of a collection of people bringing unconscious material into consciousness, through embodiment, because of each other. It is not unlike a cluster of cells, like the heart, in which each cell is doing what it must do, resulting in a pumping heart.

The Whole Earth/The Whole Body

In the next story we leave the details of personal history and see qualities of the human psyche that exist regardless of personality. If we follow the abovementioned metaphor, we move from a village story or cluster of cells to a phenomenon shared by most of humanity on earth, thus to the whole body. Almost everybody, at some point in development, fears their own death. At this time, it is interesting to note, many also fear the death of our earth.

Members arrive at a workshop full of the pain of challenging experiences that occurred in the previous weeks. Jake speaks of a persistent intestinal disease. Joanna speaks of being in another city, far away, with her mother, who is suffering from a double mastectomy. Another woman tells us of her two major abdominal operations in six weeks. Ingrid reports on her recent hip replacement. Lila describes moving again to a new house, the third move in six months. And Dianna mentions the fact that she continues to lose weight but the doctors do not know what is wrong. Judd has returned to the group after major surgery and radiation therapy, which have visibly affected his appearance. He is wearing an oversized jacket, a hat, and a large shawl. He does not speak. Exhaustion, immobility, and lack of protection seem to be shared experiences by most group members.

In our first session of moving and witnessing, eight movers sleep—two snore! The second day, six people arrive late because they were lost! Marie is one of these participants. When she comes into the studio she decides to be a witness and draws as she sees, a not uncommon mode for certain witnesses. Movers come back from the movement time and speak of their pain. Marie asks to show her drawing, but there is no time left.

In the afternoon I suggest that we return to the dyadic work to practice witness skills in an effort to strengthen the witness circle, thus reinforcing the strength of the container, and to give movers the intimacy of one-to-one work, thus reinforcing trust and safety in relationship to their material. But everyone wants to be a mover. No one wants to be a witness. The resistance to witnessing is palpable, people saying they are too tired or that they need to be witnessed and thus wouldn't be good witnesses. I choose to attempt to keep strong boundaries in the structure of our time together and so we work carefully with witnessing skills for the next few sessions. Each time we all come back together to discuss our process, Marie asks to show her drawing. Because of the amount and intensity of material in the group, there is no time.

On the third day of the retreat it is time for a long circle in which people can move or witness whenever they wish. Judd is the first to enter the empty circle. In the course of the last two days he has gradually shed his outer garments. Now we can see him more clearly as he slowly sways back and forth until he loses his balance, begins to fall, catches himself, and then begins to sway again. The witness circle feels strong as others choose to move, each coming closer to themselves in the presence of each other. The energy continues to be mostly low, quiet, and pained.

At the end of the long circle movers and witnesses speak of their experiences. Jake is angry because I rang the bell too early. Andrea is angry because Dianna spoke too long. Others speak about their exhaustion and pain. Theresa suddenly asks: "What is going on here?" Judd's fist comes slamming down into the center of the circle as he insists: "We must name it!" Lila says: "Fear of physical illness and death." Ingrid says: "It is as if we are in bardo, the gap, the place between life and death." Marie shouts: "I'm going to show my picture now!" and holds up a charcoal drawing of the bardo state, a drawing of people wandering around in black capes, not knowing. Relief among the group is visible. The collective embodiment of the fear of death makes it available for consciousness. Naming it, "holding" it together, somehow makes it more bearable. Collective consciousness again made it possible for each to understand better his or her particular role, including Bert—for whom the theme concerning fear of death had no particular meaning at this time.

Judd now speaks of his fear of his own death, describing how he feels it in his stomach. This brings a universal fear back down and into one body grounding the collective in an essential way. After all, the collective is a manifestation of a collection of individual bodies, individual lives. In this case the personal life of each man and woman grappling with the fear of his or her own death or the death of a loved one, in the presence of each other is the collective body becoming conscious.

Now, the last day, the witness circle is unusually strong. Movers are running, shouting, leaping, piling on top of one another. I see eight people in a people pile; the first morning I saw—and heard—eight people sleeping! We need our tribe desperately. We need to feel membership, especially in relationship to the mysteries, the unknown, the ways in which spirit moves.

The Universe/Spirit

The last story is about spirit, the energy inside and around the body. On our earth, most all people know at some point in their lives a fear of death. But in the universe at large, which could be called the energy inside and around the earth, death is inseparable from birth, time and space merge, material disperses and reforms, particle and wave become indistinguishable. In the universe a high order is manifest indefinitely. This order or clarity in the universe, whether perceived or not, could be understood as the witness circle, the clear presence, containing the earthbody.

The story I am about to tell is a projection of my experience as a witness, which is another way to participate in the collective body becoming conscious. As we share our experiences of witnessing the whole or being movers within the whole, we understand a little more about belonging. When witnessing this particular long circle, which occurred in Italy where twenty-five women from different European countries joined me to study and practice the form of Authentic Movement, I experienced a fullness of response to each individual as well as to a collective story.

I have named this story "The Call." Each time a voice called out, a particular archetypal aspect of the human psyche was acknowledged, accepted. In this story I saw how new energy repeatedly, cyclically accrues from life, how it is gathered, contained, dispersed back into the collective through one body, then another, then another. I saw an embodiment of my experience of our present state on this planet.

We all began as witnesses, experiencing the empty center. Slowly, one by one, some witnesses chose to move and others held the container by continuing to witness until they chose to move and movers chose to witness. And so the story begins:

I see a senior woman standing on the edge of the circle, facing out, her arms folded in front of her: a gatekeeper on the edge of the earth. At her feet, I see a woman wrapped in a blanket: a baby, new. I see innocence.

A woman walks to the center of the circle, her arms slowly lifting, calling.

I see a woman pounding, yelling, pulling her hair: destruction, despair, hatred, pain. I see suffering.

A woman suddenly stands, reaching her arms straight out to her side, calling.

I see three movers on the other side of the circle laughing, playing, tumbling: joy, beauty, love. I see freedom.

A woman begins turning, calling, a long steady call.

I see a woman standing, holding her hands in front of her as if she holds a thick tube reaching from the floor to the ceiling. She moves very little, but tension visibly builds in her body, her focus strong and steady: energy accruing in one body. She releases the tension, pounding her heel into the floor: a body as vessel shattering, birthing new energy, which is sent into the earth through her heel. I see transformation.

A woman lies flat on the floor, calling into the earth.

Women clap and sing in rhythm with the pounding heel, and come to their feet, one by one, stomping and chanting: new energy is dispersed, flowing into many bodies.

I see one woman, crouched at the feet of the dancers, hiding her face: the one not ready.

A woman suddenly moves backward to the wall, screaming: fear of the unknown manifest as the new energy escalates.

Another woman, acknowledging fear, meets the screaming woman until the terror evaporates: fear of the unknown shared and thus contained. These two women—who is leading, who is following?—slowly reenter the circle. Now a third woman walks with them. They walk so slowly.

The second woman continues, out the other side of the circle, arriving at the open window, calling out into the hills: a call to the gods for help.

A woman calls out from the other open window on the other side of the room: in response, in support, calling the gods for help.

I see a woman lying near the edge of the circle, silent, unmoving: the one who does not know what to do.

A woman sits on the floor with her legs open, breathing harder and harder: labor before a birth.

A woman wraps her legs from behind around the birthing woman. She pushes her pelvis forward, into the back of the birthing woman. Now she reaches up, out of her efforts and calls, a call for new life.

A woman is weaving shapes in the air with intense focus, directly in front of the woman who sits with her legs open: the cosmic midwife.

A woman moving around the entire outside of the circle, stepping into long deep strides, droning: the cosmic shaman, containing it all.

Again and again, I see a woman sitting on the floor with her legs open breathing harder and harder: labor before a birth. Will new life occur? This birth is not about an individual who will save our earth. This is the birth of the collective body.

Now I see a woman sitting in a corner, raging: anger, frustration, violence, hopelessness.

A woman crawls toward her, waiting, listening at her feet. I see compassion.

The clock tells me to lift the bell and let it ring. It is time to rest. It is not time for the birth. How is readiness determined? For now, like children, we are in the process of remembering something we once knew long ago and simultaneously, we are glimpsing our potential for discovering something completely new, something we have never before experienced. In the meantime, we are loving the best we can.

Toward the Unknown
A Conversation between
Janet Adler and Annie Geissinger

Annie: You recently told me you have been digging toward the roots of the discipline of Authentic Movement, to understand its origins—even of the name itself.

Janet: I was thrilled last year to find the words "authentic movement" in a book from the 1930s written by the dance critic John Martin.[1]* I believe he is the first person to use these words—as he described the dancing of Mary Wigman. I know Mary Whitehouse referred to Martin's work in the 1960s when they were both teaching at UCLA, but I don't know if they ever communicated with each other.

Annie: In 1981 you named your first school for Authentic Movement, The Mary Starks Whitehouse Institute. How did your work relate to Mary's at that time?

Janet: At that time, the work I was doing was definitely and deeply connected to what I had learned from Mary, because it was centered on the experience of the mover, in the presence of another. What I did not realize was that, for me, the name Authentic Movement included the phenomenon of witnessing as well.

I don't remember Mary using the term "witness," and I have not

---

*John Martin (1893–1985), writer and teacher, was the first full-time critic devoted to writing about dance, specifically Modern Dance. Janet quotes the full passage she refers to here in her book *Offering from the Conscious Body,* xv.

been able to find it in her writing. She called herself an "observer" or "teacher" when I moved in her presence. She gave no instruction about sitting to the side of the space because it is my understanding that her students didn't observe each other—although as her work developed she did write more about her responsibilities and experiences as an observer.

The name, for me, also included the conscious relationship between mover and witness. I didn't think about how I was using the term or that I had capitalized the two words. I just thought of it as the name for what I wanted to explore with my students. I assumed then that whatever I was doing was what I had learned from Mary.

Annie: When do you think the differences between your work and Mary's began to emerge?

Janet: Looking back now, I think the significant difference began right then—in the first year of the Institute. It is inevitable that my own personality and my own questions growing out of my studio experience at the Institute would create a different direction for me. This direction was mostly concerned with my need to explore the experience of the witness, so I began very early to invite students to witness each other. My questions about witnessing grew out of my experience of Mary as a witness, out of my readiness to study containment, and I imagine also grew out of my desire to enter more consciously the heart of relationship—because studying witnessing meant studying the relationship between mover and witness.

Annie: In *Arching Backward* you describe the evening when you first opened the Institute, *and* first experienced the "energy" of the mystical initiation. Do you think your experiences of that initiation were related to the changes you were making in the direction of your work?

Janet: Yes. Of course I couldn't have known at the time how deeply, how mysteriously the initiation and the opening of the Institute were connected. I can see now that my experience of initiation marked a dramatic shift in my work. The presence of the students simultaneously created what I experienced as an energetic web, as well as some kind of container.

This particular gestalt must have allowed the embryonic form for the discipline of Authentic Movement to kick about. At the same time, as I experienced the embodiment of this energy, my own body was racked with what could be called labor pains. I didn't realize then that I was participating in bringing into form something that was not only grounded in Mary's teaching but also in my direct experience of the numinous.

Recently, and with some relief, I realized that in the past seventeen years of studio work, beginning with the Institute, I was committing and recommitting in the deepest inward way toward bringing into form the manifestation of what I received within my experience of initiation.

Annie: Can you say more about this inward way?

Janet: It did not come through specific words or specific visions. But in the initiation, I often felt as though my body itself was being kneaded by the energy of the potential form, kneaded because of a form—a way of work—that I could never quite see.

Now I see it. I see that this obscure inner guidance was nonnegotiable and inevitable, leading me toward the unfolding of a practice, a practice that relies on the creative force at its center, the very soul embodied; a practice that organically requires the presence of another.

Realizing this now helps me understand why my experience of the evolution of this discipline has been both so painful and so gratifying. I didn't consciously know that the teachings that I received in my initiation were pushing through toward conscious collective embodiment in this world now. Yet in my teaching groups there were always new and often burning questions. I rarely felt as though I knew how to follow these questions other than moving blindly but surely into the next chamber, never knowing what we would encounter there. And it had to be *we,* not *me* alone, because the embodied discoveries *required* a circle of beings. Because the teachings were about an individual's relationship to the whole, we needed each other in order to stumble toward embodied wholeness within ourselves as individuals, within our relationships with each other one by one, within the collective body, and within our individual relationships to the divine.

Relationship in any form teaches us about our capacity to accept, endure, and survive suffering, our own and every being's: thus the creation of our developing compassion. Our compassion completely depends on our experience of each other, our relationship to the whole. I needed others to go with me, which meant enduring great fears: fear of being misunderstood by others, fear of inviting others toward experiences that I couldn't first know, and fear of betraying myself.

Annie: What do you mean by the fear of betraying yourself?

Janet: Changing the format from dyads to the collective body work was excruciating for me. You were part of a group in which we were making that change. I'm sure you remember—

Annie: Yes, the first time I worked with you. Moving in the group brought up intense fear for me, a feeling of being flooded, lost, and helpless. I remember I was afraid to move without the assurance of being witnessed by one person throughout.

Janet: At that time, after listening to you speak about your needs, I vividly remember where you are standing and how you are moving. I "see" a portion of the wall behind you fall away, opening the space, widening my perspective, reminding me that I must not betray myself, my unexplainable need to keep going, risking that you might not feel seen. And I felt a certain agony as I let go of my own need to give you personal witnessing as long as you needed it. At another time while teaching in the collective work, I remember knowing that I had to be silent as a witness and no longer offer verbal witnessing. But I didn't really know why. That was a painful risk.

Such moments, especially those most challenging transitions from dyads to collective—or from speaking to silence—or from movers and witnesses talking to each other in a collective, to writing and then reading to each other—each risk challenged my capacities to endure. And by the end of our days together (whatever group it was), realizing we had made it through, I felt liberated! Those were the gratifying times, when we'd safely crossed the threshold and I knew again there was an inherent order in the organic evolution of this path to which I was inescapably bound. Each of these crossings required the commitment of individuals, the resistance of individuals, and the trust of individuals.

Annie: For me, that retreat ended quite dramatically, the life force inside of me reasserting itself emphatically, as if grabbing me and forcefully pulling me up out of a flood. And it's very moving to hear your story about that, and how it affected you, especially relating to the fear of betraying yourself. Because one of the teachings for me of Authentic Movement practice is the understanding that I must be true to myself, that we each must hold our places as fully as we can, and that seems to be the deepest, most important way we can serve each other.

Janet: Yes, each of our contributions as mover and as witness is essential, unique, and inextricably connected. We each take our turn, but only because of the others who took their turns, teaching us, showing us, enabling us to move closer to our own emerging questions. It touches me very much to think of this lineage, which in my perception is more like a vibrant web. I think of the years when I was Diana Levy's teacher, and then the years in which Diana was your teacher, and now I am your teacher and you are the teacher of another. I like that this shape is not so specifically linear.

As my own students well know, I believe that it is imperative for a student to try everything that is offered by their teacher, to take what belongs to them—what they need from the work with their teacher—and, when the time is appropriate, let the rest go and move closer to their own unique way. One of my greatest joys is to witness some of my most practiced students discover new and suddenly necessary ways of working—importantly contributing to our experience of political consciousness, ritual, sandtray, performance, the creation of new and timely mythologies—and in doing so, taking their turns participating in the development of the discipline.

Annie: Can you speak about another teacher who affected the direction of your work, John Weir? I believe you first mentioned his influence when Neala Haze and Tina Stromsted interviewed you in 1994, in the *American Journal of Dance Therapy.*[2]

Janet: Yes. It was only then that I realized that John's work, as I experienced it in two workshops in the late 1960s, was such a central part of the discipline of Authentic Movement as it developed. If I summarize the gifts given within the awe of the mover/witness phenomenon, Mary's most precious gift to me concerned the opportunity to safely enter the mystery of moving and being moved. And John's great gift was a contextual framework for my experience as witness.

When I opened the Institute, I said right away, "The mover is the expert. The mover speaks before the witness. The witness doesn't refer to any material before the mover has. We must own our own judgments, projections, and interpretations. The only way out is in and through." I said all this—John's words—as if it was an integral part of authentic movement. I don't fully understand how John's way of thinking and speaking about one's experience suddenly and simply dropped deeply into my teaching about witnessing and moving.

At that time I had not been in touch with John for probably ten years. But I was so affected by his way of perceiving and speaking about the self that I must have unconsciously imbibed his language system and assumed it was all part of authentic movement as Mary had taught me. In many ways John's "percept language" was not unrelated to Mary's developing understanding of her role as an observer, but John created an entire conceptual system, primarily based on his study of transference within a Freudian framework.

John wrote very little, but in my research last year, I was ecstatic to read for the first time a chapter he wrote in a book early in his career and to find the word "witness" in his writing about group process. He refers in a couple of paragraphs to verbal sharing as a kind of witnessing. He describes witnesses as people who can offer accepting observation of other group members who are reliving early trauma, showing approval and respect. I must have heard him use this word in his teaching, and am so grateful because I have always loved this ancient word. I needed this word to reflect my exploration of the experience of the one who longs to see clearly.

Annie: Can you say more about John Weir's work and how you came into contact with it?

Janet: John, a master group leader, is a psychologist who is now in his 80s. His work focused mostly on physical experience, with strong emphasis on self-awareness, self-ownership. His profound insights into the psychological development of the self, his philosophy—I see now in his writing—encompassed an understanding of the inner witness, of ritual and ceremony, each reminiscent of spiritual practice.

He and Mary worked briefly together at a couple of his workshops in Maine. It was at John's workshop that I first encountered authentic movement, taught that particular summer by a student of Mary's. There was no question about the power of that workshop for me, and the safety there. I was twenty-eight years old. I awakened to both of these realms—percept language and authentic movement—within a period of two weeks.

Annie: Wasn't John's work primarily influenced by Freud? Yet many people associate Authentic Movement and Mary Whitehouse's work with Jungian thought.

Janet: What I call the ground form of the discipline of Authentic Movement—the dyadic work—seems to me to have at least equal roots in the contributions of both Freud and Jung. Freudian developmental theory, with emphasis on psychophysical phenomena, seeded my own early work with autistic children. Those experiences preceded my contact with John Weir's work, which grew from Freud's understanding of the unconscious and the central power of the original relationships with parental figures. Though I find important aspects of Freud's work incompatible with my way of understanding the full spectrum of a developing life, by opening the door to the unconscious, Freud simultaneously unveiled the body standing dense and magnificent, right there at the threshold.

Because Mary's work in Jungian analysis greatly affected her discoveries about the body's wisdom, she introduced authentic movement within the framework of Jungian thought. Jung's understanding of direct experience and the remarkable ways in which he sought meaning in relationship to it—exploration of the rich, vital shapes and essential stories of the archetypes—are familiar to me because of my discoveries in authentic movement with Mary, but such a process is not at the center of my own practice.

Annie: What has brought about your recent realizations concerning your discernment of the sources of your work?

Janet: A student of mine, Patrizia Pallaro, has been editing the forthcoming two volumes about Authentic Movement, reviewing Mary's articles, Joan Chodorow's articles, and mine for the publication of volume one. She respectfully pointed out how the discipline of Authentic Movement—my own course of inquiry—is different from, though inclusive of, authentic movement. I realize now what she means, although I never intended to participate so intensely in the development of a discipline. With the gifts of my teachers undifferentiated within me, I was trying to follow what always felt like an intuitive call toward the unknown.

Annie: So Patrizia was able to see your development in this work, from a movement therapist to a teacher of a practice in which dyads evolved into the collective body work.

Janet: That's right. I was a movement therapist when I studied with Mary Whitehouse in 1969. When I left and moved to the East Coast, I continued to explore authentic movement in a part-time private practice. So I entered the work from a psychological perspective. And I continue to believe that a witness has to have enough consciously embodied experience of her own psychological development and understanding of developmental psychology to really be able to stay in correct relationship to the psychological material of her mover, even if she is not going to process it by engaging as if she were a therapist.

As the teacher/witness in my practice of the discipline of Authentic Movement now, my responsibility is to continue to attend to my inner experience in the presence of any of that content, any material that is awakened, explored within the experience of moving or witnessing. My intention is to practice toward an emptying of myself, which paradoxically means consciously entering the fullness of myself, my feelings, thoughts, sensations, and so on. This is specifically different from "holding" the psychological material for or with the mover. Though one can move in the presence of a therapist or of a witness in a dyadic or group format, what the therapist's or witness's experience is and how that experience is articulated can be quite different. In this context, the differences are distinguished by intention.

Annie: I'm wondering who, or what way of understanding direct experience in the body, impacts your thinking now?

Janet: It is my practice in the studio that takes me further into this exploration, this study of nonsymbolic, also a nondualistic way of perception, more metaphysical than psychological. I need to attend to the exploration of intuitive knowing, a phenomenon that includes insight, but not projection or interpretation.

I become increasingly attracted to the complexities of the experience of the inner witness, which I'm realizing is the core of many meditative practices. A primary distinction between these practices and the practice of Authentic Movement is that in meditative practices, the inner witness develops without the conscious commitment to another, a mover or a witness, during the actual meditation time. In the discipline of Authentic Movement, the presence of another during the actual practice of movement or witnessing is essential by definition.

Recently I have begun to study Buddhist texts more seriously. Not long ago a new friend, who is a Zen priest, moved and I witnessed. When we spoke together afterward, she asked: "I wonder if the discipline of Authentic Movement is the feminine form of Zen?" That engaging question and others we discovered in later conversation are of enormous importance to me; they gesture toward another root system of the discipline.

Annie: I wonder how your mystical initiation relates more specifically to this practice of Authentic Movement in the collective work. What leaps to mind is experiences of "energy" in the collective work, the times when it feels that a whole story is unfolding among the movers, or a whole ritual is being enacted, of course without anyone knowing ahead of time what that would be—and yet everyone is playing their precise part. Or times when in either big or very minute ways, synchronistic, even miraculous things seem to happen. Are these experiences related to your experience of initiation? Is this the same "energy" you experienced?

Janet: Yes. I would say what you are describing is mysterious, highly ordered, and reflective of that ineffable time and space when intuition and clear seeing become one in the experience of enough individuals, at once. This feels definitely related to energetic phenomena. This could be called spontaneous ritual. Understanding how each experience is a part of the energetic phenomena of the whole collective—or even understanding what it means—is less important to me than my desire to practice safely together, which requires trust in each individual's commitment toward practice with consciousness. I believe that collectives becoming conscious must prepare to safely hold that which is too great for an individual to hold alone. This can be done by continuing to practice the guidelines of the ground form.

I imagine that in group work, psychological safety has something to do with the potential of the collective to safely hold each individual psyche. But this possibility is completely dependent on the development of each individual's inner witness—if it is "good enough" to safely contain and to express enough of his own psychological complexes in the presence of others. For each individual to come toward correct relationship to the whole, there must be enough "good enough" inner witnesses. I strongly agree with Thich Nhat Hanh when he says the next Buddha will be the Sangha—the community of practitioners. We must become responsible for our own light, our own shadow, and no longer project these out onto others. We don't need more gods. We need elders, and guides, teachers, therapists and witnesses, rabbis and priests, to help us find the gods within ourselves as we journey toward conscious participation in the collective body.

Annie: Though you did not have a circle of practiced witnesses around you during your initiation, I wonder if what you experienced might become more common for others practicing Authentic Movement. Do you think the practice somehow invites that type of energy?

Janet: The practice offers an invitation, a constant invitation, toward surrender of will. We can never know what might appear as this happens. As we're on that edge, teetering, about whether to surrender or not, I think the biggest question is "Am I safe? Is this appropriate?" The boundaries and the freedom created by the practice make possible an expansion of one's experience, which includes energetic phenomena. It is not uncommon now that a person practicing experiences a strong, first-time embodiment of the energy—completely unsolicited. This can be the beginning of an initiation experience or an isolated moment that might or might not recur at a later date.

Annie: Do you think the energy is seeking the container that is created by the practice?

Janet: I don't know if I would say that the energy is seeking a container, but because the container is consciously being developed with more and more integrity, I believe it is inevitable that the energy would be experienced by certain individuals within the vessel formed by the collective body. I know this energy as impersonal and inherently good, as a gift. The challenge is, how to come into correct relationship with it. I see this energy coming into the culture more rapidly, more often, and, I believe, with more opportunity for conscious reception. This was not the case even fifty years ago. Now there is an increasing number of people offering their stories of direct experience of the numinous in books, in schools, and institutions concerned with energetic phenomena. Our culture is just beginning to include, and even occasionally accept, such phenomena within an individual's range of experience.

Annie: Thomas Merton quotes a Tibetan saying in his *Asian Journal*: "The milk of the lioness is so precious and so powerful, that if you put it in an ordinary cup, the cup breaks." To me this is about the question of the relationship between what we contain and what kind of container we have, or are. To hold something so precious and so powerful, what is the cup that is *not* ordinary? What cup would not break?

Janet: I am not familiar with that particular saying, but surely some containers are stronger than others precisely because of the practiced intention of individuals toward embodied consciousness. This is one way to look at it.

Another way to look at it is this: what if we say that all cups break, even the strong, extraordinary ones. Then our task is to learn how to come into relationship with the broken cup. The suffering that comes from the breaking of the old form—the self or collective as one has known it—makes the true changing of that form possible, and thus creates the potential for authentic compassion.

Some people who practice the discipline of Authentic Movement might say that the circle should never be broken, that it is only "sacred" if it stays whole. My sense is that we must always intend to pay full attention to our experience as witness and mover, and that inevitably the circle must be broken, and that's what really creates the strength of it. You know the kind of china that's very fragile? It's the kind we rarely use, for fear of breaking it. But the cup that's made of clay, that's been worked and mended—the potential wholeness of that cup comes from fragmentation, not wholeness. This is like healing. Wholeness doesn't create wholeness, in my experience. It is fragmentation that creates the opportunity for wholeness, and this includes the opportunity for continued fragmentation. So, even though the practice guidelines come out of experiences in the studio, trying to follow them "religiously" makes me think of the china cup. The form becomes too fragile, and not useful, and not . . . warm.

Annie: I remember speaking about this once with Alton Wasson.* He was talking about being rigorously attentive to what is true, to your experience, as opposed to being rigorously attentive to form; that is, making sure everything is done right. It's a misplacement of the rigorousness.

---

*Alton Wasson is co-director of Contemplative Dance and an honored teacher of Authentic Movement.

Janet: Yes, I agree. The rigor of the practice can be created by our longing—longing for the clear, silent awareness. This longing helps create the guidelines. The guidelines help create safety. Safety invites trust. Trust is essential for transformative work. I long for enough trust to be able to see what I am ready to see, hear what I am ready to hear, know what I am ready to know; I long for enough trust to be as I truly am. So the guidelines can help us work more truthfully. But if the guidelines inhibit the freedom to risk working truthfully within the safety of the practice, then the work becomes like . . . like what?

Annie: Well, maybe like religion. That's what comes up for me. It becomes like religion where we may search for some essential teaching, but then get caught up in rules and regulations, right and wrong ways of doing things, and the original impulse gets lost or forgotten.

Janet: What is your religious history?

Annie: I was raised as a Protestant Christian. But I left college to live in an ashram for about a year. I had unexpected, powerful experiences there that helped me understand much more about my relationship to a larger truth. I thought those experiences were the result of the practices and guidelines offered by that community and path. I was young, eighteen years old. I thought that in order to continue to have this new relationship, this huge new understanding, I had to follow these rules and guidelines—that the connection was in the guidelines. It took a long time to realize that I had to find my own way, to realize that on a deeper level, the specifics of the practices had nothing to do with what I was searching for.

I think this is what happens with religion. The question of right and wrong ways to do things just starts to completely override the original impulse to connect with the divine. What's the right way to stay engaged with the experience of the truth? And how do I find my own specific way? In Authentic Movement practice, the guidelines are so simple. They have offered me tremendous freedom to explore this question. And the guidelines are so clearly in support of the original impulse, offering a safe place for it to be expressed.

Janet: Antonio de Nicholas writes about the distinction between the prophetic voice, which comes through the religious structures, and the poetic voice, which comes from mystical experience. The prophetic voice says, "This is where you stand. This is what God wants. This is how to behave." But the poetic voice is talking about how god might be directly *experienced* in the body—another way of knowing. I'm thinking of these two voices within your experience at the ashram. Maybe there are times when we need another voice to guide us toward discovering what we already know but have forgotten: our true nature, our poetic voice. And then what we need is a safe context, an appropriate place, in the presence of another or others, to welcome it.

Annie: Is this what we're trying to create in the discipline of Authentic Movement—the safe and appropriate context?

Janet: Yes.

Annie: Do you think it is important for us to learn about other places and cultures where the poetic voice is honored? It strikes me how, after your initiation, you delved into studying mysticism, working toward your doctorate in mystical studies. Was this to find a context for your experience?

Janet: Yes, exactly, exactly. I needed to find if, and where I belonged. Some people know a lot about the context and then have the direct experience. Others, as in my case, have the direct experience and then go in search of a context. But it doesn't matter—I think that, as human beings, we simply need that relationship to the whole. For the whole to be vital, I think we must each have the freedom to uniquely—at just the correct moment in all time, all space—step into the unknown. As our direct experience is made conscious, this stepping instantly and forever changes each one of us, and simultaneously expands the whole.

Annie: I just love that part about "uniquely stepping in." That is it! That is what I want, the freedom to uniquely step in.

CHAPTER FIVE

INTUITIVE KNOWING

Introduction

By Bonnie Morrissey & Paula Sager

As the Discipline of Authentic Movement unfolds, individuals become a part of a woven reality, simultaneously knowing the clarity and aloneness of their separateness and the essential warmth, the compassion emerging from the direct touching with the ones who are near them doing what they are doing. There can be moments in which the graceful blessing of unitive consciousness can be known, a direct experience in which the boundaries describing all relationships, within and without, dissolve.

JANET ADLER,
OFFERING FROM THE CONSCIOUS BODY

Throughout her writings, Janet gives voice to the evocative nature of longing as an impetus for growth. Within inner development, longing is the compass that orients us toward that which at first can only be intuited. The Discipline of Authentic Movement honors the phenomenon of intuition as active from the outset, hidden within the blend of impulse and choice. Over time, in an integrative process because of developing consciousness, intuition becomes a more trusted guide, becomes *intuitive knowing*, embodied clarity emerging from an invisible source.

Beginning in 1993 and guided by her own longing to be in service to all that is moving through her, Janet makes space in her life for an annual month-long retreat, which becomes a necessary and invaluable support for her intensive teaching practice. Each January for twenty-five years, she begins the year with "a return to the well." She describes these "narrow passages" in solitude and silence as an experience of energy "that had to be received and integrated, somehow insisting on resourcing me with what I needed for all that was to come."[1]

In the 1990s, while continuing to travel to teach larger and ongoing groups, Janet grounds her primary teaching practice in her Northern California studio with individuals and smaller groups. By the turn of the century, she concludes her European and East Coast teaching commitments, offering heartful farewells to her students in these established groups. Some trek westward to join her newer groups of usually six to eight students, which she organizes in hopes of inviting a collaborative exploration of intuition in relationship to specific areas of interest. These groups included themes such as mystical text, mystical dance, kundalini, the process of initiation, Jewish mysticism, Zen, and the practice of psychotherapy.

As Janet's small groups flourish throughout the first decade of the 2000s, she engages in a progressively deeper study of the ritual form, replacing the long circle with the *declaring circle,* encouraging a new and clearer commitment to choosing one role, mover or witness, within a round of practice. Alongside a more focused commitment to one role at a time, she invites an intensified precision of tracking. Janet continues to encourage movers, as they speak from the voice of their inner witness, to locate their experience precisely within space and time, while also inspiring them to attend to more exacting and meticulous details of physical movement and accompanying inner experiences. Movers refine their ability to enter and articulate "one place" in their sequence, speaking from their embodied experience with increasingly honed attention.

During these years of smaller groups and enhanced focus, the role of the *moving witness* continues to support consciousness within the collective body, as movers establish a more reliable and consistent ability to track and articulate their own inner experience in relationship to other movers, through perceived closeness, distance, sound, touch, and energetic phenomena. The role of the *silent witness* also evolves, as witnesses are invited to more actively study the contents of their embodied experience of witnessing. Silent witnesses speak together, after the moving and witnessing ritual, in a separate space that offers complete freedom to explore the contents of their own experience while protecting movers from possible projections. Consistent practice within the roles of moving witness and silent witness helps students prepare for the role of the *speaking witness,* in which they may offer verbal witnessing to a mover after the mover has spoken. Students clarify their own inner boundaries, strengthening their ability to *contain* inner experience, and learning to choose more consciously when and what to speak, as well as when to remain silent.

Each of these refinements in the evolution of the discipline becomes possible because of the smaller group size, inviting a more intentional descent while cultivating the art of concentration. As students plumb more directly into the intricacy and fullness of conscious embodiment, their awareness practice deepens. A more concentrated presence of attention in each individual creates a widening space of energetic potential in the collective body, within which direct experience and the phenomena of intuitive knowing are more likely to occur.

In her second book, *Offering from the Conscious Body: The Discipline of Authentic Movement* (2002), an evolutionary arc of embodied consciousness becomes evident as Janet organizes her view of the development of the inner witness through three sequential spheres: the Individual Body, the Collective Body, and the Conscious Body. She outlines the territory, the challenges, and the practices of discernment that are called for in each sphere, and she depicts the trajectory of development that flows from duality toward unitive consciousness within and across all three.

Each student of the discipline follows their own unique and nonlinear path through these realms. Janet reminds us that unitive experiences may be known right from the beginning, and psychological material can arise at any time. Within this spiraling through experiences of embodiment, the development of the inner witness clarifies toward witness consciousness, and the inner witness may come to be known as witness presence. As a developed-enough inner witness accrues in each student, the capacity for consciousness increases also within the collective body. Qualities of benevolence and the embodied hum of energetic potential are more palpable and consistently available within the shared space of the group. Because the evolution of the Discipline of Authentic Movement is a mystical practice primarily born in the individualistic culture of North America, the experience and articulation of personal narrative tends to precede the experience and articulation of collective narrative, which tends to precede the direct experience of emptiness, absent of narrative.

We begin this chapter with an excerpt from *Offering from the Conscious Body*. In "Waiting for Direction," a long-time student in one of Janet's groups, experiencing energetic phenomena, returns to her for individual work. Within a series of meetings, his well-developed inner witness, from years of tracking, becomes "a more vivid and loving presence" as he discovers a new strength arising out of his experience of vulnerability. The intentional choice to face the truth of our own woundedness and to cultivate an ongoing relationship with vulnerability requires surrender in the presence of one's inner witness. Willingness to suffer *consciously* is a source not only of authentic strength but also of both empathy and compassion. These qualities, expressed through tenderness, sensitivity, and humility, immerse us in a stream of compassionate awareness that may pervade collective bodies and thus enter a world very much in need of such energy, such consciousness, such witnessing.

In her next essay, "From Seeing to Knowing,"* we are drawn more deeply into the inner life and maturing practice of witness consciousness.

---

*"From Seeing to Knowing" was first presented as a paper at the C. G. Jung Institute of Santa Fe, New Mexico, in the spring of 2003 and was later published in *Spring* "Body and Soul, Honoring Marion Woodman," no. 72 (2005): 251–265 and *Authentic Movement: Moving the Body, Moving the Self, Being Moved—A Collection of Essays Vol. 2*, edited by Patrizia Pallaro (Philadelphia: Jessica Kingsley Publishers, 2007), 260–69.

Janet describes movers and witnesses gaining facility in distinguishing between merged states (absence of an inner witness), dialogic states (inner witness in relationship with experience), and unitive states (inner witness fully present in direct experience). She draws a contrast between "seeing" and "knowing," explicitly addressing the kinship and differences between imagination (a symbolic experience) and intuitive knowing (nonsymbolic), a direct experience she describes as "an intuitive wisdom occurring as veils lift."*

In an extraordinary passage reflecting decades of embodied practice and study, Janet articulates the distinctions between symbolic and direct experience. Describing a mover sitting on the floor, holding her foot, Janet offers four ways this mover may experience an image, guiding us through subtle nuances of the imaginal realm unfolding toward intuitive knowing, as imagery dissolves. Additionally, she offers two further ways in which embodied experience may manifest directly.

In both her studio work and her writing, Janet's focus continues to shift away from associative and symbolic aspects of content and story. As she delves with more persistence into the study of direct experience, she guides students ever more deeply into the detail of what the body can know in the present moment. In clearly distinguishing content from process, students are invited to open and "descend" toward the embodiment of direct experience, individually and within the collective body, becoming more receptive to intuitive knowing, to the direct touch of energetic phenomena and the manifestation of unitive experience.

In 2006, Janet moves with her husband across the Canadian border to Galiano Island, where Philip designs and builds their home, a painting studio for himself, and a studio space—the *kiva*—for Janet. Traditionally

---

*The terms *seeing* and *knowing* are central to understanding the development of the inner witness as an evolution of embodied consciousness. Janet uses these words in various ways within her speaking and writing, with or without quotation marks. She helps us recognize a spectrum of seeing, from the optical seeing that is materially or physically based, through imagery and toward the vibrational seeing sourced in energetic phenomena. Similarly, a spectrum of knowing emerges, from the purely mental to the fully-developed intuitive.

a kiva, sourced from Pueblo, Hopi, and Navajo First Nations Tribes, is a chamber, usually round, built wholly or partially underground, thus holding the power and deep body memory of earth. Dreams, visions, and other energetic phenomena are invited and received by and through individuals within the ritual space and time of the kiva, and shared afterward with the tribe or community.

During her initiation, searching for support, Janet visited and worked briefly with Jaichima, a Huichol shaman woman in Sedona, Arizona, in part of what is known as the Four Corners of the United States, where Pueblo peoples have lived historically and continue to live. There, during an especially intense time in her initiatory process, Janet sat alone in a kiva, tracking her experience, as visions poured through her body. Her kiva on Galiano Island honors that time, that experience, that ritual space that held her, and the indigenous people who offered support. In preparation for the release of this book, though Jaichima is no longer living, Janet reconnected with Jaichima's brother Rutury, also a shaman, who offered his blessing of the naming of her space, which flowed from this intersection of culture and tradition.

As years pass and her teaching in the kiva continues, Janet begins to see and further articulate the full picture of her experience of the development of embodied witness consciousness. She envisions a timeless iconic image formed in the space where two circles overlap, and she recognizes a name for this shape in the tradition of sacred geometry—*mandorla*.

In her essay "The Mandorla and the Discipline of Authentic Movement,"* Janet honors the mandorla as a vibrant alchemical form and a template that can hold the fullness of the evolving discipline. With the whole trajectory of development now visible, she surrenders to a complete and public acknowledgment of the practice as mystical by capitalizing the *d* when referring to the Discipline of Authentic

---

*"The Mandorla" was first published on the Discipline of Authentic Movement website and later published in *Journal of Dance and Somatic Practices* 7, no. 2 (2015): 217–27. (This essay can also be read in German and French on the Discipline of Authentic Movement website.)

Movement, an important culmination of the manifestation of the form. Evoking a physical space and a shape through time, the mandorla reflects the full arc of the developing inner witness, providing a nonlinear and developmental map, a shared visual language for students and teachers. As students cycle from the ground form of one mover and one witness to the expanded form of two movers with one witness, toward small groups with multiple movers and witnesses, the blessing of feeling seen matures toward the longing to see another and toward an integrated felt sense of membership within the collective body. Roles unfold in a natural way within the discipline, and witness consciousness evolves within movers and within witnesses, eventually meeting in nonduality: mover consciousness and witness consciousness become one.

As enough consciousness coalesces through each individual, one by one, the collective body manifests a clearer, more palpable consciousness of its own. Alignment of the self within the whole continues to refine, as reliance on content or symbolic material falls away, allowing movement, sound, light, and vibration to arise within a palpable energetic field. Conscious membership within such a field may appear first as synchrony and then develop into spontaneous ritual. Because of a deepening practice involving formlessness, within the immense potential of a field of emptiness, the phenomenon of ceremony may naturally arise. As full participation in the intimacy of direct experience manifests, all witnessing coheres toward *integral witnessing*. Each former role and way of witnessing becomes integrated and can be experienced as intuitive knowing within ceremony. Moving, witnessing, speaking, and listening within a "shared energetic field of awareness" become a culmination of what is possible within an embodied collective of individuals guided from within, in conscious relationship with each other and the whole.

In "Intimacy in Emptiness: Ceremony,"* her most recent essay and the final offering of this chapter, Janet writes from within her experience of

---

*An earlier version of Janet's "Intimacy in Emptiness: Ceremony" was presented at the First International Gathering of Circles of Four Faculty at Werkhoven, The Netherlands, in May 2017. This is its first publication in print.

the now fully mature discipline. Her voice leans toward the incantatory, toward spoken prayer, in which each word carries a vibratory resonance. Her words interlace with the words of other individuals participating in a collective experience of *ceremony*. Speaking and listening after moving and witnessing, voices weave together as one expression, each voice contributing a distinctive and important thread.

In the early 1980s, within her initiatory experience, Janet was shown the evolutionary possibility of individuals collaboratively participating with others in consciously embodied collectives. She writes, in October of 1984:

> . . . Thoughts of what to do, how to participate in the embodiment of becoming collective, becoming conscious, interfere with a flood of visions, of people moving and witnessing in continuous circles, of people awakening into clear presence. (see "Becoming an Initiate," page 58)

Throughout decades of teaching, grounded in the immediacy of the studio work and her role as primary witness, Janet's intuition guided her in response to this question. One by one, each student arrived with willingness, "wandering into [their] interior wilderness" in her presence (see "Intimacy in Emptiness: Ceremony," page 222). After years of inquiry within the collective experience of large groups of students, Janet reflects: "And it had to be *we*, not *me* alone, because the embodied discoveries *required* a circle of beings" (see "Toward the Unknown," page 166).

Janet describes ceremony as "a mysteriously timed elegance of interconnectedness," a choreography of movement and stillness and sound and silence in alignment with the life energy of spirit. This may be experienced by participants as embodied wholeness, and it may manifest in numerous ways such as emptiness, presence, clarity, silence, infinite space, intuitive awareness, unitive consciousness, light, vibration, oneness, devotion, love, awakening, sacred geometry, a sacred rite, or the unfolding of prayer.

Waiting for Direction
Excerpt from *Offering from the Conscious Body*

Waiting this evening at summer's end, I am watching the dogs on the hillside roaming through the prickly grasses, recently scythed, still golden. The tall man arrives with peaches cradled in the cup of his shirt. We leave them lined up on the bench outside the door and come into the studio, settling near the low table on our cushions. The intensity of his inner experiences in the dance group led him to discussions with me concerning his wish for individual work. I light the candle as he makes eye contact and moves into the space, working for ten minutes. I call his name and he opens his eyes, looks at me, and returns to his cushion. Now he speaks his experience.

> I walk to the center of the room. My arms leave my sides and arrive away from my body, palms out. I am standing, waiting for direction. My right foot leaves the floor, moves slowly forward, and arrives once more on the floor. Standing, I am waiting for more direction. My palms leave the outer positions and arrive together in front of my face, move down over my face and torso, and wait for further direction. My left foot leaves the floor, moves forward, and arrives. My right foot leaves and arrives. I am waiting. I leave the center, arrive at the window, and wait. I am seeing that the way of the inevitable is paved with leavings and arrivals, with stillness and movement. So simple.

This kind of inner witnessing is a blessing. The edges of the pools become more subtle, liquid, and disappear. He is not only tracking his movement and inner experience seamlessly—his inner witness is becoming a more vivid and loving presence. Because of his clear shift from personality into presence, as his witness today it is unnecessary for me to offer him anything other than my presence. May my presence be enough.

The tall man arrives for continuing individual work but the evening hour is now dark as the seasons have moved. He lights the candle, speaks with me about how these new experiences of presence are affecting his life at home, at work. Though he tells me of an increasing worry about his responsibility in terms of his work because of deep exhaustion, he speaks of more peace within himself. He also speaks of an absence of an old and familiar armoring in relationship to his growing sensitivity to disorder, traffic, television, and conflict. He feels a particular kind of vulnerability emanating from his experience of a deepening presence within. He is gratefully glimpsing a new experience of strength that he begins to associate with the vulnerability.

Walking to the center, he turns and makes eye contact and closes his eyes. His inner witness:

> I stand and wait for direction, becoming a boundaryless field of pixilating vibrations. My upper torso suddenly jerks. I hear a high-pitched sound in my head. The vibrations become louder in my spine and neck. My neck tilts to the left, my fingers become locked in specific shapes. My lower back aches. My stomach feels flat, pushed against my spine. I feel another jerk, this time more in my shoulders.
>
> I feel my body floating upward. My feet are becoming unwieldy, huge and itchy. I feel as if I am not breathing. I would like to walk out of this now, but I can't. I am lashed to this spot but without ropes or emotions. I am not paralyzed, but I am not actually able to move. I feel another jerk. This is where I cannot see myself. I am leaving my body. I open my eyes, in gratitude for the presence of my outer witness.

My inner witness:

May my presence be enough.

After twenty minutes of work I see this man very, very slowly begin to make the long walk to his cushion. Here he tells me of his experience, again with clarity and patience. He speaks of his willingness to surrender to these sensations. We talk about what he describes as sudden jerks in his body when he moves, which he has begun to notice in the last month. I tell him the Sanskrit name for this phenomenon, *kriya*. Kriyas are spontaneous, automatic movements that can occur anywhere in the body. Though often experienced as sudden jerks, they can also be vibratory or smooth. We also discuss the phenomenon of his fingers extended into certain forms in relationship to each other. The Sanskrit name for this full shape of the hand gesture is *mudra*.

We speak at length about the moment in which he becomes aware that he can no longer consciously stay in his body and the moment when he opens his eyes. Now his practice becomes focused on such moments. What precedes these moments? What is he doing right before he realizes he is leaving his body? What happens as he is leaving his body? Because the content is new, because he is experiencing awe and some fear, effortful tracking—just as he practiced in the individual and collective body work—becomes essential again. He must commit toward remaining in his body consciousness while he is experiencing other ways of seeing and knowing, no matter how strong the pull is to leave, no matter how awesome the experience that calls him away.

I prepare the space for the tall man by sweeping the floor and lighting a candle. There is a knock on the door, and I gesture to him to come in as I walk toward him. He makes it clear that he does not want to speak now and goes immediately into the work. I see him walk to the carpet, look at me, and close his eyes. He works for thirty minutes.

His inner witness:

> This space has become sacred for me because of sacred experiences
> that I know here. Standing at the edge, I brush off the bottom of my
> right foot with my left hand. Now I brush off the bottom of my left
> foot with my right hand just as I do before entering the enclosed
> garden behind the temple. Entering my sanctuary, my body becomes
> an antenna. I vibrate. The kriyas come and go. I see myself clearly
> here. Empty, I know clear silent awareness.
>
> As I float up and get smaller, I hear a song inside my head as though
> I am singing it, but I don't know this song. I have never heard it before.
> It's a tragically beautiful song in minor key. This song transports me
> more deeply into the vibrations. This is real, really happening to me.
>
> Cautious, I can't see as clearly now but I am ready to leave and I
> must come down. I don't want to open my eyes to do it. I will myself
> down by focusing my inner gaze on a tiny and bare winter tree that I
> see, illuminated by snow, white everywhere. I know I must return, open
> my eyes. More kriyas. The ache in my back becomes terrible. I am
> nauseated and weak. My stomach is churning. My feet are burning.
>
> Now focusing on coming down, I'm being painfully, aggressively
> shoved back into my body. Arriving on the floor, I lie for a long time
> flat on my back, my hands on my stomach. No one will believe me.
> Can I believe me? I open my eyes.

We make eye contact as he turns toward me. We see each other here
for an extended time. When he crawls back to his cushion there is
more eye contact. Because of the depth and duration of his practice,
my verbal witnessing becomes less necessary. At times in such a situation, the details of the experience of the witness can actually clutter
the energetic field. Increasingly the witness becomes clear silent awareness in the presence of energetic phenomenon. My presence becomes

my offering. My prayer is my longing. *May my presence be enough*.

. . . The tall man wants so badly to sing me the song he hears during his experience and cannot. He wants so badly to describe his experience. He says he is clear when he is there and knows exactly what's happening, though he feels now he cannot articulate this experience well. And when he tries to articulate it he feels not only frustrated but as if he is betraying the experience. When he doesn't try to articulate it or somehow bring it into form he can feel painfully alienated and, at times, less human.

Because of the extraordinary quality of direct experience, sometimes even with such a developing clarity, a mover's mind questions if he is making up something, imagining it, or somehow creating it. Exploring the tension between doubt—"No one will believe me. Can I believe me?"—and belief—"This is really happening to me"—often leads to a deeper acceptance of what he knows to be true. He knows this experience is real because of his conscious experience of sensation that accompanies his movement.

The tall man can increasingly stay in his body while these experiences occur. Now he includes in his work the task of enduring what at first can be a very challenging transition back into a more grounded embodiment. This can be demanding, exhausting, not only because he must choose to contain the energy rather than open to it but because he is in fact moving from one energetic field into another. Such a changing within space and time becomes easier as practice develops. The rigor of the practice is required as he learns how to experience other dimensions of reality while maintaining a witness presence.

In this discipline we continue to discover that mover and witness, moving self and inner witness, individual body and collective body, body and word are all at first experienced as separate phenomena and then known in moments of grace to be the same. Usually energetic phenomena are first experienced as separate from ordinary consciousness. With committed embodied practice it is possible to discover that ordinary and extraordinary experiences can exist in an integrated way.

From Seeing to Knowing

I witness a mover with eyes closed sitting on the floor, cross-legged. I see this woman lifting one foot up onto her other thigh. As it rests there, she brings her fingers of one hand to the underside of this foot, pressing the skin gently. I see her other hand scooping under her foot and with those fingers, delicately caressing her toes. Tears are falling down her cheeks as she sits, one woman, one form, in the midst of our universe simply holding her foot. As witness, I too become riveted to her foot, and my own heart aches with such tenderness as I see, as though I am feeling, the tears streaming down her face. Soon, when she returns to her cushion, with eyes open, to speak her experience and to listen to mine, I hear the voice of her inner witness as she speaks of a "rush" of feeling, of love for her foot. I hear her words and know the silence around them. I see her lift her foot and know the stillness around her.

The discipline of Authentic Movement concerns a mover's longing to be seen by an outer witness, and the longing of a witness to see a mover.[1] Most of us know a great longing for both within our nature, to see ourselves and to see each other. How simple this can sound, how complex, incomplete, and mysterious this is. I once heard a mover say to her witness: "When I see you seeing me, I stay nearer to myself."

The core of this work is the evolution of the inner witness manifesting within the development of mover consciousness and the development of witness consciousness. The mover begins, safely in the presence of an outer witness, by learning to become aware of her impulses to move, which ones she chooses to follow into movement, and the accompanying experiences of felt density in her body that are created by sensations, emotions, or thoughts. This process of an emerging inner witness invites clearing of the inner chambers, the places imbued with personal and collective memory, often trauma and suffering, often places created through the presence and the absence of love.

Such work, so many years and years of work, though in direct service to the soul, is usually compelled by the personality, the incomprehensible but vivid combination of genetic coding and personal history. Such work becomes a necessary blessing as ground for other ways of embodied knowing.

Through this process of clearing toward presence, veils lift. Because the strengthening inner witness clarifies and expands, the individual becomes more able to consciously recognize, honor, and trust the body knowing, an intuitive wisdom occurring as veils lift. In the discipline of Authentic Movement, I find the term *direct experience,* which originates within the mystical traditions of monotheistic religions, to best describe moments of purely embodied awareness for movers and for witnesses. This term is proving helpful as we attempt to bridge such experience as it moves from body through language toward consciousness. The studio work increasingly demonstrates qualities of a mystical practice. What occurs in this practice has occurred similarly in different ancient and contemporary mystical traditions.

There is a call toward entering emptiness. With eyes closed and with focus inward, there is an intention toward staying present, toward practicing the art of concentration. There is practice toward the rigor of impeccability in tracking inner experience. There is a longing for a language that could describe direct experience, that which is indescribable. Ritual occurs, becomes necessary. The blessing of clear silent awareness can become known. There is a deep desire for daily life to manifest such a blessing, such awareness.[2]

The privilege of growing such an inner witness demands hard work as well as an awareness of the blessing of grace. Growing an inner witness directly creates opportunity for transformation from the most delicately woven, poignant personal story, a narrative that feels completely unique, into a boundless space where the thirst, the longing for healing, ceases as the awareness of the experience becomes universal. What follows are words from a mover as she tracks a visual image created by embodied experience of both "the mass" and "the stem," a developmental journey in which she discovers presence in "the direct stream."

I know that the "mass" has been something that I have felt to be a part of my body for years. It is a hunger that isn't for food. It is shrouded in wads of gauze, dampening and muffling its cry. I keep moving so I don't have to answer, because somehow in moving it is quieted.

Recently while moving, it announces itself as a "mass of desire." I hear very distinctly the cry for recognition, for filling, and it has to do with being enough, being worthy, being okay to ask for something, anything that I want and to act on that need, desire, request.

Today actual movement into and out of the area brings sensation to it that is new, more weblike, maybe tingling. The "stem" under the mass appears and has to do with something else . . . something that seems like a very mysterious thing. I am standing there and all of my being knows that a particular alignment of my spine allows me to be a part of the energy matrix that creates our manifest world rather than slightly out of the path of it. This sensation is a radical shift in consciousness or being. It's a little like feeling my body as a tuning fork in some way, and when I can receive clearly through my body, my ego kind of goes away and yet I still am.

Somehow I have stepped into "the direct stream" and it can just pass through me. I haven't dissolved, but I am a part of . . . and the great hunger is gone! This picture helps me understand the quantum level shift of experience that I sense when my "stem" gets lined up with my "mass." Oh brother. I do feel like this is a huge opening for me into what I can now believe in as my understanding of

Spirit and the Trinity. I feel like I just got baptized or something. Or maybe it's communion, because I have a responsibility to act on this knowledge.

As this mover works with "the mass," she is not merged with her experience because she is tracking sensation, emotion, and thought that are occurring directly in her body, creating a dialogic awareness. When she is in the "direct stream," she enters a unitive state for what she later describes as an eternal moment. In moments of such grace as has just been described by this mover, the inner witness is fully present as awareness and yet such presence in no way divides or complicates knowing—knowing becomes intuitive. Here there is an experience of nonduality, in which there is no separation between the moving self and the inner witness, and yet it is the development of the inner witness that makes such an experience possible. In this practice we are moving from embodied relationship with associative phenomena toward direct experience of energetic phenomena.

As egoic layers of the mover and the witness become consciously embodied enough, spaciousness becomes palpable and seeing becomes so much more than looking with the eyes. Seeing oneself, seeing another become synonymous with knowing oneself, knowing another. Direct experience creates intuitive knowing.

> The process of seeing represents a spiritual act. Here, intelligence does not mean reason or discursive thought as we think of it but intelligence as an organ of direct knowledge or certainty, a pure light of intelligence that goes beyond the limits of reason alone.[3]

Such a particular kind of intelligence, clarified by van Loben Sels,[4] is certainly germane to the phenomenon of awareness. I often return to Deikman's clear discussion about such experience within his inquiry into what he calls the *observing self*.[5] He insists that we cannot observe the observing self, that we must experience it directly. He names the absence of any defining qualities, boundaries, and dimensions: "awareness is the ground of conscious life, the background or field in which all elements exist"[6] and "behind your thoughts and images is awareness, and that is where you are."[7]

Where you are, where I am, here you are, here I am: these words can reflect a developing intimacy with our bodies, our temples. Dilip Roy, a disciple of Sri Aurobindo and The Mother, writes of yogis who accept life in its entirety, including the body, which they call the temple of God. His description of direct experience is refreshing: "I found myself ensconced in a blind darkness. All of sudden, there was a great stir above my head. I could see nothing in the gloom, but heard a voice distinctly say: 'Direct hit, direct hit, direct hit.'"[8] This direct hit is different from the experience of the moving self and inner witness being merged or in a dialogic relationship. Direct experience is synonymous with surrendering images of self, of an identity of self as one has known it. In such moments, some movers and witnesses speak of moving into and through the archetype of God, or the symbolic nature of God, into a clear silent awareness, an infinite emptiness. This emptiness is named by mystics, by Buddhists, by shamans, by human beings who have wandered and who do wander through our world inquiring into the mystery of our presence here, into the nature of fear and its relationship to awe within the exquisite and inherently ordered reality of our lives cycling.

Rabbi Akiva (as cited in Epstein) describes man's desire to "dispense with the mental idea or image of God, and by transforming himself, experience Him."[9] Meister Eckhart writes of wanting "to penetrate the simple core, the still desert into which no distinction ever crept—neither the Father, the Son nor the Holy Spirit."[10] He encourages a detachment from self, from the image of self so that one can unite with the formless being. Thomas Merton explains a Zen perspective:

> one is Buddha and that Buddha is not what the images in the temple had led one to expect, for there is no longer any image and consequently nothing to see, no one to see it, and a Void in which no image is even conceivable.[11]

A contemporary scholar of mysticism, Smoley (as cited in Miller, 2003), speaks about direct experience from the perspective of the esoteric traditions. He discusses "higher realms" that have an objective existence, that can be known and experienced. "Some say these levels are more real than the ones we experience in ordinary life."[12]

How do these places feel more real? They are known to be completely so in the body. In the discipline of Authentic Movement, we intend toward practicing an awareness of embodied detail, felt by the senses one by one, sequentially marked, regardless of the content or the source of what is becoming manifest. A mover speaks:

> I know God only because of this body that I am in. This knowing occurs HERE as I stand and open my hands, tilt my head back, bend my knees. I hear a soft but high-pitched sound, not vacillating, but consistent and strong, as my skin becomes porous. My boundaries evaporate as I notice a quickening, now a pulsation, now subtle vibration traveling from my heels upward, through my yoni, my throat and out the top of my head. I am upward, no downward—I am everywhere and nowhere.

Antonio de Nicholas, another contemporary scholar of mysticism, writes: "The mystic is not stopped from practicing religion in a different way, by the use of faculties other than the cognitive."[13] "The primary text of a mystic . . . is his human body."[14] Hillman (in his commentary on the work of Gopi Krishna), referring to Krishna's kundalini experiences, writes:

> Did these events actually take place in his body, in his cells, nerves, organs? Or did they take place in the yogic body? . . . The chakra system of the yogic body is not supposed to have any objective existence in physical space. Yet the psyche insists on this body language and body experience so that what is logically impossible is indeed psychologically not only possible but felt to be true . . . his physical body was for him the material place of projection of immaterial

events and there in the "body" they were experienced by the senses and felt to be "real."[15]

But how to speak, adequately enough, these ineffable experiences that are called many different names in different cultures, each with profound similarities and astonishing uniqueness? Speaking what is ineffable creates an instant contradiction. Though it can feel impossible to speak these "direct hits," in these moments of unitive consciousness, the human psyche longs to, and even feels it must find words, especially when such experiences are new to the nervous system, new to developing consciousness. But speech and language are primarily symbolic phenomena.

In the discipline of Authentic Movement it is the intention of the mover, when returning after the moving experience, to speak with the witness, to practice toward speaking the experience, not speaking about it. We practice offering the words in such a way that there can be a felt shift from the words carrying symbolic meaning toward the words energetically becoming the vibrations that they are, and thus directly being the meaning themselves. Practicing in this way opens pathways for a natural process of integration, which reduces the tremendous intensity of the longing to speak such unnamable forces as they become directly embodied.

I hear a witness speak these words: "I see you turn and I feel compassion." As I listen to this particular witness speak in this moment, the word compassion is compassion itself, not a symbol for it. I intuitively, directly receive the compassion. My experience here as a listener is distinctly different from other times when I hear someone say they feel compassion and I am brought into an experience of the word instead of knowing a direct experience of the word.

Until recently it has been mostly mystics who have felt challenged and yet compelled to try to speak and write such experiences. Now, as these experiences are occurring more often in our culture, we are receiving words from people who do not necessarily think of themselves as mystics. Within the process of finding words, that bridge from body to consciousness, it is completely natural to wonder: What does this mean? How can I understand it? A mover speaks:

> When I find myself bringing too much effort toward meaning, "she" is trapped, the feminine is trapped. I am trapped. This is not about meaning. This is about trust. I want to stay with the contextual rather than the conceptual. I want to stay in my body.

In the discipline, we are studying the distinction between symbolic experience and direct experience. Direct experience evolves without a particular philosophy, without analytic inquiry, without narrative language. We are practicing awareness of the grace of direct experience when it occurs. The meaning, if any, occurs beyond the experience itself, cannot be known until after the experience of conscious embodiment. We are trusting that insight will appear within an inherent, synchronistic order of inner process, developed within the intuitive realm. In the meantime, we are intending toward practicing the cultivation of embodied presence. When this can happen, conceptual or symbolic ways of knowing float back into the wings of our consciousness, there to support, confirm, and enrich the intuitive knowing.

The following words have lived inside my desk on a faded yellow card for twenty-five years. They clarify and sustain my developing questions concerning the ways in which imaginal or conceptual experience differs from intuitive knowing. Direct experience is an intuitive experience.

> Intuition provides the insight that sees through the filtering screen of thoughts, images and feelings to the formless content of experience. Once you recognize the permeable and transitory nature of this screen, you can subjectively differentiate intuition from imagination. The distinction between intuition and imagination is precisely this: pure intuition is knowledge that comes out of the formlessness and silence, whereas imagination gives form to the formless and is con-

ceptual in nature. When one imagines something, one is conceiving of it, no matter how abstractly. Thus, imagination is the vehicle by which intuition finds expression in life.[16]

The utter force of imagination is of course ancient, boundless, and one of our greatest and most mysterious inner resources. At times while moving or witnessing, when the fullness of a gesture is apparent and the heart, oh the heart wants to break, the mind craves meaning. In such moments, imagination can erupt. The visual image can seduce, persuade one into associative phenomena. Such images can be experienced as limitless in quality, texture, context, content, light, color, sound, movement—limitless in possible meaning.

Here the mover or the witness can consciously choose to commit, riding it into the deep nature of the conceptual mind, or choose specifically to be with the embodied experience, aware of the image but not engaging it. In the studio now, more and more individuals are choosing the latter, staying true first to the experience of conscious embodiment. When the body can be trusted enough because of the presence of a strong inner witness, and when the heart can be allowed to break, it becomes possible to open into another way of knowing, of being released directly into the core or formless source of the gesture.

Almost one hundred years ago, the philosopher Bergson (as cited in Barrett and Aiken) offered his perspective:

> Philosophers agree in making a deep distinction between two ways of knowing a thing. The first implies going all around it, the second entering into it. The first depends on the viewpoint chosen and the symbols employed, while the second is taken from no viewpoint and rests on no symbols. The second can attain the absolute.[17]

> An absolute can only be given in an intuition, while all the rest has to do with analysis. We call intuition here the sympathy by which one is transported into the interior of an object in order to coincide with what there is unique and consequently inexpressible in it.[18]

How can the mover find his or her way into the direct, inexpressible nature of a gesture? What does this mean to enter a thing, to enter an experience without the trusted accompaniment of the conceptual mind, yet with conscious presence? I do not know explicitly how to answer this question, but I have been studying it, deeply, for many years now. Just as the Zen masters can move us closer to what a thing is by telling us what it is not, I can say that to enter a thing, in this context, is not to merge with it, not to be in a dialogic relationship to it, for example, as in wondering about it from a place of curiosity, but to somehow become one with it, because of it.

I do know that a particular hue of vulnerability is necessary, a readiness to open into a completeness of not knowing, into true surrender. I know that a mover feeling intuitively that he must enter a specific moment "now" tells us that timing has to be related to such a choice. I also know that when such choices are made—and I believe to truly enter a thing, an experience, requires conscious choice—one is initiated into a new way of knowing and in such a moment consciousness changes. These realities have everything to do with the practiced attunement of an inner witness. The body is the direct route to the kind of consciousness that knows a formless silence, the one which quivers at the core of all form and all space.

In this particular inquiry, I have rather simplistically isolated four ways a mover can experience a visual image from an intention to remain embodied. Of course, the subtle nuances of similarity and difference between and among them all more closely characterize the true spectrum of the developing inner witness. Though it is equally engaging to follow these journeys of image within the experience of an outer witness, I am choosing here to focus on the mover. From my perspective as both a mover and an outer witness, the content is secondary—no matter how remarkable, archetypal, or unusual the implied meaning—to the felt, embodied experience as the image is being "seen." It is the energy that is moving within the body, the energy that creates the image, that concerns authentic change, not the story that the image implies.

The first two ways occur when the mover is either moving or still.

In the first way the mover is seeing an image outside of herself, an image that is not experienced in her body. If we return to the woman holding her foot as she sits on the floor filling with emotion and gratitude, she now becomes aware of a visual image. This image has a two-dimensional quality and exists over there, away from the mover, perhaps a picture of the mover. There is no felt connection between the image and the mover's awareness of her body. When such a picture appears, it is natural to wonder, "What does this mean?" Here the mover is reminded to try to stay within her body sensation while simultaneously being aware of the image.

> As I hold my foot in my hands, I see myself sitting in a cave by the sea.

In the second way, the visual image that becomes apparent also begins over there, outside of the body. If awareness of it persists, the mover might notice that it is infused with perhaps texture or movement and choose it to become part of her embodied experience as she begins to feel the multidimensional, alive qualities that resonate now inside of her. The mover learns to discern whether she is experiencing the image as it enters her body from the outside and she begins moving it or she is consciously going toward the image that she sees, entering it, now moving it—bringing her conscious body to the image that she sees.

> I see my hands leaving my foot. My right hand reaches forward, grabbing a stone ledge that is appearing just above the surface of what looks like ocean water. I am pulling myself up, climbing into a sea cave. I sit inside this cave.

As the body and the image meet, there can naturally be even more interest in the personal meaning of a sea cave, the mover's history with such an image, the relational history with this image between the mover and the witness, the mover's family history with this image, and so on. Here the mover's mind becomes curious, and because of the vividness of the light, the colors of the water and stone, the weight of the body changing planes, perhaps she would like to know more about this spontaneous series of sensations, emotions, and thoughts. This mover has many choices, one of which is to just stay with the embodied experience as she consciously moves into the image or the image consciously moves into her and trust that meaning, if any, can appear as intuitive knowing when the gestalt of her entire being is ready.

The third way in which an image enters the work of a mover comes when the movement itself creates the image or series of images. The body actually spontaneously forms or shapes the sensations arising within the image. The person is moving with focus, with presence and trust, when suddenly she is not seeing an image but she is inside it. The mover is directly knowing an image, becoming it. This mover has many choices, one of which is to just stay with the embodied experience and trust that if there is meaning it will appear as intuitive knowing when the gestalt of her entire being is ready.

> I am sitting, holding my foot. My hands leave my foot and I reach forward in a certain light, like dusk. My hand touches stone, cold and wet. I can feel it and it is as though I see it, because it is gray in color, kind of striped, but I don't see it with my inner eyes.

> I know it because I am here, in it. I pull my weight up onto the stone ledge, lifting each leg, kneeling into a smooth place, wet, but just on the surface. I am turning my body around and sit with my legs crossed inside a sea cave. The curved wall behind me comes around to its edges. I can see the ocean beyond me, wide, becoming vibrant, but again not with my inner eyes. The light is dusk light, dusk light and I am here, opening, opening my arms round in front of my torso.

> Here I am.

This experience is very different from choosing to enter or be entered by an image outside of the self. This is not an experience guided by visual stimuli but instead by intuitive knowing. The mover does not "see" the cave by the sea, yet she knows it in vivid detail. When this kind of experience happens for a mover, she is most likely shifting from a personal toward a transpersonal experience. The content of the image is not personal. There are no emotions here, which is very common for movers when the experiences do not seem to be sourced in the uniqueness of personality. The centrality of egoic and associative material begins to disperse.

In the fourth way, the mover is inside an embodied image, moving the shapes of it, which is similar to the way discussed above. But in this way, the mover follows the body as it forms the images, moving in and through them into an experience in which there is no longer any form, into no self, no thing, into a direct experience of emptiness:

> I am inside a sea cave on the edge of a tidal flat. I am sitting on stone. The walls are smooth stone, curving, shaping a space, an empty space, a space of light. My arms come around in front of my torso. I am holding emptiness, I am holding light. I am becoming emptiness . . . emptiness and now light.

There is another way, this one dependent on an absence of image from the beginning. In such experience there is a vivid awareness of the body, within an elegant sense of placement in space, yet no guidance from body shape or image. It is the body knowing without any symbolic reference, narrative language, or egoic perception that direct experience is manifest. If any words are uttered after such an experience, they seem especially in this situation to be shaped by intuitive knowing, not symbolic formation.

In these last two examples, the image of the cave as well as all associated sensations integrates. The known image of the self dissolves through a felt permeability of all membranes. The inner witness becomes clear, silent, only aware as the mover awakens into a unitive state, into an experience that is known by the mover to be sacred. Time and space are apparent as infinite. One person in such a moment weeps and knows the word gratitude, another awe, another humility. One begins spinning in silence. One speaks of union with the indwelling God, one says he is being nothing. Another simply sits without words, without desire, need, or impulse. There is no meaning in these direct experiences of emptiness. The meaning is the experience itself.

And there is still one more way I want to name, a way of knowing image that can accompany movers and witnesses: the way of visions. Visions do or do not create experience of literal emptiness. They inevitably leave the mover or witness in a particular inner place in which the sense of personhood is expanded. They can occur out there, away from the personal body, or here, fully within. They can be created by the movement with the mover inside of them or they can evolve outside of the moving body. What distinguishes visions from the other ways named above is primarily the stuff of which they seem to be made.

Vision imagery is made of a quality of light, sensed as though the forms, the colors, the movement are forged by an electrical energy. For many this energy is experienced as sensations of burning, burning line and color, movement, and sound directly into the body. The intensity of the burning can range from being experienced as terribly painful, physically, to completely painless, as though there is no physical body to feel the burning. And, last, the content of the images, as well as the thematic development when there is a series of them, reflects an absence of the laws of gravity, logic, form and shape, time, velocity of travel, as such qualities can be known in or near the earth realm. Here again, the content, no matter what it is, is secondary to the literal changes in body consciousness, in the way of knowing intuitively what is true.

Visions can be experienced as direct manifestations of the formless source, the eternal force, the "no thing." Daniel Matt's words, in a paper that means much to me, are appropriate here:

> The word *nothingness*, of course, connotes negativity and non-being, but divine nothingness is a positive quality. God is greater than any *thing* one can imagine, like no thing. Since God's being is

incomprehensible and ineffable the least offensive and most accurate description one can offer is, paradoxically, *nothing*.[19]

In closing, I return to the patient of Robin van Loben Sels, who refers to what I understand to be her inner witness, that completely mysterious yet essential inner force that can be known as one of the greatest blessings of all:

> Some place else in me kept witnessing all this because I could not, I was ended, what I used to know as "me" had cracked wide open. I let go, but the witness held it all, unmoved and unmoving, something attending nothing and everything. I felt the force of its attention: clear, open all the way through, always.[20]

All such experiences of intuitive knowing emerging from conscious embodiment can bring some new sense of responsibility, as the woman moving from "the mass" to "the stem" to finding herself in the "direct stream" tells us. True commitment to a parent or to parenting, to a partner, to a work, to our earth body or to our own bodies, is an experience of love. It is love that explodes silently or brilliantly, wildly or sweetly from the source of direct experience. We know love when we directly experience the seer and the seen as one, the knower and the known as one, and we are whole. And it is such love that permeates, hones, and makes genuine our responsibility to such a blessing.

The Mandorla and
the Discipline of
Authentic Movement

Authentic Movement, compassionate witnessing of moving becoming conscious, is a process grounded in the relationship between a mover and a witness. Different teachers of Authentic Movement offer their evolving perspectives in unique and diverse ways. The Discipline of Authentic Movement, a mystical practice centered in the development of embodied witness consciousness, is one way in this growing field of exploration.

The inseparable root systems of the discipline are mystical practices, healing traditions, and dance. Portal to healing wounds of the heart, portal to direct experience of the numinous, the moving body invites an awakening—summoning the human soul toward a return, a reunion with the eternal.

An embodied mystical practice, which invites the possibility of transformation into new ways of knowing, must include the light and shadow of personality to become integrated into a contemporary life. In the early years of the developmental process of an individual's inner journey toward such wholeness, psychological and energetic phenomena experienced in the body are distinguished from one another. With continued practice and study, the personal realms and the transpersonal realms are not experienced as separate.

In the discipline, in an empty studio, in the presence of an outer witness, an individual beginning as a mover discovers, journeys through hidden recesses in personal time, personal space, to become a more conscious witness of herself and then of others. In this untidy, uneven, unpredictable process, an embodied relationship, particularly with imaginative and associative phenomena, moves toward direct experience of energetic phenomena integrating, becoming intuitive knowing.

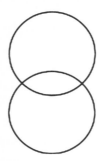

The Discipline of Authentic Movement, the process itself, remarkably finds home within an ancient shape called a *mandorla*. The essence of this iconic shape further illuminates the studio practice of mover and witness. Created by two separate circles (or mandalas) joining by overlapping each other, the shape of an almond or an eye, a yoni, a flame, or a bud becomes apparent in the center (see above).

The mandorla—often described as a coming together of heaven and earth, of the divine and human—appears throughout the world in the history of art, architecture, and religion and is remarkably evident in the imagery of various mystical traditions. It appears, for example, in the Kabbalah, in the early Egyptian drawings of sacred geometry, in Buddhist texts, and in Christian symbology.

Early Christians used the mandorla to make themselves known to each other by one person etching a small circle in a wall and another person, perhaps encountering the drawing at a later time, etching another circle slightly overlapping the first, thus creating connection.

In the discipline, the mover longs to be seen in her true nature, to be known by the outer witness. The outer witness longs to see another clearly. From this place of essential human desire for intimate, loving connection, the mover's circle of being overlaps with the outer witness's circle of being as they commit to practicing the discipline together.

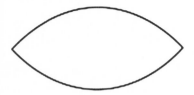

The mandorla, its emptiness mirroring the emptiness of the studio space, can simultaneously represent the relationship between the mover and the outer witness and the mover and her inner witness. Within both dynamics, the energy represented in the drawing above by the empty space between an upper arc and a lower arc can create a tension between the two arcs. This tension can be experienced in the studio work as a boundaried energy field.

In this field of awareness one may feel a quickening, called, compelled to remain in the empty space represented by the two curved arcs, not knowing. Both the mover and the witness may choose to surrender toward being in the empty studio space in the presence of each other. At the same time, the mover may choose to enter more fully her inner world. Such allowing, relinquishing into that which is mysterious, must be met by each with true will, a conscious intention to stay present enough.

Vital forces especially within the interiority of the mover are reflected in drawings, carvings, and sand paintings of the mandorla. In some traditions, the shape invites an awareness, a memory of the feminine aspect of life as a sacred womb, the concealed, hollow place in which spirit incarnates. Some describe this liminal space as an enclosure that emanates light from within.

In this way of studying the mandorla as a visual representation of the Discipline of Authentic Movement, it is as though a ritual space is carved by the outer edges of the shape, evocative of the longing toward clear seeing. In the studio, the outer witness sits to the side of the space with eyes open. Eye contact between mover and witness before the mover closes her eyes and enters movement and again in the hazy space of opening her eyes as she returns, each time marks a beginning and an ending to the ritual, marks an honoring, a gratitude for the presence of each other.

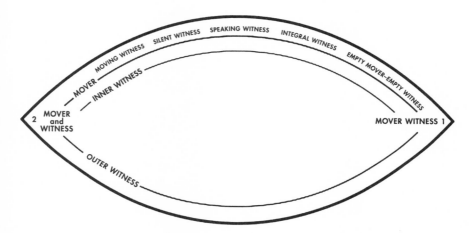

In the drawing above the emptiness within the mandorla is filled with representation of embodied consciousness: gestures, words that echo the practice of the Discipline of Authentic Movement as it exists in the studio space as a developmental but nonlinear process.

Looking into the mandorla is one way of perceiving the wholeness of a journey of the development of embodied witness consciousness. Yet a visual portrayal of a process can separate phenomenon within it that is not always experienced as separate. A drawing can make concrete or unmoving that which has beauty and integrity or it can elevate it into the fluid force that it can be known to be.

On the far left of the drawing above, where the two arching lines of the mandorla intersect, the number 2 represents duality, the beginning of a shared journey between two distinctly separate beings, a mover and a witness, each filled with their own utterly precious and infinite detail of a self. The outer witness, who has had her timeless turn in the immersion of her own mover's journey, welcomes the new mover arriving. On the far right, the number 1 represents grace, unitive consciousness within the mover, within the witness, and within their relationship. MoverWitness.

The upper arc in the drawing of the mandorla marks the path of the mover. The middle arc just below the upper one reflects the path of her developing inner witness. And the lower arc designates the path of the outer witness.

As can be seen in the left half of the drawing, the mover passes through yielding, elusive membranes, entering different witnessing roles, each one sourced in her evolving relationship between her moving body and her inner witness. In the presence of an outer witness, she commits first as a mover, and when it is time, she practices as a moving witness, and again when it is time, as a silent witness. When it is time, she steps into the honor of becoming a speaking witness. She immerses herself in the requisite ground form of the discipline in which egoic work is based within the individual body, work that deepens empathic resonance.

As can be seen in the right half of the drawing, because of the evolving, deepening experience of the mover's inner witness, when it is time she enters yet another witnessing role as her practice guides her toward experience of an integral witness. And at times, she becomes an empty mover–empty witness. Intuitive knowing and authentic compassion, compassion that cannot be willed, deepen her presence as shown by the arc of the mover descending toward wholeness.

For a mover, timing—a readiness for transferring her position or direction of focus to another role in the practice—is marked when the experiences and the skills of the current role have been absorbed, integrated enough. Back and forth, there are always times when individuals naturally choose to return, to reenter an earlier role in response to specific inner material. And there are times when an individual is present in a role further along the arc, one that spontaneously arises in relationship to a felt experience of an absence of density. Always present but not always accessible, direct experience of the numinous can occur at any time within the journeys of movers and witnesses. Such experience becomes safer as the inner witness clarifies and strengthens, because of extended practice in the ground form.

The process of the development of the mover's inner witness, reflected by the arc just below the arc of the mover, is the heart, the innermost gem of the discipline—

> *descending*
> *into movement*
> *or into stillness*
> *not knowing*
> *a moment occurs*
> *a lucid moment*
> *when the mover*
> *becomes*
> *aware of herself*
> *in time and space*

This is the beginning of witness consciousness within the studio practice. An experience of an inner witness, an indwelling light, a quality of attention becomes known.

The lower arc in the drawing of the mandorla designates the path of the outer witness, the one who consistently carries enough trust in herself, in her mover, and in the bones of the discipline. She commits to consciously "holding" all, that which is visible and that which is invisible, as she tracks her mover and simultaneously her own inner experience in the presence of the mover. Because of the mover's trust in her, the outer witness is gifted with a deepening and continuing practice toward presence.

When the mover's experience comes to an end, she is invited toward a conscious transition from moving to speaking with her witness. Sitting with her witness, she learns to speak her movement, in present tense, rather than speaking about it. She learns to choose what to speak and what to contain. The witness listens and responds by choosing what to speak of her inner experience while witnessing and what to contain.

In this way, language bridges experience from body to consciousness. For both mover and witness, the intention toward the practice of more conscious speech is central to the development of the discipline. Moving and witnessing, speaking and listening—this is the way of the work—

> *again*
> *again*
> *and again*
> *only two rituals*
> *interdependent*
> *moving and witnessing*
> *speaking and listening*

Mover

Clarifying the mover's journey through the named roles in the drawing of embodied consciousness widens, makes more whole, an understanding of the studio experience of each mover becoming conscious within a developmental process.

The experience of being the only mover with only one witness for as long as necessary is essential within the development of the discipline. In the beginning with no outer or inner instruction, no agenda, the mover enters the emptiness.

This mover stands. Her right foot turns slightly inward. Her head lifts and tilts to the right. Her left arm extends, reaching back and up. Her palm opens—

> *and so begins*
> *entry*
> *into a passageway*
> *shaped*
> *by the visible*
> *body*
> *moving*

into the invisible
the inner life
of the mover

The mover's awareness of her experience—tender or painful, shining or opaque, saturated with felt sensations, emotions, thoughts, and images—becomes honed. The body form literally becomes a place of enclosure in which direct encounter with density occurs. As trust in her outer and inner witness deepens, the mover continues toward opening into the unknown, discovering movement that is ordered from within, that is truthful, authentic. A loneliness imbued with all that is already known and all that might be known, at times transforms into a felt experience of coming home. Her inner witness accompanies her moving body with increasing attention, acceptance, and permission.

The mover opens to the possibility of tenacious movement patterns sourced in personality complexes. She opens to the possibility of encountering unresolved trauma bound within her nervous system. As she chooses to turn toward the fire of persistent inner material, the rigorous, demanding, sometimes tedious task of tracking inner experience is faithfully practiced—

directed by
an inner longing
for clarity
for transcendence
capacity to hold
express or contain
all that arises
from within

At identifiable thresholds, penetration of fear or of awe—of an utter vulnerability—becomes the source of a growing strength. The risk of experiencing the ineffable fear of a death of oneself as one has known oneself to be can become the gateway into a transformation, into new ways of knowing.

Moving Witness

When the mover feels seen enough by one outer witness, she begins to see herself more clearly, more empathically. Naturally there is room inside the mover now for a companion, the presence, the human warmth of another mover in the studio.

The teacher/witness invites two movers to move in her presence at the same time, each with eyes closed, each becoming a moving witness for her fellow mover. First blindly, not yet ready to actually look at the other, the movers share the witness, the empty studio space, the evolving questions that organically emerge in dyadic work. They can hear each other, and if they consciously choose, can touch or be touched by the other, or they can move together. Returning to the speaking and listening ritual, they continue to practice and study conscious speech, now learning more about the ways in which they experience the beauty and at times the challenging complexities of another, of the other mover's personality and presence.

Silent Witness

Each mover first becomes a witness of herself and then of another. Under the guidance of the teacher/witness, when the two moving witnesses are ready, one by one, they choose to sit to the side of the space and see the other moving. As the movers take their turns as silent witnesses of each other, they are invited to track their inner experience, no longer from the perspective of a moving witness, but now from the perspective of a silent witness with eyes open. The teacher/witness offers speaking witnessing to the mover, while simultaneously modeling the specificities of thoughtful speech for the silent witness.

By tracking her inner experience as an outer witness and then privately speaking with her teacher—protecting herself and her mover from a responsibility for which she is not yet prepared—the silent witness enriches her understanding of her own personality, recognizing the origins, the complexities of her projections onto the mover, her judgments and interpretations. She learns to discern, to distinguish between herself and the mover, between obscurity and clear seeing. She and her teacher/witness know when she is ready to experience the great responsibility of being a speaking witness.

Speaking Witness

A speaking witness commits toward presence while witnessing a mover, presence afterward in listening to the mover speak, and presence in speaking in response. Readiness to be a speaking witness, based on moving, moving witness, and silent witness practices, means readiness to offer witnessing to one mover within a dyad, and when it is time, to offer witnessing to more than one mover. The format of the dyadic work grows into triads and quartets, small groups in which all participants increasingly practice as movers and as speaking witnesses. Speaking witnesses learn to discern—

> *what to contain*
> *what to speak*
> *how to speak*
> *how*
> *to feel connected*
> *while speaking*
> *how*
> *to empathically*
> *accompany*
> *the mover*
> *sitting*
> *in presence*
> *eyes open*

Speaking witnesses participate in a larger collective, committing to membership in circles of witnesses for many movers. Embodied witness consciousness within each mover and each witness is a shared longing for embodied collective consciousness. Ritual practice clarifies. Each ritual begins with individuals, one by one, declaring whether they will be an outer witness or a mover for the duration of the ritual. Many witnesses at the same time share, see the detail—crystalline—of many movers moving inside the witness circle. Witnesses become aware of an aesthetic, a mysterious yet vivid perception, a recognition of a sensitivity that seems to emanate completely naturally, timely, from within a mover or group of movers. Each witness experiences her own inner response as she witnesses and when she chooses, she speaks from that place in the speaking and listening ritual that follows.

Integral Witness

With a continuing commitment toward presence, as though arriving in a clearing, the experience of the speaking witness expands, matures into that of an integral witness. For the first time the offerings among participants in the speaking and listening circle are not just based on experiences in the moving and witnessing circle. An integral witness, modeled by the teacher/witness, is one who witnesses, listens, and responds by speaking consciously from multiple perspectives. She responds to whoever speaks from whatever original role in the preceding round of the moving and witnessing practice. Feeling seen, seeing herself, and seeing each other one simultaneously—

> *participants forget*
> *who is the mover*
> *who is the witness*
> *everyone speaks*
> *everyone*
> *listens*
> *to each other*
> *echoing what matters*
> *welcoming*
> *spontaneous invitations*
> *to speak in response*
> *no effort*
> *now*

Empty Mover–Empty Witness

Unbidden, direct experience of vibration, light, insight is known by the mover, by the witness in her presence. One knows all suffering, all joy.

There is nothing to do. There is nothing to say—

> *emptied*
> *a mover*
> *a witness*
> *see*
> *are seen*
> *in silence*
> *in still presence*

The moving body and the inner witness become one. Such moments of freedom, of transparency, of a porousness, infuse the empty mover–empty witness with a wholeness within themselves, mirrored in the presence of each other. It is not necessary for one to feel seen by another when direct experience of the indwelling Witness transforms into authentic presence.

A mandorla can begin as a small form, created by the overlap of two larger separate circles. Through the development of witness consciousness, it can be seen in the drawing above how that seed ripens as the individual circles of a mover and of a witness each mature, growing the mandorla larger and larger until it disappears into only one bright and clear empty circle, a mandala. This progression can be understood through the inner journey of a mover becoming conscious, becoming whole, and simultaneously through the journey of the mover and the outer witness, their relationship becoming conscious, becoming whole.

The above drawing, the undulating river of mandorlas, with no beginning and no end, is an evocative image of what can be imagined as a chain of ascending and descending arcs of movers being seen by witnesses, seeing themselves and seeing others, each moving toward what is true because of direct experience in the presence of each other.

An integrated awareness of wholeness, a capacity to translate, transfer the way of the work outside the studio and into the world becomes accessible to movers and witnesses.

It is only through consciously embracing such a transition into moving through a daily life, witnessing, speaking, and listening with a clearer presence, that the commitment to such vigorous and satisfying work within the shelter and protection of studio practice becomes wholly complete. Woven into the practice of the discipline in the studio is a consistent awareness of the longing for embodied presence when buying mangos from a vender at the market, when stepping up and into a bus, when speaking with a loved one at home about wet boots inside the door.

Because of the development of witness consciousness, an inherent order is evident in all that happens between the experience of duality and unitive consciousness. Longing. Time. Endurance. Trust in a process, in oneself, in the other. Trust in all that remains veiled as a potential source for the unfolding of witness consciousness. Looking again into the mandorla as one way of perceiving the wholeness of a developing journey of embodied witness consciousness—

an empty studio
a witness
a mover
an inner witness
bound by love
by gratitude
so deep
for the seer
for the seen

Intimacy in Emptiness
Ceremony

In the kiva I see
a horizontal line with no end
vibrating across the room
in both directions
out that window beyond the sea
and through this window
piercing
the mass of the boulder
crossing in the center
the vertical axis reaching
up down into nothingness
two bright lines
marking the bones
transparent
I see it know it directly
the diamond
a quality of light emanating.

Here I know an ancient union
devotion embodied
a presence of light
because of our source
and we become exquisitely intimate
with such abounding emptiness.

In the beginning of the practice of the Discipline of Authentic Movement, in the presence of an outer witness, at an unanticipated moment, a mover, wandering into her interior wilderness, enters an experience of "being moved." It is here, acknowledged both by the mover and the outer witness, that a glimpse of what might later be recognized as energetic phenomenon is apparent—mysterious and directly known. Here can begin an ancient journey toward a possibility of unitive consciousness.

Energetic phenomenon clarifies, through love, a pathway to light. Not sourced in personality, paradoxically, it can at times support healing of core personal wounds. In each soft turning of the spiral in the development of the discipline, we can consciously choose to cultivate a relationship to energetic phenomenon, thus bringing us new ways of knowing.

Within such a commitment, we inevitably experience the essential nature of the utter fact of separation, an unavoidable process, one that must precede and most often follow unitive consciousness. We enter the phenomenon of separation by beginning with a mover and a witness, two separate roles within the guidelines of the core practice of the discipline. Because of a winnowing process beginning in dyads and evolving into group retreats, the potency of the light and the shadow of our personhood—original roots that have shaped us, been shaped by us— become conscious. Within such a phenomenal journey, the presence of a great blessing can grow into a loving inner witness, honed and polished:

intimately guiding
sheltering and liberating
a knowing becoming
a potential union
of mover consciousness
of witness consciousness.

Trust in the compassionate presence of each inner witness is grounded within the wingspan of the collective becoming conscious. When enough of us as individuals experience a generosity of such presence enough of the time, this shared experience within a group reveals a mysteriously timed elegance of interconnectedness, a synchronicity:

now no longer asking
am I a mover?
am I a witness?
we might ask
may I be present enough?
as ritual practice
deepens
celebrates
a new shape
ceremony.

Ceremony is an original force, a human need, an old dignified destination for communing in this earth realm. We enter ceremony—or ceremony enters us—because we recognize each other. We choose each other: offering, receiving the challenge and the welcome of what is true. This gift of truth in any ritual practice can be at times synonymous with the gift of perceived beauty, an aesthetic sensibility that emanates from the intrinsic "choreography" of authentic movement within a clarified vessel of beings grounding the process of clear seeing.

What began for a mover within the intimacy of a dyad as a need to be seen becomes, in ceremony, an experience of embodied devotion. What began once for a witness as a need to see the other clearly can more often be experienced as the grace of clear presence in ceremony. Each role—moving, moving witnessing, silent witnessing, speaking witnessing—integrates with all others. Every one of us is now an integral witness, one who sees and is seen, who listens and who speaks from a shared, refined source.

An Organic Evolution

How does the specific and organic evolution of embodied consciousness within each one of us clarify so that our inner witness now includes integral witnessing? This distinct form of witnessing not only makes ceremony possible, but it is the kind of witnessing that can—must—translate through the doors of studio practice and into our daily lives.

The journey of shared practice, both within fifty years and within one studio hour, is the impeccable journey of the inner witness of each one present. Such a rigorous and continuous commitment to this evocative process is necessary for sustained engagement as an integral witness.

Developmental aspects of the practice, each one preparatory for participation in ceremony, include:

+ the two rituals, interdependent, intertwined—moving and witnessing, speaking and listening—becoming less separate
+ the years of practice within an intimacy of dialogue—those protected, precious, and enclosed places of safety for the meeting of one mover and one witness—both within solo and group work
+ echoing of another's words often beginning in the first group experiences, in recognition of one's own experience, not intended to be in service of the other
+ the process of embodying one's own personal narrative and recognizing it as distinct from every other person's narrative as well as distinct from transpersonal experience
+ an integrated consciousness of emptiness, cultivated from the beginning of practice, both before and after moving
+ the generative practice of a declaring circle in which we make a covenant with ourselves, naming our role for the duration of the ritual
+ distinguishing the experience of belonging from the experience of participating in a consciously embodied collective

Integral witnessing can prepare us for the fullness of what collectively emerges in ceremony, an experience of becoming an empty witness.

Often such a blessing occurs in response to being in the presence of empty movers. In both phenomena,

> *transparent and pure*
> *benevolent*
> *empty presence becomes*
> *a knowing, a not knowing*
> *what is seen*
> *what is unseen*
> *wordless*
> *boundless*
> *compassion.*

Preparation for ceremony requires an abundance of dedicated practice in discerning judgment, projection and interpretation from intuition. But intuition alone is not necessarily in service of personal growth until

> *intuition identified*
> *becomes conscious*
> *refines*
> *becomes intuitive knowing*
> *a sacred light*
> *within the life*
> *of an inner witness*
> *within the process*
> *of self-emptying*
> *a trusted*
> *accessible guide.*

Because of an energetic reciprocity with those who participate in ceremony, the shared space can be experienced as sacred, both within and around us. An essential ingredient of sacred experience can be a direct knowing of an innocence.

we are born
into this realm
innocent
through a narrow passage

dying
maybe again
a narrow passage
and a longing to leave
with an open heart
with an innocence
(if privileged)
forged through
consciousness
emptied
into vastness
not knowing

A growing familiarity with experience of energetic phenomena within any of the different configurations of the practice in solo, dyadic, and small group work prepares us for perceiving "portals" in ceremony that might invite a direct knowing of innocence. Thus ceremony can become a field of awareness in which an initiatory experience—a dying of oneself as one has known oneself to be—can occur, transforming a life's narrative.

As time and space collapse in ceremony, content becomes less primary. The vitality of vibratory frequencies becomes more apparent. We experience less distinction between alignment with a specific frequency of vibration within our own body and alignment with such a frequency within the bodies of others. In this way, vibratory frequencies are directly known within the collective body itself, often experienced as a unified concentration.

In this field of such convergence, does energetic phenomenon arise out of the emptiness or does emptiness become known directly because of energetic phenomenon? Either way, no matter what, awareness is always here, though not always accessible.

> *distinct from clear presence*
> *awareness—a deathless vibration*
> *resounds within*
> *beyond our consciousness*
> *and silence*
> *an ineffable sound*
> *among us*
> *affirms*
> *not an absence*
> *of sound of word*
> *thought or spoken*
> *not a pause*
> *but, yes, a place*
> *eternal, inexhaustible*

It is the inevitable way of the Discipline of Authentic Movement to continue to evolve toward unknown experiences that hone us, hone the practice itself. Now it is as though movement, stillness, sound, silence—directly known—accrue within the field of awareness, alchemically maturing into an experience of expansion beyond known inner boundaries.

Moving and Witnessing in Ceremony

> *standing in a circle*
> *in silence each one*
> *an integral witness*
> *no longer in service*
> *to movers*
> *empty space appears*
> *in front*
> *behind above and below*

no bell but an inaudible
invisible invitation
among us
no eye contact, only clear focus
into the emptiness arising
intuitively one by one
or more than one at once
we step forward moving
eyes closed or opened
or stay standing
marking witness presence

an infinite treasure
a wealth of personal
and collectively embodied
gestures forming
each as if when needed
organically appearing
some known before
many others emerging
for the first time
waiting for this moment?
intimately directly known
by all witnesses
inner and outer
as witnesses become movers
now movers arriving
into witness presence
liminal boundaries
seamlessly crossed

no bell announcing
but an inaudible, invisible
consciousness of timing

a shared awareness
of each one present
and ceremony ends
as we emerge
lucid
one by one
out of and into
the capacious
empty
silence
with no need to return
to our original place
no one place in the circle
belongs to anyone

if eye contact
is chosen
an intuitive choice
no longer acknowledging
seeing and being seen
now simply
accompanying
a beholding of a light
within the other
a reflection of shared
clear presence

Speaking and Listening in Ceremony

In the transition from moving and witnessing to speaking and listening, a continuing silent immersion in emptiness is reflected in our presence as we sit on the circle's rim. Leaderless within such a liminal space, we prepare to speak and to listen.

Because words carry us from body into consciousness, the speaking and listening practices have historically developed with the same committed attention as the moving and witnessing practices.

> *timing*
> *of when to speak*
> *becomes implicit*
> *intuitively known*
> *from a source*
> *of being spoken*
> *and we enter a word*
> *a word enters us*
> *enters the collective*
>
> *and just like moving*
> *our speaking*
> *follows an emergent*
> *thread*
> *less a linear narrative*
> *more a continuation*
> *an evolving trust*
> *in words dwelling*
> *within silence*
> *space around each one*
> *words expanding into*
> *an intimacy in emptiness*

As this way of speaking develops in a collective, a sense of fluidity emerges, not unlike a certain freedom that can occur when a mover experiences no destination, no intention to understand or alter what is unfolding. Here in the speaking and listening ritual, we are responding spontaneously to words and the gestures of the one who speaks, with no intention to directly serve any other person or to shape that which is being offered. Speaking the detail of each movement as ground for what happens is often no longer necessary.

After years of experiencing memory as a distraction from direct speaking, naming a memory now can enrich experience readying to fulfill the next moment. Arising from within the present moment, memory becomes implicit, including the most recent moving and witnessing time, minutes ago. A participant writes:

> This word re-member... I feel time being woven. I am remembering... with a space between my fingers and my forehead. Between my eyes, I honor whoever comes in. I weave time, embodied memories, of past moments into this moment now. I see space as being multi-dimensional in the now of this moment sharing.

Here are different voices spoken and heard in response to the moving and witnessing ritual, reflecting a process experienced by each integral witness; in one way, resembling the art of conversation. In another way, these individual voices appear as one authentic voice arising out of the numinous within the realm of ceremony itself.

> **Ceremony begins for me when I walk into the kiva, a temenos, a sanctuary where I know sacred geometry.** I feel a freedom without eye contact to stand among all of you in the emptiness. *This is my body. This is my prayer.* I step back in reverence for the gorgeous emptiness. *I look and I look, I keep looking and wonder what I am seeing.* Suddenly there is a moment of relief when I remember that there are within each of us infinite places, spaces that will always be hidden.

> **I see you moving what I need to move so I don't actually need to move.** I cry with you . . . as if I am moving, no need to contain. I join you with no concern for interrupting you. *I see two of you make eye contact and feel in the presence of a mutual flow of energy, as though you are witnessing each other . . . There will be no need for me to offer any witnessing to either of you.* When is it even necessary to offer witnessing?

I don't know who is a witness? Who is a mover? Perception changes. I have no need to be seen as mover or witness. *I don't need witnessing, I need to be met.* I need to touch you more in ceremony, directly meeting a tenderness within me, a thankfulness. *You whisper, you grow upwards, you chant and you dance. I only need to stand, reach, touch your heart and know that I must serve.* I glimpse the new experience of no outer witnesses while I am sliding low to the ground and feel whole.

Witnessing myself, I realize I no longer name what I see or feel: hand, chin, knee, contraction, sadness. Instead I just know it. Witnessing you, I no longer name what I know to be true, as though my direct seeing of you is enough. *Everything I know I know because of the fact of my body.*

I see me kneeling, my hands over my eyes, witnessing my inner witness witnessing my vulnerability. My darkness begins to burn me as I roll onto my back. I feel such a vast silence, miraculous. I seek it. **I see a path and opening my eyes, walk into it, trembling.** I am in my place, imbued with a mysterious, violet light.

I notice when I am not present, time separates from space. **I enter cyclical time, feeling called back around into the spiral instead of a more familiar climb into linear time . . . instantly feeling less afraid of dying.** Oh THIS is eternity. **Suddenly, being turned . . . my whole body is being turned this way and I am Every Human facing extinction.** Here is light, only light. *Here is Grief, only Grief.*

I hear many voices in different ranges, sounding, not words, but forms made of vibration. *You walk toward me as if seeing me but your eyes are closed and I stand to welcome you back.* I come back, feeling received, and my eyes just open. I see you directly in front of me and sense someone to my left still moving, slowly on the way toward the edge of the circle. **Standing in the circle, my**

hands are still formed, filled from within, in specific shapes. *I allow my hands and arms to continue to move. I am not finished as long as you are not finished.* **Even when we all are standing at the threshold of the circle, recreating it again and again, the silence that is in and around all of us, all our space, all space, continues.**

Astonished, humbled by such a place in time, I experience each individual as if lit from within, in fulfillment of their own nature, unencumbered by the tenacity of personality, yet rooted in knowing themselves as whole because of being imbued within a shared energetic field of awareness.

> *grateful!*
> *utterly relieved*
> *in awe of the grace*
> *of unitive consciousness*
> *apparent among us*
>
> *a luminous resolution*
> *an ancient longing*
> *now met*

As we become intimate with abounding emptiness, other circles, perhaps in recognition, surround us. Loving spirits appear at times as we enter the mysterious invocation of ceremony. Is ceremony a place perhaps we have always recognized? We are descendants of courageous people of ceremony on the banks of that river, within those dark forests, along the edge of this sea, in studios, kivas and synagogues, theaters and ashrams, churches—in hiding and in safe light. Dancers, mystics, healers were compelled, even when it seemed impossible, commanded to embody that which is true within the offering of ceremony.

July 3

CHAPTER SIX

LINEAGE

Who Teaches, Who Learns?

Introduction

By Bonnie Morrissey & Paula Sager

How can this mandorla template ground but not paralyze, secure but not command, invite but not tempt us toward grasping hold of the mysterious nature of the actual studio practice of the Discipline of Authentic Movement?

JANET ADLER,
LETTER TO CIRCLES OF FOUR FACULTY
(NOVEMBER 2015)

The path to the kiva curves around a giant dark boulder. A series of stepping stones embedded in grass lead to a breezeway overlooking a sheltered cove. Ducks and geese fly, float, or nest, eagles swoop, and sometimes seals surface from the deeper waters. Janet will be standing here, ready to welcome us. Boots and bags are left under a bench. The doors to the kiva are open and we enter . . .

In the potent space of emptiness generated within the kiva, Janet's offerings of intensive week-long annual retreats bring an increasing focus to the questions and work of students actively engaged in teaching the discipline. Introducing the mandorla to senior students in 2012, she invites each of us to spread an empty sheet of paper on the floor of the kiva. With pen in hand and Janet's voice guiding the way, each student traces an upward arcing line from the center of the far left of the page, drawing a form into visibility. A shape appears, a gestalt holding all we have been learning over many years, all that Janet has been tracking over many decades. Within her offering of this new form, she continues to ask: "Who are you as one who is devoted to this work? What questions do you bring to your students, from day to day, or year to year? What must you offer that you trust will invite you toward new learning?"[1] Being a teacher of the discipline is always to be a student of the discipline as new learning inevitably brings new questions.

The appearance of the mandorla in Janet's psyche in 2012 and the publication of "The Mandorla and the Discipline of Authentic Movement" in 2013 mark the evolution of the discipline into maturity. During this same time, a growing interest is arising among her long-time students to nurture and preserve the distinct nature of the Discipline of Authentic Movement and to distinguish it from other tributaries of Authentic Movement, which flow in various directions from the earlier work of Janet and others. In 2013, assisted by three senior students,* Janet founds Circles of Four, a postgraduate level program to prepare committed students who wish to teach the Discipline of Authentic Movement (see Resources for website). Beyond Circles of Four, students who have worked with Janet at any time have benefited from her teaching, integrating what they received within their work in such fields as psychology, the arts, education, medicine, community organization, meditation, and other contemplative practices.

We begin this chapter, which is focused on lineage, with Janet's own preparation to teach. In "Speaking the Same Language: An Evolving Dialogue with Mary Whitehouse,"† Janet takes us back to 1969, to a small empty storefront on a street in West Los Angeles, where she receives from Mary the nascent form from which the ritual practice of moving and witnessing will evolve. Even before they meet, Janet expresses her longing to see Mary's eyes, a measure of the importance for Janet of eye contact, a relational phenomenon appearing first in her early research and then, with increasing prominence, through every phase of her developing work.

---

*The "three senior students" are Julia Gombos, Paula Sager, and Bonnie Morrissey.
†"Speaking the Same Language" was first published in the *Journal of Authentic Movement and Somatic Inquiry* June 2011 (reprinted with permission from Dr. Jaime Stover Schmidt, Editor in Chief).

"Speaking the Same Language" is an ode to the role of teacher, as well as a tribute to Mary herself. Janet remembers Mary's creative force and presence as a teacher and the radical nature of her invitation to close one's eyes and move as a way of opening to the unconscious. Her warm welcome and offering of a mutual inquiry nourish Janet's already developed attunement to the primacy of relationship, affirming the intuitive responsiveness she explored in her earlier work with children. Recognizing Mary as her teacher, Janet realizes a return to her "true nature" in the discovery of an embodied approach that will support her inquiry.

Mary's sharing of a movement practice that accesses the depths of the psyche dovetails with Janet's previous studies with John Weir. From John, Janet learned new ways of directly speaking one's experience, ways rooted in self-authority. The resonance Janet experiences within these pivotal relationships with Mary and John gives rise in the discipline to an organic process of teaching and learning, in which trust is a primary medium and intuition is a primary guide. The intimacy of relationship in which trust can safely develop creates a vessel through which healing and transformation can occur.

After returning to the East Coast, Janet and Mary continue, until Mary's death in 1979, to correspond through letters and sometimes audiotapes. Janet's devotion to the art of letter writing flourishes within her own teaching practice. In "Letter to Students" (written in 2003, previously unpublished), she writes (via email) to a group of students who are returning for a monthly series of study in her California studio. This single letter represents hundreds of letters sent to groups of students since the beginning of her teaching career. Written during the time of more intensive focus on direct experience and intuitive knowing, this letter conveys the way in which Janet lovingly embraces all possible human response to experiences of the numinous, veiled or unveiling.

A decade later, in "Ritual Practice" (shared with students in 2014, previously unpublished), Janet offers her own process of inner and outer preparation for the arrival of students traveling to Galiano Island for a week-long retreat. With attention to each detail of readying the space, ritual is embodied and commitment is renewed. The discovery of "movement that is ordered from within" that Janet experienced in Mary's studio is carried forth, manifesting in an aesthetics of inherent order. Sweeping the floor, filling the teapot, setting flowers on a mantel; each conscious action arises within a seamless relationship between self and surroundings, steeped in the practice of presence.

In her brief 1997 essay, "Questions: Teaching the Discipline,"* Janet wonders what a nonpatriarchal, nonhierarchical model of assessing readiness to teach a contemporary mystical practice would look like. Knowing she does not yet know, Janet extends her commitment to hold the question, knowing only that learning to teach the discipline must be based on the inner process of each one who makes this journey. She stays close to what she knows of the path of preparation, which, she writes, begins with "attention to *personal consciousness* and moves toward attention to *collective consciousness,* but it is the latter that deeply holds, as if in waiting, the former"(see "Questions: Teaching the Discipline," page 261). Sixteen years after the publication of this essay, her intriguing intimation of a holistic structure is realized in the birth of the Circles of Four program.

In "Emergence of Circles of Four" (2013),† Janet shares her vision of an international collective body of teachers and learners carrying forth the specific lineage of the Discipline of Authentic Movement. She introduces a new program of practice and study created for those who seek to teach "this particular embodied process concentrated within the development of consciousness." In Circles of Four, a learner is at the

---

*"Questions" was first published in *A Moving Journal* 4, no. 3 (1997): 10–11 and later published in *Authentic Movement: Moving the Body, Moving the Self, Being Moved—A Collection of Essays Vol. 2,* edited by Patrizia Pallaro (Philadelphia: Jessica Kingsley Publishers, 2007), 470–73.
†"Emergence of Circles of Four" was first published on the Discipline of Authentic Movement website in 2013.

center of a circle that includes three faculty members. Each learner discovers their own unfolding emergence of the inner witness, in their own unique time frame, guided and supported in turn by each of their three teachers. Two strands of one theme, preparation and readiness, run throughout the learner's studies as they come to experience this pattern of growth in an embodied and recurring way. A recognition of readiness at each new threshold lays the groundwork for an eventual moment of clear and direct knowing: readiness to be a teacher of the Discipline of Authentic Movement.

Just as each unique circle of four holds the potential of a consciously embodied collective, guiding and embracing the process of teaching and learning, so too does the whole organizational shape of Circles of Four hold the alchemical potential of new modes of synergistic learning and holographic process. The practice of the discipline continues to guide faculty, learners, and learners who become teachers, toward new ways of participating, within a consciously embodied collective that is collaborative in structure and international in scope. The generative relational nature of the discipline as a "vibrant energetic web" is not hierarchical; it is multidimensional, interconnected, and alive.

The remaining writings in this chapter consist of letters sent as emails to learners from Janet in her role as a retreat teacher in Circles of Four. In "Letter to Learners before Retreat" (written in 2018, previously unpublished), Janet writes to a group of learners who are preparing to travel long distances for their annual week in the kiva, acknowledging their outward preparations in leaving home and their inner preparations to arrive, ready to immerse in the ritual practice. Letter writing is central within the design of the Circles of Four Program. Within letters, the practice of conscious speech begun in an intimate dyad extends into a medium that reaches beyond a single studio experience, connecting the interweaving voices of the learner and their three teachers.

In "Letters to a Learner," from 2015 to 2019 (previously unpublished excerpts of personal correspondences), Janet responds to monthly letters from one learner. Shoshana integrates her studio experience, personal life, readings, and work with clients and students as she cultivates the voice of her developing inner witness through writing. The intimacy of these letters and the rhythmic consistency of the monthly exchange support a deepening process of inner growth. Reflected in Janet's responses, we experience this learner's exploration of balancing transpersonal experiences with personal ones. The learner is becoming more keenly aware of the presence and sometimes the absence of her inner witness. As time passes, she is drawn to silence, stillness, emptiness, and the revelation of mystery in daily life.

We end this chapter with "One Basket: The Closing of a Teaching Practice" (written in 2018, previously unpublished), a personal correspondence from Janet to a group of learners. In this writing Janet recognizes, with both complete clarity and sheer surprise, that the time has come to close her teaching practice. This unanticipated milestone is ushered in by kundalini energy, guiding Janet during retreat work with what becomes her last group of learners. Once again, an inherent order becomes visible and ritual provides a portal at this new threshold. A lifetime of inquiry is embodied through a vision appearing: a ritual of gathering, release and surrender, and the return of that which is deathless.

The synchronicity of the energy reappearing at this time is profoundly reminiscent of the first appearance of kundalini in 1981, when Janet opened the Mary Whitehouse Institute. Four decades have passed since Janet invited eight interns to join her in asking the question: "Who is the Witness?" Now eight individuals join her once again, each learner embodying direct experience of the discipline as a mystical practice.

The mystery of inherent order lives at the heart of Janet's teaching career. Within her commitment to track the evolution of this mystical practice, forty years of transitions are reliably guided by the arrival of kundalini energy. Both beginnings and endings are heralded by energetic phenomena that inform her of the precise timing of crucial and evolving inflection points. The synchronicity and uncompromising nature of these experiences teach her early on to listen, and to surrender to a wisdom larger than her own personal timing or desires. She learns to cooperate with spirit at each decisive moment, to consciously yoke her personal will to the will of an invisible intelligence, through her receiving of direct experience manifesting as intuitive knowing.

As we consider the preparation of teachers in a way that reflects the integrity of the practice, we recognize within the Discipline of Authentic Movement an invitation to both the secular and the sacred. Because of the fullness of Janet's offering, each one who comes to this way of work discovers their own specific and unique pathway in and through, wherein the experience of being moved may open a doorway toward divinity. The discipline is a non-sectarian practice that welcomes students from any background, ability, orientation, or tradition who are prepared for their own rigorous descent.

Speaking the
Same Language
An Evolving Dialogue with Mary Whitehouse

> . . . I am waiting (to know when I can come to you). . . I for some rea-
> son, cannot relate to you in the formal manner traditionally appro-
> priate for such an introduction. And yet we have not met . . . I have
> no sense of your eyes, your hands. I cannot write as freely as I seem
> compelled to want to do. . .*

These were words with which I began my autobiographical essay,
October 1, 1969, in response to Mary Whitehouse's request. In my
preparation to work with Mary, I was aware of an unchallenged clarity
within me to simply do whatever was necessary to arrive on the doorstep of her studio. I knew my decision was correct.

Just before writing the essay for Mary, I found myself suddenly—
it was a last-minute decision—a participant in a personal growth lab
at the National Training Institute in Bethel, Maine, with John Weir.
Until this life-changing experience, I did not consciously know about
an embodied path of developing awareness, though I trusted my body
implicitly. I did not consciously know there was such a realm as the
numinous, though I had often experienced it.

Mary had been the person on John's staff to lead movement sessions.
Because she had just become challenged by her diagnosis of multiple
sclerosis, she did not teach at this lab. Instead her student, Josie Taylor,

---

*All indented quotations in this piece are from the author's private collection.

243

guided us beautifully. I experienced my first encounter with what has become, through these years, the discipline of Authentic Movement. That first morning, lying on a carpet under a piano, I felt a recognition of this "way" belonging to me, to my very nature. This "way" was a clear response to such great longing within my twenty-eight years of living. Before I left, John introduced me to Mary on the phone, and so began a series of phone conversations between Mary and me in which we prepared, at many levels, to meet later that autumn.

> I feel a sense of completeness in finding what I need. It wasn't at all clear until I spoke with Mary this afternoon on the phone. I do not need a good Mother. I have been blessed with a fabulous one. I do need a teacher—a person wiser, older, who has been where I have not, but who speaks my language.

This journal recording in November 1969 reflects a beginning of my experience of our relationship, before meeting in person in her West Los Angeles studio. My commitment to authentic movement had begun. Day by day, I waited for her to tell me it was time to meet in her studio. I frequented the beach, already subliminally involved with my shadow, as is apparent in these photographs from that time. Little did I know how much unconscious material was about to surge through my body into consciousness in Mary's presence, because of Mary's presence.

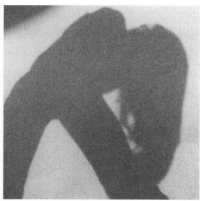

Now forty-two years later—it is time—I begin to write about my experience of Mary, our evolving dialogue. In the early '70s, soon after I had left our short, essential studio work together, we sent audiotapes back and forth to each other, sometimes speaking over the other's voice with our response. She often began her recordings with laughter—which I loved—expressing confusion and frustration with the technology of the recorder she was trying to use and how invariably the machine wouldn't work the way she wanted it to. Her voice on these tapes, especially stirring as they unwind, chronicles for me the great changes, inner and outer, she was experiencing during her illness.

This "correspondence" occurred when I was married and soon to be a new mother, living on the East Coast of the United States in the Pioneer Valley of Western Massachusetts. I can see now that she held a special place of witness for our family even though she never was in our home and never met the children. Mary knitted a baby blanket for our infant son, and I remember being so touched when she insisted on making a new one for our second baby. There are times in the tapes in which she is asking about each son, specific questions, and about me as a new mother, and I hear my own voice in response on tape, telling her, in detail, about my inner experience of the sweetness, the awe, the challenges of such an emotional and sensual immersion in the intimacy of my new family.

We also exchanged personal letters, hers often beginning in shaky handwriting with "Bracha Dear." At John Weir's lab, we were asked to use a pseudonym and without thinking, I chose the name *Bracha,* not knowing that it was a Hebrew word or what it meant until much later. John introduced me to Mary as Bracha, and that is what she always called me.

> Bracha dear,
>
> Will you take a letter just as it comes . . . ? And so I must ask you to accept just random thoughts and responses as they occur to me. I sit here knitting and wishing I were clearer headed but not wanting to put off writing any longer. I'll try.

Among Mary's letters, there is a kind response from an organization to which I had written in 1970, apologetically rejecting my inquiries concerning funding for a film about Mary's work. There is also a reading list for her workshop participants, books published from 1951 to 1967.

I have a few photos of her sitting with a shawl resting on her shoulders, the orange and yellow one I wove for her. Now here in these recent months in my kiva studio on the island, there are moments when I suddenly realize that I am sitting in my teacher/witness chair, with my arms resting on the arms of the chair and my hands folded on my lap, wrapped in a shawl given to me by a student of mine. This specific embodied configuration brings Mary to me, a soft meeting of an outer photographic image and an inner experience.

In reading my movement and dream journals from those potent months with Mary in Santa Monica, I notice so much naming of what I experienced as a return toward my nature yet simultaneously what I experienced as nascent, what actually required the following decades to mature. For example, I write the word "discipline" and then forgetting, only consciously choose this word years later when I realize, know that for me the practice is indeed a discipline.

> . . . it seems that this is the discipline I've been looking for, ready for, can be drunk on. . .

> . . . important, dark, definitely on the right track. . .

> . . . search is FINALLY directed inside rather than outside. . . .

These markings, evocative and poignant, remind me that I recognized Mary as my Teacher, having never had one of this nature before. My brief, but fecund, intense work with her during the winter of 1969 and the Spring of 1970 was essential regarding both my personal and professional growth. So much of my gratitude has been expressed in my own writings, in interviews, in choosing Mary's name as the name of the school I founded in 1981 for the study and practice of Authentic Movement,* and, most importantly, within my own continuing teaching practice.

Mary's experience of multiple sclerosis is inseparable within me from my experience of receiving her teachings, of being in her presence. She was entering this deep sea change in her life at exactly the time when we met. At times, she commented on her gratitude for the fact that we had no history together. Soon after I arrived, she spoke of the absence of previous relationship with me as comforting for her. It reminded her that I could have no expectations of her relative to "who she was before" she became ill.

Excerpts appear in particular letters from Mary concerning the dawning of her illness within her body, within her psyche:

> But it was wonderful to feel so much better after that long spell of crawling on the floor . . . it has been a very limited life . . . I would so love to be able to give something to people again.

> It is as hard to get well as it was to become ill.

> You find me at a time when my main statement is: I don't know.

> I don't know.

> I think the major point of some such illness as mine has to do with what I can get out of it in an inner sense and that leads right into the most private and intimate part of my understanding of myself that simply isn't possible to convey even to people one loves.

---

*The Mary Starks Whitehouse Institute in Northampton, Massachusetts.

What I saw was that Buff's death was the beginning of a process, a clobbering of which MS was really the last chapter . . . the whole illness has indeed been inner, no matter how outer the disability looks or shows.

Mary wrote a book, unpublished, about her experience of the sudden death of her sixteen-year-old son, Buffy. She told me on an audiotape that she did not know what she was going to do about "that book," but something eventually, she guessed.

As is evident in her writing, Mary was a woman of her time, working from her own unique history as a dancer and dance teacher. From what I experience as a place of love, her risks were apparent, her honesty in not knowing seemed available to her, and her courage to work as she felt compelled to do was clear. Her choice to invite a conscious relationship with me as I moved in her presence, encouraged my consciousness to deepen, as did the consciousness of her other students, our students, their students, and so on. Her actions were radical. She truly broke ground in both the field of dance, guiding souls returning to dancers, and also in the field of depth psychology, guiding bodies returning to those seeking consciousness.

In an interview with Tina Stromsted and Neala Haze in 1994,* I remember speaking about my trips alone as an adolescent, every Saturday for two consecutive years, from our small town in central Indiana to the city of Indianapolis, to study privately with the Sadler's Wells prima ballerina. Frightened and excited, determined and uncomfortable, I seemed to persevere until one day when, just before entering her vacuous studio, I briefly glimpsed to my right a white spinning form, propelled up and away from me. Was this a classic ballerina figure disappearing? Was it my soul refusing to stay any longer inside my body that was about to dance, once again, without it?

Once inside her studio, she showed me the sequence of steps from

---

*Neala Haze and Tina Stromsted founded and directed the Authentic Movement Institute in Berkeley, California, from 1993 to 2004. They invited Janet Adler and Joan Chodorow to serve as senior faculty.

last time and told me to do them. What were they? How could they have vanished after so many hours of practice? I could not find them in my body or in my mind. Or was it that I *would not* remember? Then came the long bus ride home in the winter dark and my going immediately to my room, where I closed my jewelry box, the one with the spinning ballerina in the center, and placed it under my bed. So died my dream of becoming a professional dancer.

Fourteen years later, in my first experience as a mover in Mary's studio, I was instantly aware of a source—my soul returning to my body moving. In the very same session when Mary and I were talking together after I moved, I was acutely reminded of what I had recently discovered in John Weir's presence: my body is the primary requisite for my search toward consciousness.

The process into which I was hurling myself or perhaps being hurled, demanded a necessary resource: the inexhaustible unconscious. Perhaps it was the strong influence of Mary's own Jungian psychoanalysis that fueled her curiosity about how the unconscious, arising from the body moving, can shape the potential for conscious awareness.

I remember at times returning to Mary after moving in her presence, how her whole face would light up and she would exclaim: "Now what was that all about?" Her trust in the body knowing seemed always to be held reverently in relationship to her wonder. She tells me on tape:

> The physical body, as an instrument of living, is the most mysterious, most awe-inspiring complex. I think it's a wonder that any of us manage, in spite of the traumas and complexes and buried things, to function.

> Do you suppose that we could get to the place where we know whatever it is that we find ourselves in, we have chosen it somehow . . . (that leads to a conversation about karma and reincarnation, you know) . . . and that we stop taking it too seriously, keep some of the energy for living it?

A former student of both Mary Wigman and Martha Graham, Mary Whitehouse transformed her dance studio into an empty space for something other than dance to occur. She sat to the side of the space while her dance students moved, many having come to her in response to injuries. She discovered, later in her teaching practice, that talking after moving was important. May we not forget the primacy of these significant innovations, now that they are assumed within Authentic Movement practices as generations of her descendants move and witness, speak and listen, in studios around the world.

As distinct from other pioneers in the field of dance movement therapy, Mary worked with adults who were not suffering mental illness. I experienced her primarily as an artist. To me she was a strong woman, a strength that I trusted because I experienced her vulnerability. She knew how to safely enough invite those of us who came to work with her, toward opening to our own vulnerability—the source of our own developing strength.

Mary did not use the term *witness*. She described herself as the one who "watches." Many of her students moved with eyes open. She could be directive from her seat or even come into the space with the mover. Sometimes she played music she chose and sometimes she asked her students to choose music. Sometimes she invited improvisation. In both individual and group work, she offered mirroring exercises or specific "movement problems" to be explored. Many of these ways were different from how many of us work today. Her teaching skills, her strong personality, and her radiance created the presence of a woman whom I experienced as wise, with pioneering vision.

In the studio, Mary was concerned with process, not results. Most days during those few intense months, I was in her studio working alone with her or in a group. And I was often with her in her living room, sitting on the floor near her chair. We taped our dialogues, each trusting in the possibility of discovering an order within her way of work, a map to guide her writing.

Almost a decade later, she spoke to me on tape about her life's work in relationship to where the "field is at present."

The way I did it could only have been done back then. What is known now is way ahead of anything I know . . . the questions now being asked are so useful and rich and were not possible then.

This humble and honest surveillance of her field of study and practice perhaps supported her intention to discern her own contributions within a historical context. The following excerpts are from letters and tapes she sent to me one year before she died concerning her intentions to write a book:

I even have had the letter from a New York publisher.

. . . as if there were value in certain things only. As if the whole point were something other than living my life as transparently as possible . . .

. . . that there is nothing against the essential nature, nothing fighting the truth, no deciding by the ego of what it will and will not permit.

I honestly don't know whether the writing was so much of the ego that it really has gone by or whether I am just afraid of it. . . it is much bigger than that . . . or whether I am avoiding a genuine part of myself.

. . . it is only a problem if I resist.

. . . as if I know nothing about THIS synthesis except by doing it.

Nevertheless, if I think of it that way, as a pilgrimage to the place where I am not, it begins to allow reflection and a seeing how it all happened, even why, and makes me gladder than ever to be here where I am right this minute.

I am having trouble getting down to where I suit myself as the source.

The impression was that the writing, whatever it is, lies way down underneath and needs to be contacted for no other reason than that it belongs to me.

. . . or is it decided by Haschem?

Being ready and able to know when it is time to end, as Mary called it, one's "public life," seemed to be part of her continuing inner dialogue, perhaps because of the interruption, the grave challenges, and maybe she would have said, the gifts of her illness:

It is a long pull to become really clear that I cannot and don't want to pick up where I left off. This is unsettling.

This week-end I gave what is certainly my last weekend workshop. . . I was able to feel that I no longer want to use the energy that way. . . it's over, over, over.

I remember my own experience of awe when she knew it was time to end her teaching practice. And I was comforted, relieved in knowing that for Mary, there was a place, a spot on earth somewhere, that always met her soul, that was always accessible within her. I am told that she flourished in her childhood summers and into her adult life on Monhegan Island in Maine:

Monhegan. . . the one place in my whole life that has a psychic continuity. . .

A decade later, in 1986, I visited Charlotte Selver in her apartment in the Zen monastery at Green Gulch Farm in Sausalito, California.* I had studied Sensory Awareness with Charlotte on Monhegan Island

---

*Charlotte Selver brought Elsa Gindler's Sensory Awareness work to the United States in 1923 and continued to develop it until her death in 2003.

one summer fifteen years before. As she was pouring our tea, her very old body curving over the tea tray, she told me that every summer when she and Charles returned to Monhegan to teach, one of her first destinations was to Mary's grave where she ceremoniously brushed the sticks and leaves of winter away from the gravestone, honoring her colleague.

In the early night of April 29, 1979, not knowing that Mary died that day, I dream the wholeness of my relationship with my Teacher. There is a long journey in which I experience the fullness of my experience of her, including some specific aspects of which I was not previously conscious. Near the end of the dream, I experience a clear communion. Then Mary sits in a grey sweat suit on a wooden meditation bench with her legs crossed. I sit on the floor facing her, with one hand on each of her feet. Her head slowly, silently drops down on her chest. Her body arrives lifeless into my lap.

Writing these words now, I remember her voice again on tape:

> There is such sense that falling into the collective pattern of any solution to life is only a stopgap—that the real experience of loving and living, finding one's way, in the end, is individual.

There is no published book written by Mary about her work, no film that she produced before she died. "To get to this authenticity a sacrifice is involved. . ." These are Mary's words, and maybe it was Mary's book that had to be sacrificed.

Instead of her book, for me, there is something grand, living well with an integrity at its roots, growing now across the world, regardless of the psychological, spiritual, or artistic contexts within which it is offered. Such vital work exists because, with a ferocity of her commitment, Mary Whitehouse opened a profoundly creative portal into authentic explorations within the unfolding realms of embodied awareness.

Letter to Students

Sebastopol Studio
Northern California
September 4, 2003

Dear Ones,

The light is already shifting and I see you here, walking through the door, sitting on the carpet, moving and witnessing on the wooden floor. I am so eager to see you again, our work beginning to feel a bit more seasoned, more grounded, and with a specific group energy that I find very engaging.

. . .

Mary Oliver has written a wonderful, book-length poem entitled "The Leaf and the Cloud." If you find and read this poem, you will come across a chant-like stanza about veils. As she names the veil that never lifts, I am drawn to her acceptance of inner places we will never have the privilege of going, to her compassion about this and even her sense of a precariousness about the possibility of going there. I am then invited ever so gently into a hope: the potential of entering the light that can be experienced in front of or behind those membranes, a light that can be known as impenetrable as well as capable of evaporation.

I am aware of our understanding that we are moving toward a more "spiritual" focus in our work together and eager to learn how such yearning will be actually manifest in the studio

254

work as well as in the discussions. Coming back together after a break is always for me exciting because we have been less connected, less knowing of the whereabouts of each other, less aware of what has been happening. Where did you go? Was it an external or internal journey . . . or both? How did you fare? Are you in the midst of it or glad to be back or disappointed about returning prematurely? How are you?

Until we meet soon, I send love,

Janet

Ritual Practice

one evening

stepping through the kiva doors
stepping the next two steps
down
bowing now crossing the space
I sit on the hearth near
the plate of stones
stones carrying the mysteries
from then to now

placing paper kindling
birch logs in the fireplace
opening the flue
sweeping the floor
the soft wide broom
back and forth
back and forth
now kneeling and sliding
covering the floor
round and round
my hand on a soft oiled cloth

shaking it outside
and I walk to the lilac tree
the sea sound below

I see
the bald eagle
circle and swoop
as I cut long branches
walking more slowly
now to the hose and filling
the tall vase with water
arranging the stems

back inside the kiva
placing the vase
on the mantel placing
a new candle
on the celadon plate
filling
with matches
the round celadon pot
the one with a lid
just next to the candle

turning the silver clock
nearby turning time
slightly toward
my chair
lifting out of the niches
each of the eight
large candles clipping
their wicks checking
their height cleaning
the white
plate on which they stand

folding the sea-blue
blanket placing it

in front of my chair
laying the brass bowl
of a bell
on the green
stone footing the ringing stick
next to it for me to reach
to the left of my chair
just near the few
violets in a tiny vase still
blooming

back in the kitchen now
I find
the glossy wooden tray
choosing
the white tea set each cup
the pot the black iron
base beneath it a tea light
inside
carrying the tray
outside I clip mint leaves
from the earth
dropping them
in the tea pot
continuing back to the kiva
placing the tray on the window seat
near my chair

outside the doors now
emptying the stone bowl
of sea debris water
one bright purple
shell chipped
hearing the eagle call

the shrill of it shaking
my heart or is it my hands
as I wash
the paw prints away
from the glass doors
now sweeping the breezeway
the stepping-stones
the ones that make a pathway
for coming and going

the next morning

lighting the flame on the mantel
the fire beneath it and turning
I stand at the boulder window
a first seeing of people stepping
on the flat stones curving
around the boulder
appearing
in silence

they take off their shoes
enter the kiva she pauses
placing one leg resting it
on the other knee as
it bends and she brushes
detritus from the sole
of that foot now the same
with the other
and she stands her tears
acknowledging her arrival
choosing her place within
the forming
within the circle

I close
the curtains at the door
turning into the kiva
now crossing the space
and stand by my chair
feeling and seeing fire
lilacs the soft green of silk
curtains the boulder the sea
the tall trees I hear the creek
running
here is the image above the sea window
the white round light radiating
within the dark boundless space
and I ring the bell once

I see the eyes of each person
one by one
standing
directly knowing emptiness
before us and we become
witness mover we become
more truthful
we become more whole

Questions:
Teaching the Discipline

From my perspective, the discipline of Authentic Movement is a PRACTICE. This practice is about relationship and therefore is developmental. Thus the witness/teacher learns directly through the experience of practice as a mover and practice as a witness, daily, weekly, year after year after year. In addition, in-depth therapy in which one's body is fully participating as well as in-depth study of psychological phenomena strengthen the preparation toward the responsibilities of teaching others.

Practice is strengthened by an intuitive recognition, a trust in this particular way. Practice is strengthened by a deep knowing that time passing is absolutely necessary. Certification of hours of practice does not necessarily mean that a person is prepared to teach others. If the witness/teacher has not embodied mover and witness consciousness "enough," how can he/she safely guide another to do so?

Commitment to such preparation develops readiness for the responsibility of teaching the discipline in several different formats of practice. Because this is a discipline growing from Western soil, practice of the form begins with attention to *personal consciousness* and moves toward attention to *collective consciousness,* but it is the latter that deeply holds, as if in waiting, the former. Experience as a member of a collective body invites movers and witnesses to learn about their relationship to the experiences of merging with the whole, being separate or in dialogue with the whole, and being in a unitive state with the whole. Here the work includes questions of belonging, betrayal, political consciousness, all in relationship to the deep responsibility of embodied collective consciousness. The intention to guide the development of each individual as mover, as moving witness, and as (seated or standing) speaking witness suggests that the teacher has studied and practiced group process.

Relationship between the individual body and the collective body becomes a source from which questions of spirit emerge, enhancing conscious exploration of the experience of merging with the divine, being separate and in dialogue with the divine, or being in a unitive state with the divine. Are these experiences the same as knowing the divine within another, within the whole, within oneself? How does a teacher prepare for this aspect of the work?

The depth and complexities of this discipline are apparent. Who is prepared to teach it? Who is prepared to supervise teachers? In many meditative disciplines, a hierarchical structure determines who is ready to teach others. We have few external models that might lead us into the unknown territory of another way. It does not feel appropriate to me to use what has been a primarily patriarchal framework to discern readiness to teach [the Discipline of] Authentic Movement, perhaps because the process has evolved from the feminine aspect.

Avoiding the traditional framework does not mean that we yet know the new way. At this time, I choose consciously to endure not knowing the best way. My practice teaches me that each mover, each witness, one by one, must endure the experience of not knowing—and of knowing—when and if one is truly prepared to teach others. Only in this way can action reflect practice. Questions from the witness/teacher, asked in support and guidance, are essential in the time of assessing readiness.

The risks of such ethics are clear: misuse of the freedom of personal responsibility to self and to other. I acknowledge this risk and continue to trust in the integrity of this discipline. For these reasons, I now extend my own commitment toward individuals who are choosing the discipline of Authentic Movement as their primary teaching practice. I wish to be in greater support of such awesome work concerning knowing one's readiness. Those who choose to struggle in depth, over time, with such a challenging ethic are those who I personally wish are, will be, teachers of the Discipline of Authentic Movement.

Emergence of Circles of Four

Often it seems as if authentic movement has always existed, but somehow for reasons that I don't understand, it has been my chosen task to witness, to record my experience of its unfolding, its inherent order made increasingly visible. Similarly, I wonder if all gestures already exist within the pregnancy of the empty studio space. Because of the presence of their witnesses, maybe it is the movers' responsibility—or is it their longing—to enter these gestures, bringing each one in exquisite detail into the light of consciousness.

In these forty years of my commitment to the Discipline of Authentic Movement, a way of life clarifies as a devotional practice. Immersion in it depends upon an experience of relationship, an evolving relationship with oneself, another, the collective, and that which is invisible, unnameable.

Circles of Four is an international postgraduate-level program of practice and study for those wishing to become teachers of the discipline. . . . The formation of this collective is an offering back, in gratitude, to each student whose dedication to this way of work is reflected in their teaching practice. In collaboration, because of the commitment of each one in my presence and in the presence of their colleagues similarly dedicated, a form strengthens, a practice is honed. Circles of Four was created not only to acknowledge and to clarify study and practice that is necessary to teach the discipline, but most importantly to welcome, to offer the discipline to those individuals who recognize this particular embodied process concentrated within the development of consciousness.

One subtle but consistent thread that connects years of engagement in the evolution of studio work is an emergence of questions arising, as if from a timeless, underground stream, always moving. These questions articulate and, in so doing, guide the arrival of new boundaries necessary to contain the experience of not knowing, of risking, of trusting what can become intuitive knowing.

And a fresh question appears: How will an international postgraduate-level program be held and sustained by a collective body of teachers without a director? I remember when the Mary Starks Whitehouse Institute, the first school committed to the practice and study of Authentic Movement, began in my studio in Northampton, Massachusetts, in the fall of 1981. The experience of embodied individual consciousness emerging was dominant at that time. The actual journey we each would be making toward membership in a nonhierarchical web was not yet known to us.

Forty years later, there exists a vibrant, international collective body of individuals practicing, studying, teaching the discipline. A way of collaborative work is becoming increasingly available to those in search of a mystical practice sourced in embodied awareness, to those choosing an experience of evolving witness consciousness that includes both the personal and transpersonal phenomenon that grounds clear seeing.

We can now perceive the wholeness of the complex and liberating journey of an individual's development into membership in an embodied conscious collective. For this reason, our learning organically extends into a program of preparation that is precisely a collective body, *a circle of four,* the learner and three teachers. Circles of Four is a formal reflection of the wholeness of such a passage, in service to each learner, to each teacher.

In a dream, months before the emergence of Circles of Four, I am holding an infant with an ancient face. Carrying her over a bridge, I hand her to many individuals, many people with their arms open, receiving this mysterious discipline that I love. And all is well.

Letter to Learners
before Retreat

Dear Ones,

Now one week from today we will all be finding each other once again, seeing each other's eyes, touching and being touched by each other, listening to each other, speaking and not knowing, and moving and discovering and feeling new and old emotions and lighting the candles and blowing them out.

I wonder if any of you are familiar with Lalla, the fourteenth-century mystical poet from North India? Maybe I read you her poems last year? I keep her near, so now I send you one of her offerings from a little book called Naked Song:

> *Sir, have you forgotten the promise*
> *you made in your mother's womb,*
> *to die before you die?*
>
> *When will you remember*
> *what you intended?*
>
> *Don't let your donkey wander loose!*
> *It will stray into your neighbor's*
> *saffron garden. Think of the damage*

it might do, and the punishment!

Who then will carry you naked
*to your own death?**

As you prepare to travel such a long way, I invite you to
remember that all that you are in moment-to-moment time is
enough . . . as you fold your shirt and roll your socks, check
three times that you have your passport, and answer one last
email.

There is nothing you must prove or perform or embellish or
plan. Not knowing is the way of this work.

Cultivate your intention toward committing to the study and
practice of the discipline in the presence of your colleagues,
of my assistant, Angela, of me, toward a loving, developing
devotion to the evolution of your inner witness.

Sending my love and all good wishes for an easeful journey,

Janet

---

*A selection from *Naked Song* by Lalla, translated by Coleman Barks, published by
Maypop Books, 1992. Used by permission of Coleman Barks.

Letters from
Janet to a Learner

June 2015

Dear Shoshana,

O my, what a beautiful first letter!

As I read what you have written, I am moved by the way you are working with polarities both in the studio with Thea and in your life, especially at a time in which there is so much loss, change, suffering for you. I am sorry you have lost so many loved ones and in such a short time period . . . your dream of marrying Death feels so poignant.

Your words discovered in your solo studio work: "I'm seeing that every moment is for me like a door to the vast unknown truths," and that you are exploring this also in your dyad, feels core within my own understanding of the development of mover consciousness. This is exactly, with the skills you are learning in tracking each moment, how the inner witness grows and can grow with awe, just as you express it, and with compassion.

Your studio work with Thea regarding the experience of "blocking" felt experience can also, as you discovered, invite precious insight. Your words: "In this way I opened to some dark spaces in my personal life . . . light and shadow becoming conscious."

And as the personal work becomes more conscious, there is more space, more access toward actually entering transpersonal material. Energetic phenomenon can become a more conscious part of our daily lives as we encounter it safely and appropriately in the studio work.

Your letter feels like our—your whole circle's—next step in conversation, in correspondence, as part of the newness of the weave of your deepening work within what I feel to be your clear and strong commitment to the discipline. I am very happy to be a part of this journey all together.

Blessings,

Janet

July 2015

Dear Shoshana,

I am interested in your naming your focus on the development of your inner witness and how you learn about it from the different perspectives within which you find yourself moving. As I read of your words about security and container, I immediately think of the pelvis . . . ground, home, bone, always present . . . for me a center of our human anatomy. Is it a place that can hold all, I wonder . . . even this, or that, or could it possibly hold even that?

And yes, your words about your three languages. I am drawn to this question of translation. Some of my students for whom English is not their native tongue say that when they practice the discipline they think, feel, do it all in English! That this way of work is in their cells in English. Others must return to their native tongue when the content is deep and complex and then find their way back to English through translation. In the process of translating Offering from the Conscious Body *into other languages for publication, when I have been invited to be involved, I am thrilled as I learn so much about the specificity of each word and how different it can be in different languages, but also, at times, we discover similar roots in the sound and shape of the words. Rich, rich terrain.*

Here on the cove as well: "cool and caressed by the sea."

Blessings to you and yours,

Janet

September 2015

Dear Shoshana,

I am moved by your words about the relationship between personal and transpersonal experience . . . how you recognize the difference. I appreciate your reference to how I was trying a while ago to write about this stunning possibility concerning the same movement patterns as a portal that can lead to personal or transpersonal work. Often in my experience, the same gesture series can actually open into specific past trauma as well as energetic phenomenon, bringing these two phenomena somehow closer together, which can indeed be how we experience them. I look forward to discussing this further with you.

Your referring to your journal entry about the golden vase, becoming a Buddha: the sphere of light in your hands and then the lotus. Yes, in terms of process within the practice of the discipline, it seems for many that in certain parts of our journeys, the only way to directly know the light is by committing toward conscious descent into darkness. Your words about Om mani padme hum, are striking to me . . . your experience of it recently and then your naming compassion as an embodied experience.

Again I am interested in your reflections on letting your words appear directly from the experience. "The words find themselves" as you say, just as the movement can find itself. What is this mysterious way as though we are guided and if so by what? Is this the inner witness manifesting through embodiment becoming conscious? Yes, describing about the experience is different than directly speaking it as we try to do in the practice. I hear you naming—both in talking and in writing—how this way of describing it seems more closely related to the personal work for you and the direct speech seems to come from transpersonal experience.

Knowing you are a fairly new learner in this process, you can help us help you as we all learn about the art of letter writing, another opportunity to find the voice of your inner witness, this time to write it. We are finding that it is indeed an art and one that magnificently reflects much of the process of the discipline. As we invite learners to send these monthly letters through email, we are all learning how to hone and develop this way of connecting.

Now looking forward to your next one, I send more blessings,

Janet

January 2016

Dear Shoshana dear,

I like this image of you facing your wardrobe, with some doors open and some closed. Dark and light.

I hope as you read this that you are now very well again from your illness—a time when you write of your dreaming more than moving. How beautiful to read of your being drawn toward your body temple. I can understand the excitement, the hunger, and that, yes, you also know some anxiety or fear.

You write of your body, or parts of it, being made of light. As you write you include the full range of your emotional response, including, importantly, how you know it to be "normal."

Your question about your relationship to will and surrender within your inquiry concerning knowing how to balance transpersonal experiences with personal ones, especially as a young mother, is profound. This poem comes to mind called "Dark Angel" written by an unrecognized author of the First Nation people:

> *Not knowing the way*
> *I move forward on the way*
> *with hands outstretched*
> *with hands outstretched.*

These two genres of experience actually do integrate over time, but it seems that this is not in conscious time and we cannot will it. It happens as we continue to recommit, commit again and again, toward the development of our inner witness, our way of choosing to try to be present—whatever the content may be. Process always seems stronger than content no matter how devastating, brilliant, dazzling, or withering the content may be.

Thank you for your words regarding your experience of your hand made of light. This is clear, moving, honest. I recognize you here, the you I am coming to know as we come closer to meeting on the island in the Spring.

Janet

February 2016

Dear Shoshana,

Reading about the realm of words in your letter tells me more about your relationship to them historically. I am happy to know how your recognition of words as a very alive force within you has been a deeper part of your path. I trust this and welcome your words, circling first or just landing at once . . . appearing from a place of intuition or from at times perhaps your executive function. Yes, they clarify distinguishing experiences among the one who moves, the one who witnesses, the one who writes, the one who sees, the one who loves.

I appreciate that they appear having survived a process of translation . . . which for me always makes such words especially moving. Now I remember working years ago with a large group of students, all but one speaking English as their first language. We all waited a bit breathlessly each time this woman began to speak because somehow her words felt so concise and clear, as though each one was being chosen in that very moment, and then spoken with the same care.

Are these precious moments when we cross over a threshold, an invisible line? A place in time and space that welcomes us into that which is newly known and perhaps always known . . . a paradox so inviting.

Soon and with love,

Janet

April 2016

Dear Shoshana,

I receive your letter as a burst of Spring energy . . . each part: your walk in the forest, your deepening commitment to this practice arising not only in the studio but suddenly when you are doing what you are doing, and of course when you are watching the flowers . . . and! when you know you are becoming part of a whole, not so alone with the depth of your inner experiences.

First the listening: Yes, I am aware of a fullness, a readiness, a willingness to take in what is being offered to you as you listen to a colleague or teacher . . . and as I listen to myself witnessing you listening, I feel quite wide, with an awareness of no boundaries . . . a spacious, deep welcome.

Now your moving: Here in the kiva I am a beginner as your witness, just learning the precious details of each gesture you make, and again how focused I feel as I see you make them, one by one. I look forward now as a teacher in your circle to experiencing a widening of your gesture repertoire, learning more each time we meet about your own path of discovery of new shapes inviting new inner rumblings.

Since I have recently been with you and so fully enjoyed all that we exchanged, I will stop here. Now I look forward to your next offering. I am wondering what you are reading that supports your current questions in the discipline? I am wondering how your own questions within your practice of the discipline connect with any questions either of your children are working with in their "practice" of daily life and all that it brings to them? And I am wondering how your own questions connect with any of your clients?

O may you be well . . . and your family, each of your children, your husband, and all who you love,

Janet

June 2016

Dear Shoshana,

I am moved by your discussion of the relationship to trauma and energetic phenomenon: your client's readiness to surrender here, yours to be present for him, and your naming courage in relationship to all that is dark, all that cannot be seen. And yes, vital and of course necessary for the inner witness to grow and strengthen, widen and truly become compassionate enough in such unbidden moments.

Your words about your own tendencies, so natural, so universal:

> *O, I know them so well, the ways to switch to some more secure space, the fluttering of the thoughts, sudden not feeling, dark clouds that quit the movement. The experience of an internal fight between something that the body brings me to and some other part of myself that wants to avoid it.*

You write beautifully about the "tenderness" of our internal defensive processes, how we protect ourselves from "touching and following embodied memory" until as you say, with the support of a commitment to the truth, will and surrender can integrate enough in very certain moments into and through the portal that actually opens. Those very certain moments have always been of great interest to me. What is the timing that brings us to such a gate: enough presence of the inner witness, enough presence of the outer witness, enough compassion from both and then a poetics of mystery . . . something that cannot be controlled . . . risk and blindness, trust and readiness, sometimes terror and helplessness? Or is it an experience of faith within the vastness of not knowing?

And it is, just as you write, in such unforgettable moments in a mover's life of reliving trauma, that the outer witness is called to be exceptionally present for many reasons, but especially to support the mover in not enduring more than her or his inner witness is ready for. This really reminds us of the importance of the relationship between mover and witness—length of time in working together, amount of trust—as crucial foundation for the readiness of the mover to turn into the embodiment of traumatic experience. I imagine you know much about this in your psychotherapy practice.

And then yes, sometimes the transpersonal realms appear.
And yes, such experiences can appear in support of avoiding
personal trauma, creating a bypass, or can appear in support
of egoic work that can strengthen a capacity or readiness to
endure the reliving of trauma. So much to track and I am
confident in your sensitivities to do so.

Sending love from the cove and all the baby birds now becoming
teenagers,

Janet

July 2016

Dear Shoshana,

How I enjoy each time receiving your letter. I like the way
you work with one question and open it so fully. This time
the question of the inner witness: where is she located (I have
never found mine located in a specific place in my body), how
do you know when she is absent, is the pelvis involved, and the
difference between awareness and observing. Thank you for such
a full inquiry in this direction. And I appreciate your words:
"Discerning all that."

I have a book here in my library called The Observing Self, *by*
Deikman . . . one of those books that was part of a response to
my own questions at one time about witnessing. I don't know if
there is anything now relevant in it for your studies. Of course,
Buddhist studies and our inquiries in the discipline are very
connected in many ways and relevant and thankfully accessible.

Yes, observing what is arising and embodying what arises are two
different things. I am interested in your inquiry into two such
different ways. Perhaps they both lead to the same outcome? But
in the discipline we are choosing embodiment for sure, and yet

the mover can always choose not to embody a specific gesture. So conscious choice is part of what becomes quite complex in this business of choosing embodiment, as you know.

I wonder if there is a difference between sensing—and maybe this is an intuitive thing—and knowing directly. And is there a difference between an empty mind and clear presence? Empty mind in this way of looking at it is not usually really possible as we live our daily lives within our culture . . . as wife, mother, teacher, daughter, therapist. Presence certainly is, thank goodness. Do you ever have experiences of empty mind that you might locate in any of these specific realms? Do you ever have transpersonal experiences that tend to arrive into the empty mind?

May you and yours be well.

Sending love,

Janet

October 2016

Dear Shoshana,

I have read Nancy's wonderful response to your October letter and resonate with all that she writes. I am especially moved by her drawing attention to your word tenderness. Ah there it is again! Yes. It is clear to me how with the depth of practice to which you have committed regarding the development of your inner witness: you can name, you can acknowledge, welcome, even celebrate all the moments when your inner witness is "clear, is light, is receptive, compassionate, out of time." And then how clearly you name when this is not true.

Yes. When we do feel we are moving forward on our path with a clear enough inner witness navigating our way, one that can be more loving to ourselves and others, it can feel like a sudden, almost shocking moment when we have lost connection with that benevolent presence within. We act in ways that can feel utterly disappointing, even embarrassing as we "notice" we are once again reacting or unkind or not in alignment with our true nature. Maybe it is here that the gift becomes humility as of course we are just people wandering around trying to see ourselves and our loved ones more clearly, with a more fulfilling, authentic embrace. And the saddest thing is that just as you say, such confusion usually appears in the midst of our most primary relationships.

I am quite taken by the clarity of your distinction between your work with your inner witness within your practice of the discipline and within your meditation practice. How privileged we are to be able to choose two such different paths that, as you say, can have the same outcome.

Now the light changing, the colors becoming warm on the trees and the ground . . . all familiar signs of feeling called inward toward exactly what you are writing to us about . . . toward an experience of the presence of relationship to that which begins as invisible, veiled, but becoming ready to be known, to be seen. I seem to wait, in a quiet way, all year for this particular depth and breadth of inner work because of the seasons changing.

Sending love,

Janet

November 2016

Dear Dear Shoshana,

Your words have a richness, beginning with the vividness of the attic and its amazing history for you. How wonderful that it is still there for you to return to at different stages of your life, from childhood to knowing it as a bride and then where your first child appeared and now, a place within which you draw your circle around you and write to us.

Witnessing.

Witnessing.

Witnessing.

I deepen as I read about your way of entering and living into this mysterious process called witnessing that can be filled with emptiness or filled with joy or creative problem-solving or loving or sadness or confusion or light. Sometime will you tell us a bit about witnessing a client with whom you especially resonate or who challenges you or who invites you toward their relationship to emptiness?

And this time I especially love reading about your children. Do you have a photo of them that you might share?

Sending love,

Janet

December 2016

Dear Shoshana,

I now turn toward my annual silent January retreat so I will not be responding to your letter next month, but will fold my response to your January letter into my response to your February letter.

> *And the emptiness turns its face to us and whispers,*
>   *'I am not empty. I am open.'*[1]

All good wishes and sending love,

Janet

February 2017

Dear Shoshana,

I am deeply moved by your last letter to your teachers. Nancy's response is full and loving, marking much of what you write and what I also feel. So I will respond in another way. Hooray for having more than one teacher!

To be able, to be ready, to consciously choose to hold the amount of darkness that you experience within and around you, recently and historically, is remarkable. As I read, I feel as though I am in a ritual with you:

> *You and Thea are sitting in the very center of the kiva:*
>
> *I see you just across from each other, legs crossed, and you are holding your toes, your torso slightly bent forward. (I wonder if you remember this position here last time? Perhaps I have marked it before in your presence and if so it is because of my continuing inner experience as I see you.)*
>
> *Now in this ritual within my imagination, there is one candle on the floor between the two of you. You each are rocking forward and back, ever so slightly. (This particular way of moving, the Jewish people call davening.) I hear old music, mostly string instruments. The light all around you is soft.*
>
> *In my experience, you are each feeling directly connected with the other and with some larger presence. Now I hear another nearby and open my eyes and see Nancy sitting exactly as you two are, davening as you are, equal distance from the central candle and each other. And now I am davening, as I sit equal distance from the central candle and each of you.*

A paradox: Your circle has been here all along in a mysterious way. We are holding both the subtle and the harsh realities of manifest and hidden darkness with you.

I am noticing my response to your words: "compassion for who holds in his personal or cultural history the burden of guilt." I resonate with you here. Not instead of the victims, but in addition, I have always been concerned for the ones who somehow enact the darkness, causing such great harm to others but also to themselves, of course. Sometimes my experience of this can be confusing for others to understand. I wonder how you work with your own awareness of this compassion for the guilty ones.

And how totally precious to "meet" your family! Your children are beautiful. And now I have a sense of you and your husband together . . . Thank you for this introduction.

Sending love until soon when we will be in the kiva again together and with your colleagues,

Janet

March 2017

Dear Shoshana,

You write in your letter this month how gratitude emerges when you enter a time alone . . . silence and space. I am touched by your acknowledgement of the three of us in this way. I am touched by your depth and sensitivity to the vastness of such realms. You might enjoy the book The Philosophy of Emptiness *by Gay Watson, a book as I might have already mentioned, that has been a great gift to me this winter.*

Yes soon now and more love,

Janet

⬭

April 2017

Dear Dear Shoshana,

I like your way of naming authentic wishes at the end of your letter. Spring is arriving here on the island but still so cold. Everyone mutters about this, longing for the warmth of the sun. It seems the trees and flowers bloom anyway, without that warmth, and this interests me.

As I read your April letter, read about the relationship between your intense place of silence within you and simultaneously your experience of such presence, I feel a kind of liberation . . . and gratitude that both can be true for you at once. And I am grateful also that you choose to connect with us, your teachers, from this significant place.

Your continuing inquiry into the phenomenon of suffering and the strength of compassion also interests me. I am glad to read of your inner connections with Ani Choying Drolma again. Isn't it remarkable how we are touched by others and touch others in such mysterious ways, not knowing directly who it is really but recognizing them immediately through their words or drawings or music? And maybe you have had the privilege of being in the presence of this person?

Again, thank you, dear Shoshana, for connecting with us from this place, on your knees, your opening of your skin into vulnerability and more openness . . . your clarity, your light.

Sending love,

Janet

⬭

June 2017

Dear Shoshana,

Thank you for such a moving letter. As I read it, I imagine Nancy and Thea also reading it and then I am reading their responses as I prepare to write mine. You write: "Now I feel I work from a different place . . . Very often I used to contact the world from some other place, reflecting, rescuing, serving others, keeping my truth to the side." As I read this, I am aware of the wonder of how new insight, like you are experiencing now, can feel almost shocking sometimes as we know it in relationship to the old way . . . if only we knew then what we know now! And simultaneously, the gratitude for the new knowing, an excitement maybe about how this is already changing your life. I am touched in reading: "I needed time for that opening." Such wisdom in realizing this . . . how necessary time is for certain nervous systems maybe. It certainly makes sense when such changes are so authentic, as yours clearly are.

Authentic change always amazes me. Usually, in this way of work we cannot will it, only cultivate it. And as I hold your letters and remember your kiva work, it is apparent that indeed you do cultivate the development of your inner witness, your consciousness, and you do suffer in the process, not knowing if or when insight will arrive or an authentic shift will be known. Here again is the mystery of timing with which we cannot interfere, only bring awareness to, which you do so beautifully.

You name your ability to help, to save others that you have always known. What a gift and now, especially what a gift to have such resonance with others' suffering without or with less of what you name as a covering over of your own personal truth. I wonder how that original gift will transform with more of your own truth available at the same time. How grateful I am that you feel compassion for yourself in this process of "liberation, love, and courage." To now turn with this awareness, this compassion, toward the question of teaching the discipline, feels timely: "I can start with gratitude and a sense of readiness. And now I also feel the Openness for it!"

Summer time always feels like a sensual time . . . more skin available to the warm sun, water, sand . . . I think of you and your children enjoying all of this together . . . a certain joy in perhaps you and your husband seeing the children moving through summer time and summer space with maybe some of that liberation you are now feeling as well.

Sending love,

Janet

PS: I am so enjoying the singing of Ani Choying. Thank you for remembering to send it to us.

July 2017

Dear Shoshana,

I want to begin with the ending of your last letter as it moves me so much:

> *Other words that come to my mind describing the new quality are softness, pliancy, trust, and Love. I perceive in my heart constant round openness full of tender Love. Love that is not necessarily an emotion, is not the opposite of anger, it includes and encloses all.*

The infinite nature of what you name, a love that encloses and includes all can be profound ground for a daily life, one that includes marriage, children and work and parents and travel . . . shopping and disappointment, sadness and joy, crisis and surprise and fear and wonder . . . ground that we can cultivate toward a deepening readiness, ability, and presence . . . a place from which we can respond, a place from which we can offer.

I wonder if evolving experiences of emptiness are arising in relationship to all that you name. It does come to my mind as I read your letter. Here is what Gay Watson writes in her conclusions about the phenomenon of emptiness, and I like now sending this to you as it makes me think of your life and what you offer in this and other letters at times:

> *First, a philosophy of emptiness must be close to experience, embodied experience. Next approaches to emptiness are therapeutic, signifying a way to deal with anguish, a path to living better. And third, a philosophy of emptiness is centered in awareness rather than evasion.*[2]

Does this make sense to you and if so what might you say in response?

Sending love,

Janet

December 2017

Dear Shoshana,

I am always happy in receiving a letter from you.

You name noticing with Thea that the focus of your individual work is shifting toward teaching and this seems timely and wonderful to me. I am interested if you and she will be continuing solo work at this time and if so, perhaps less often? As witness from afar of your relationship, I have always felt such respect and gratitude for how the two of you have woven such a deep weave together. And knowing how Nancy works, I feel great joy in realizing that you might be working with her more.

And stillness. As I read, I am remembering my own experience of you in the kiva in stillness, a trusting of an authentic arrival, or is it immersion? As you write about such an inner place this time, I am wondering if you perceive any difference in this experience since your deep work last year with personal history, some of the dark places that perhaps you went "in and through"? It seems each round of returning to any fragment of unresolved personal history liberates, allowing us a more direct encounter with the mysteries, which include the phenomenon of stillness, just in the way you write about it.

I am glad to read of your time with your fellow learner. This kind of peer dyadic commitment you two made can only strengthen each of your work, and of course it will strengthen your entire kiva collective.

I am grateful for your response to my question regarding "embodied memories in relationship." It is hard to even imagine the two pregnant women you refer to, and how they are together in such dire circumstances. Perhaps you are one in your generation who is carrying memories from the Holocaust in a certain way because of who you are, your particular sensitivities. In doing so I am clear then that you are offering something essential to your country, to the world, and of course I am interested in how this "carrying" impacts or has impacted your soul, or choices that you make within moments, or your daily life in general.

May the winter light in the bare trees offer more space, more invitation, for the depth of your inner work.

I send love,

Janet

February 2018

Dear Dear Shoshana,

One thing that continues to interest me about your journey is the relationship between the depth and profundity of your inner life—stillness, meditation, solitude, time with your trees—and how these experiences influence, arrive into your offering to another or to a group. I look forward to learning more about this perhaps in your kiva work. I have such confidence and trust in this particular direction from inner toward outer . . . a direction perhaps you know so well?

I notice in this last letter your naming the places on the front and on the top of your head. Again I look forward to meandering toward that awareness, if indeed it appears in the kiva work.

And I feel happy in reading about your work with Thea and also your preparation to engage with Nancy and your assisting with her teaching. All seems to be moving so authentically toward a newer experience of being a learner in Circles of Four.

More in depth perhaps in response to one more letter before welcoming you here once again on the island.

I send love,

Janet

May 2018

Dear Shoshana,

Reading about preparations for Thea's arrival in your country . . . I send all good wishes within this journey you both are embarking upon. And then I read of your supervision work with Nancy in what feels already like such a solid way. Yes. I am touched to read a bit about your experiences here on Galiano in retreat work . . . the depth of your movement work, how you write about your female body, about your womb . . . "The Earth. The Cycle." And I appreciate your writing a bit about your experience of the surprise of our last day with my absence.

I am not sure, but as I read, I am imagining that you write about subtly perceiving what is true in terms of the changes in

*my life and my work at this time when you were here. I am not
surprised that you intuited this immediately . . . not exactly
what is happening, of course, but your sensitivity to "other ways
of knowing." So I understand that there is a relief in knowing
what in fact you were sensing was real within me. If indeed
this is what you were writing to us about in part of this letter, I
want to acknowledge it because for those of us who do have such
sensitivity, often it can be unclear what we are "picking up."*

*For some this way of being, as you know, can be a gift and also
sometimes a burden . . . sometimes a real challenge because we
don't always know what is happening, just as you write: "I felt
some kind of confusion, lack of clarity, appearing from time
to time." I wonder if you would be willing to share in another
letter how this capacity supports, confuses, challenges you
in your teaching or therapy practice. Now that you are more
formally teaching the discipline, I would be interested to learn
more about how you experience your intuition, for example, in
relationship to your mover's work, how the issue of timing for
instance is handled when you feel you know something that the
mover maybe does not yet know? Again your words:*

> *And I find out how confusing it is sometimes for me, perceiving
> something important underneath and not being yet able to name it.*

*And even as a parent, or friend, or even as a learner with three
teachers, how do you experience what I am here calling intuitive
knowing?*

*And now I send you love from green and sunny Galiano. Isn't
this new springtime green indescribably evocative?*

Janet

June 2018

Dear Shoshana,

I am very engaged by the discussion among you, Thea, and Nancy about the relationship between intuitive and cognitive. It would be interesting to learn more about how these places arise within your clients and students—similar perhaps to your experiences and of course different.

And here perhaps you are maybe naming again your psychic abilities? Thank you for the clarity that you describe when your "irritation" arises. Is this different from what you are specifically discussing regarding clear and cloudy? For those of us who are primarily intuitively directed, such inquiry as you are making seems imperative as our "intuitive way" feels so natural and apparent . . . yet it is not always helpful because projection, judgment, and interpretation can unconsciously interfere. I am also interested in the need for balance with our cognitive function, especially as a teacher. For example, if a teacher has very developed gifts in the realm of intuition and has a student who is primarily mental, and the teacher desires to meet the student where they are, this can sometimes require stretching within for the teacher in order to include another way of processing experience. A big question: How to come into alignment with oneself in the presence of another without betraying either of us?

> *And mostly in the studio practice I do trust myself and also I trust the profound wisdom of the person I work with.*

Me too; I am, of course, trusting your way and it is a way that includes inner reflection . . . which is why I trust it!

I am interested in reading about "words flying out of your mouth." Isn't this kind of experience totally mysterious? And I am intrigued to read of your urge to draw when experiencing cloudy moments. This feels like a wonderful idea, and one that was a part of my teaching and personal practice of the discipline for many years . . . clay, pen and ink, colors, pasting . . .

in response to moving and to witnessing. Maybe this would be something to further explore when you are the mover, though I don't know how much you might have already been doing this. As you know, sometimes drawing brings us closer to the direct experience than words and thus becomes enough and/or a bridge to clear language.

Dear Shoshana, I send you much love,

Janet

July 2018

Dear Shoshana,

I am happy in reading more about your experience of the retreat with Thea in your country. There is a breadth of experience you name: such few words—from joy to exhaustion to immersion in stillness and silence—the stars near.

As I look at the photos you have sent, suddenly I see both the great beauty near your home and at the same time, I see the energy of this beauty and know it to be everywhere in the world. Your little niece, her body in the sand, becomes Everybaby. The water, Everybeach. All water. Your perception as the one who chooses and marks these moments. All seeing. And the clouds, yes, All clouds Everywhere.

May this time of peace stay with you.

I send love,

Janet

September 2018

Dear Shoshana,

I enjoy reading in your most recent letter how you lace the "theme" of transition into other parts of your life, beginning with your own authentic experience of it, and then in your family time, your clients and patients, and especially how you describe this in your time with Nancy.

The phenomenon of transition continues to intrigue me as it will always for me remain mysterious. Having already left where you are but not quite yet arriving fully into where you will be—that space which can be short or long or timeless— the vibration of it seems necessary and often challenging, a reminder to me of the potency, the inevitability of change always occurring, even when not quite visible.

In reading your words about this, your consciousness of it, how you have been tracking yourself through it in different situations, feels fabulous. This is the best we can do, what you do—trying to bring a loving enough inner witness presence to all that arises.

Sending now love from me to that loving inner witness of yours,

Janet

October 2018

Dear Shoshana,

Once again, I am moved to read of your inner experiences as you witness yourself "strengthening my inner witness" with your family, your clients, and nature, including the one tiny bird drinking, trembling, bathing. Maybe this is what it is all about after all . . . seeing clearly that which is present.

It matters to me that you write about accepting more and more that which you know intuitively, directly, and now with less complexity around such a gift. I so appreciate how you write:

> *And I trust. This is for me the grounding in which I start to trust myself and this experience of mine, while working with another person in this very delicate, special place of this door open. Integrating, making space for it and connecting it with love and care to the very normal, everyday life.*

Sending you love now,

Janet

November 2018

Dear Shoshana,

I am immersed in writing about ceremony now, rewriting an essay I offered to the faculty at our last Samaya gathering—all about ceremony now after these two years passing in which the faculty especially has been deep in inquiry and practice related to what might be occurring all the way over on the right side of the arc of the mandorla. We want you, as a learner, to know as much as possible about this, yet again, mysterious shape of the collective becoming conscious. It is perfect that Nancy will be offering a retreat for several people from your kiva learner's group in which you will focus on ceremony and integral witnessing.

And I read in this current letter as you write about your time with Nancy:

> *We walked together to some level and then said that further I would go further by myself. And I went, to the top.*

Yes, maybe this is indeed what might be happening for you at this time of intending to complete your work within your circle of four "on the way for the Blessing" . . . a time of a certain kind of separation having "walked together to some level" and then the experience of going by yourself—and I need to add—to the top of your path at this time.

I feel near as I send love and full support,

Janet

January 2019

Dear Dear Shoshana,

As the new year arrives, my heart is opened by your loving message concerning the newness of your Blessing arriving. Yes, it is so clear to each one of the four of us that it is time for you to be welcomed into the next step of your teaching practice, which we each want to support as does the whole faculty.

I hope you can come to the kiva in July as a beautiful possibility, as a part of this next step, both for you and for your colleagues. I want the other blessed teachers, the ones who have completed their work in Circles of Four, to know you and you to know them and what better way than entering the practice of the discipline together. And also, there will be more time for us to work together again, for me to learn who you are becoming now . . .

Shoshana, your tender words:

> *It's my best transforming I've ever experienced 'til now.*

And now I offer them back to you within the context of the depth of my gratitude for your commitment to your evolving inner witness, to the development of your embodied consciousness, within this shared practice because it has been an utter privilege for me to be one of your teachers.

With love,

Janet

◯

April 2019

Dear Shoshana,

Your last letter! When such finality appears before me I always feel astounded. What? How could this be? What happened? An end. Yes. And as you often have inferred, a beginning.

I like experiencing how you bring us directly into your moving/ meditation practice and how they now integrate. Yes.

my back straight

As I read these words, I see you stand erect and walk through a portal into the world, a world I believe is awaiting you in a very specific way at this very specific time of completion, of readiness. The shape of the doorway is an arc, much like that of the mandorla but taller and not so wide, more intimate. But similar enough that I find myself naming it . . . as if somehow, the very arc of it, knows you. It is made of clay, earth color and not perfectly smooth, more with a texture I find so inviting.

As you reread all the letters, written and sent, yours and your teachers in preparation for gathering them into one form, I too am doing the same thing. What a joy in knowing this parallel path right now!

Go well, dear Shana, until we three gather around you for your blessing at Samaya* next month, in the presence of the whole faculty, with love,

Janet

---

*Samaya, a retreat center in The Netherlands, was the location of the First and Second International Gatherings of Circles of Four.

ONE BASKET
The Closing of a Teaching Practice

The kundalini energy arrives, unbidden, the night before we complete our retreat. I receive a vision, a teaching, entering my being with its familiar force, emptying me, bringing me to a halt, demanding all of me again. It arrives as direct experience, announcing an ending.

I vividly see each one of you, eight of you learners present in this retreat, and simultaneously I recognize you as students and learners in all of these years of sharing my love of this way of work, this way of life:

> *Dusk. I begin to gather*
> *your shawls left behind*
> *on the furniture*
> *where you sit*
> *in our living room*
> *at the end of each day*
> *sharing questions*
> *sharing gestures.*
>
> *I see this shawl*
> *my shawl today*

wildly purple
in my arms here
as I keep walking
round and round the room
my arms filling
with all the shawls
I have ever worn in studio practice.
I can feel the weight
of them now draping
over my head, my shoulders.

Heavy, somehow they land
in a basket
next to another basket
filled with remains
of candles I loved lighting
in all the studios.
And another basket
this one filled with dead blossoms
from each bouquet
I loved preparing.
And more baskets, each a different size
and shape, holding objects
reflecting forms, faces.

I see each of you lift up
carry one basket
as you all walk down
and across the lawn
onto the beach

where you ritually place them
at the edge of the water
where the tide will meet them
sweep them out to sea.

With no time passing the vision brings a new morning light, and I see the one basket that held the dead blossoms returning emptied of death, oh just beginning to fill with new life, fresh flowers.

CHAPTER SEVEN

WITNESS CONSCIOUSNESS
INTO THE WORLD

Introduction
By Bonnie Morrissey & Paula Sager

a spark of fire
into the palm
of each hand
burning
right through. Hands
are wounded
all hands, all people
　　　　　Janet Adler,
　　　　　Arching Backward

The seeds of a lifetime may ripen, burst, and deliver themselves to the world in many ways. The seeds of a mystical practice may do the same. Through the Circles of Four program, each faculty member, learner, and teacher who has completed the program participates in the evolution of the Discipline of Authentic Movement in unique ways. New teachers step forth, arriving in service to their students, guided by their own inner questions. Some of these teachers will grow toward becoming faculty members, further nourishing the program. An expanding international collective body of teachers of the discipline grows, now without a director, as Janet gradually and graciously withdraws from her central role. She continues to mentor and participate in the collective body of Circles of Four as it evolves, seeking and discovering more collaborative, less hierarchical ways of being.

As our devotion to this work matures, can we remember why we practice? As each one of us steps out through the doors of our protected studio spaces, returning to the intricate detail and complexity of our daily lives, the guidance of our strengthening inner witness may manifest in ways both simple and profound. What does it mean to offer a conscious gesture, a conscious word toward what matters in our lives? What are the fruits of witness consciousness in each life, and in our world? Always we wonder how to bring developing witness consciousness from the studio into our everyday lives, in which we witness ourselves and others move through time and space. Without this essential process of translation, the Discipline of Authentic Movement is incomplete.

In 2006, two-and-a-half decades after her experience of initiation began, Janet arrives at another significant doorstep, another transformative moment in her life, as her mother faces increasing health challenges. After long consideration, Janet's mother decides to fast as a way to meet her own death. We begin this final chapter with "Witness to a Conscious Death,"* an essay in which Janet tracks and documents this momentous loss as she attends her mother, who makes deliberate choices regarding the timing and manner of her departure from this life. This essay is an account of an awesome depth of intimate relationship within a journey of separation and grief. "Maybe we are taking turns," Janet says, referring to the conscious delivery of one by the other: mother birthing daughter into life, daughter midwifing mother toward death, and her mother nods yes. Janet companions her mother to the rim of death, to the edge where each must proceed alone. Here is one woman's story of witness consciousness in the world.

As in her initiation, ritual grounds the significance of this journey for Janet and for her family. With utmost care and without sentimentality, candles are lit, wine is sipped, blessings are given and received, a shroud is hemmed. An atmosphere of ceremony may be perceived,

---

*"Witness to a Conscious Death" was first published in *Natural Transitions* 3, no. 3 (2014).

entered. Gesture and word both emit from and help to maintain a sense of lucidity and presence. "Like her death, my grief will be inevitable," writes Janet.

In the next essay, "Suffering,"* a previously unpublished work, Janet names a perennial paradox: we are separate beings and we are entirely interconnected. "That man's starvation," Janet writes, "is not my own hunger. And simultaneously I directly know we humans to be the same." How utterly human it is to turn away from suffering, our own and that of others. All great social movements are born and develop from courageous individuals turning toward suffering, toward our own pain, and toward the pain of others with compassion and a deep longing for the guidance of insight and wisdom. To turn toward suffering, Janet reminds us, is not merging, not losing ourselves in the suffering of the world, but finding a way to come to terms with bearing the realities of incarnation, including the experience of that which seems unbearable.

Janet writes that the depths of suffering can be experienced as a separation from our source where we are "as far from unitive consciousness, from our original light, as a human being can be." She recognizes this place, and turns toward it in herself, surrendering toward her own suffering within the immensity of suffering in the world, without any demand for relief. Longing to see each other more clearly, learning to love, through relationship we learn "about our capacity to accept, endure and survive suffering, our own and every being's" (see "Toward the Unknown," page 167). Perhaps because of her long commitment to this inquiry and her willingness to surrender fully to the embodiment of her experience, Janet finds her way in and through this conundrum, able to reside more consciously and more closely with that which seems intolerable in herself and within the world.

In such transformational moments, the inner witness becomes witness consciousness. The grace of direct experience and intuitive

---

*This previously unpublished essay was adapted from Janet's presentation for her Bat Mitzvah in 2014 at Temple Emek Shalom in Ashland, Oregon, officiated by her son, Rabbi Joshua Boettiger.

knowing enter the world as a quality of presence, seeking to permeate all density. Janet's prayer, flowing above and under the surface throughout her writing, affirms her wish: "May the quality of consciousness that is emerging collectively within our world outweigh the quantity of unconsciousness that suffers on our planet. May all suffering become compassion" (see "Presence," page 33).

As we move closer to the generative edge of mystery, the energetic body becomes more palpable and vibrates in synchrony with something invisible that is yet unknown, something new that may be received. The infinite nature of the inner and outer worlds can become the same. Each one of us may savor a more lucid yet humble awareness regarding when we are truly present and when we are not, perhaps the most we can hope for in a lifetime. It is possible to become paradoxically both clearer in our knowing and more easeful with uncertainty, marks of resilience, health, and empowerment.

These essays carry us nearer to the fruition of our practice, wherein the beauty and power of witness consciousness may manifest as medicine, as a healing force. Within a space of devotional awareness, the mandorla tips up and is lit, a candle flame burning as compassionate presence inside the circle of all beings.

Witness to
a Conscious Death

Many die too late, and some die too early.
Yet strange soundeth the precept:
Die at the right time.

ZARATHUSTRA

Preparation

Our Mother led her life very fully, especially in her relationships and in her work as a visual artist. As I matured, she discussed with my brother, Larry, and me, her clarity about not wanting to live beyond her capacity to have a clear enough mind, to enjoy dignity, self-control, and a reasonable absence of pain. By the time she was in her late sixties, she showed me the bottles of pills in the bathroom cabinet, supervised for her by Dr. Sherman—a gifted, warm, and deeply kind physician who understood her fears . . . not of death, as she said, but of "dribbling away." I witnessed the second time she spoke with Dr. Sherman in her home when she thought that maybe her failing eyesight or increasing pain from osteoporosis were warnings toward choosing to end her life. Both times he urged her to wait, feeling that she was not "suffering" enough to make such action appear ethical.

Six months after Mother is celebrated in her beloved Chicago at her ninetieth birthday party, she fears that in another six months she will need round-the-clock care. She is becoming blind. She is in pain while standing or sitting. Now she commits to her own death. She feels ready. After repeated failed attempts to find support from physicians and/or hospice, when Dr. Sherman realizes how persistent she has been, how profoundly disappointed she is now with no support, and how she intends to go ahead with her plans regardless of doctors or hospice, he decides yes, he will be there for her and will ask a colleague to help with prescriptions, if they are necessary. Mother seems elated.

With loving intentions, she writes letters to her grandchildren and great grandson, explaining her plans. Having always said that she never could die by stopping eating and drinking, as she loved this part of life so much, this is the very path she chooses, as this is the only one she knows in which no one else can possibly be incriminated . . . no pills in applesauce, no possible finger prints of another on any supporting object, no helium tanks and plastic bags.

Once she decides, doubt appears, as it often does once we commit to anything that matters. Even though she has repeatedly reviewed the whole picture, including her feeling that this is a good time to die because no one in her immediate family is in crisis, she turns back one last time and asks: "How can I do this to you and your brother?" I tell her that for me, I will be devastated whenever she dies, now or later. She cannot indefinitely prevent my experience of her absence. Like her death, my grief will be inevitable.

For a long time, years and years, it had been understood between us that I would be Mother's midwife, do whatever I could in support of her way of dying. I trust her decision and commit to her and to her commitment to this process, with careful inquiry into any judgement, projection, or interpretation I might have regarding her choice. I find no inner obstacles, no hint of confusion about what she tells me. And paradoxically, I am aware that my experience of *her* dying, *her* death, the absence of *her* presence, phenomena about which I know nothing, are ahead of me, unimaginable, literally unimaginable. For now, I need to stay connected to her, honoring her truth.

As autumn appears, Mother impeccably attends to all of the ways in which she is connected to life. Larry's children and grandson come to her in her home in southern California to say goodbye. She welcomes visits and phone conversations with relatives and friends, trying to explain her plans. Most refuse to listen, voicing strong judgment. She thoughtfully organizes her finances and legal matters and continues to care for her roses in the garden, her family of birds needing seeds every day, her correspondence . . . one by one, completing. She slowly begins to eat less, preparing. Mother is resolute. Many say: "Of course, Posy, you can always change your mind once you begin." She smiles and nods and I know that she knows that nothing will change her course of action.

Thanksgiving

Our sons, Joshua and Paul, arrive at their Grandmother's home a few days before Thanksgiving. She directs them first in rearranging her bedroom for her final exit. She knows exactly where she wants the furniture and how it might be moved. They shop with her for the last family meal of turkey, dressing, sweet potatoes, greens, and a pie. It has been agreed among us all that this meal will not be elaborate, just the basics and just what we love. Mother especially loves leftovers, and most of all, Thanksgiving leftovers.

My husband, Philip, and I arrive next and we all cook together the day before Thanksgiving. We have asked Mother if we could do a ritual before the meal begins to help us hold awareness of what is happening, suggesting a simple shabbat service, though it is a day early. She sweetly agrees, trusting that her wishes for an absence of what she calls sentimentality will be honored. We get dressed up a bit and meet at the card table in the living room at four o'clock in the afternoon.

Mother arrives in shiny black pants covered with iridescent, brightly colored butterflies! We begin the ritual with lighting the candles, sharing the challah bread, and drinking some wine. Mother says, yes, she would like to read the *vidui* prayer, which in Judaism is spoken by the one dying or the rabbi before death. We listen to her read the English version of this prayer, carefully translated by our son, Rabbi Joshua, so that God never appears in it . . . since Mother has little patience for a God, or for that matter, for prayer.

As she reads, I see color drain from her face. I hear her voice shaking, as she acknowledges that she is choosing to die.

In the spirit and tradition of my fathers
and mothers, I offer this prayer:

Please, forgive me for that which I need
forgiveness, for that which may still be
heavy on my heart. Forgive me for the ways
that I have missed the mark throughout my
lifetime. Forgive me for the times that I
have caused others pain. I did the best I could.

And please forgive those who caused me pain.
Forgive those who hurt me intentionally or
unintentionally. May there be forgiveness and
release.

May it be possible now to experience a full
healing: an opening, an allowing, a great
compassion for myself and for others.

I acknowledge before my ancestors and the
great mystery before which I stand, that my
life and death are out of my hands. May I be
sheltered in the shadow of great wings.
May I be protected and guarded on this next
journey, as I have been protected and guarded
on the journeys that have brought me to this
point.

Protect my dear loved ones, with whose souls
my soul is bound.

After reading the prayer, one she has never seen or heard before, she wonders out loud if she is indeed taking her death in her own hands, as if this might not be an honorable way to die. We speak of her decision to die as another choice on her path. How the process will unfold and how she will actually stop living will not be in her hands. She seems relieved.

It is customary on shabbat for the children to receive blessings from the parents. Mother says, yes, she would like to do that although she states her lack of comfort with words in such a situation. Reassured that words are not necessary and accepting that we would also like to bless her on her journey, she is ready to continue the ritual. The four of us stand around her as she sits in her white chair in the living room. Weeping with her and exquisitely present, we each speak a personal blessing as we place our hands on her body. Staying present, now she rises, reaching her hands out over all of us . . . these hands that I know . . . I know these hands, now trembling as she speaks to each of us. I can't say how we all stop crying or how we arrive at the Thanksgiving table.

The meal begins. The light feels softer and warmer. Somber and deeply connected, we ask to hear some stories that she always loves to tell us. Before pumpkin pie and ice cream, I thank her for choosing a path in leaving that in no way will confuse any of us in terms of responsibility, directly engaged or not. After dinner we go back to the same card table where Mother brings a little paper bag of audiotapes of Joshua and Paul's voices when they were little boys, recording stories for their Grandma and Grandpa in celebration of their birthdays. Mother and I lie on her long couch, each at an end, reaching for the other's feet. Philip and Joshua sit on chairs across the coffee table, and Paul sits on the floor near his Grandmother's head. As we listen to the tapes, I hear the voices, deeply know them, from another time, time past, inaccessible, irretrievable, and simultaneously I know Mother's death is immanent, not yet accessible, soon to be irretrievable.

Transition
The boys and then Philip leave, and Mother and I have the next four days alone before she begins her fast. When we are hungry, we eat small portions of leftovers and whatever else is around. We sort through her lush, soft sweaters, water the plants, and wonder if we should refill the

hummingbird feeder. She remembers one more check to write to her favorite charity, Planned Parenthood, speaks on the phone with Larry, and putters in her ceramic studio.

On the patio after lunch one afternoon, I ask, as I have before, about any fear that she might be feeling. She answers: "I was so afraid of childbirth and then I realized that most women have experienced it. Every single person has or will experience death. It can't be that bad." Laughing, she continues: "I am really looking forward to it . . . my next great adventure."

One evening at the kitchen table before bed, Mother asks me if I have received any visions about her dying. I tell her: "When the opening of your art exhibition two years ago ends, and Philip and I fly back home to Northern California, I get into the tub before going to bed. I see my legs open and come up in preparation for birth. Now I see you, Mother, coming out of my body with no pain or rumple, no drama or obstacle. You lay flat on your back, wearing the blue outfit that you wore at your opening. Your hands are folded over your heart. You float into infinite bright light, merging effortlessly, not a glimmer of disturbance." Mother looks right at me and says: "Oh, I get it." And then she gestures with her right pointer finger moving away from her body in front of her, curving down and now pointing back at herself, smoothly arriving and pointing upward next to her face. I say: "Maybe we are taking turns." She nods. The house feels clear and deeply quiet. A sacred space is emerging.

Sunday evening I ask her if she would like me to light a fire in the living room, put a cloth on the card table, bring the candles, and make a beautiful last dinner. She is clear that she prefers to sit in her chair in the kitchen with the plastic table mats, the photos of her family all around her, her tiny coffee pot nearby . . . everything just as it is. We literally eat the very last spoonfuls of Thanksgiving. When we are finished at 8:00 p.m., I see her lift her glass, drink one sip of water, get up and take one chocolate truffle from the cupboard, and walk toward her ceramic studio. Maybe I am a half of a second delayed in my awareness that I am actually witnessing her last receiving of food and drink. I remind her that she had not planned to begin until tomorrow morning. Is this my resistance? Maybe she would like some water before bed? She gestures with her hands, swinging them with the tops of her fingertips under her chin, out and away from her face, and simply says: "I want to get on with it."

The First Six Days

I sleep on the other side of her big bed in her bedroom. As we awaken Monday morning, we simultaneously and silently roll toward each other, our outside arms reaching straight up and clasping in the middle of the bed. She speaks: "I will always be with you."

Once dressed, Mother goes straight to her studio, and with a serious look of focus and intention that I recognize, sits at her work table, finds the radio station she wants, and begins working with her hands. This is a seminal moment for me, one of her greatest teachings. It is her creative work toward which she brings her attention, to which she commits in this moment and again and again in the first days of her journey. She does not, in what might be the most difficult moment of her journey, talk to me about her feelings, ask me how I will navigate my days when she is gone, tell stories, or disclose long-held family secrets. No, instead, I see her lift the tool, shape the material, move her hands into gestures that I recognize as actually a part of me, ones that perhaps have been a part of her since she began art classes at age nine.

She enters her creative work as a vessel, a strong vessel to hold her as she crosses this archetypal threshold, choosing to move through with awareness. It seems that her creative work anchors her, is the process, the way that contains this unimaginable turning, turning directly into her commitment to die. I stay near her. We talk a bit as she intends to finish three small sculpture projects.

This day, I forget when, Mother stops answering the phone. Sometimes I follow her from room to room as she touches tops of tables, objects, makes associations with people in her life, quietly reminds me to phone someone, write someone, call someone. She returns to her studio work after a nap. When she naps, I rearrange the kitchen and realize suddenly that I am in charge of this home, our Mother's home, the one she has been in charge of throughout my life. I put all food away into the cupboards. I place a green plant in the center of the kitchen table . . . in place of the round, marble plate that held her vitamins, little packets of Equal, salt, pepper, a tiny bouquet of yellow pansies. The lawyer comes in the late afternoon for a final visit. Jerome, her best friend, comes in the evening.

On Tuesday the hospice organization agrees to visit, ready to participate because now Mother is in the active process of dying. Mother is this organization's first experience with a person choosing to die by refusing food and water. As the intake nurse, Alice—deeply kind and present—leaves, she tells us to dial 930 any time for our case manager, Brenda, who will always respond.

Later in the day a man, who is working for hospice, brings metal and plastic equipment to the front door. Mother seems relieved to move into a hospital bed where she says she is more comfortable. We set it up next to her own bed where I will continue to sleep. We decide to take the telephone out of the bedroom. I witness myself unplugging it, picking it up and carrying it out, out where? . . . the primary vehicle for our intimate and constant communication since I left home at age eighteen.

By the time Larry arrives, late Tuesday evening, Mother needs help walking. Her body edges appear softer, less clear. Her hand gestures are slower. She tells us with such joy: "I'm not hungry! I'm not hungry!" Because she is not receiving any of the sensual pleasures of food or water, we ask our family and friends who are calling and wanting to help, to each send flowers. And so begins Posy's Garden.

Wednesday morning the doorbell rings. A bouquet of long-stemmed gladiolas is left in the entryway. Soon the doorbell rings again and then again, each time announcing the arrival of more flowers. Larry walks Mother into the living room and out to the sun-filled patio. On the round table there, I open the boxes, cut the stems, and place them in vases. While gently holding her hand, Larry reads her the loving cards. He places some bouquets in her arms and, smiling, she touches the flowers, fingering each petal. As we take the flowers to Mother's room, I experience a fragrance, a feeling of fragility, a tenderness unbearable. May my presence, however it is received, be enough.

It is Thursday and I am feeling a shift within. I notice that I am less and less able to literally be away from her. Smiling broadly, speaking softly, gently holding my hand, she says: "There is nowhere in me that doubts this decision."

When she sleeps, I sit at the foot of her bed in the big chair that she asked Joshua and Paul to place there for me. I am very slowly hemming a large silky aquamarine piece of fabric which, guided by my description, Paul chose and brought here from San Francisco. I have seen it for months in my mind, covering her dead body, covering the metal table, when she is being wheeled out of her home. Hemming the fabric helps me prepare. This will be Mother's shroud. Now she awakens and I moisten her mouth and lips with sprays and sponges on sticks. She asks to see what I am doing, the cloth I had told her about. I show her. She lightly touches the fabric, expresses gratitude, and falls back asleep.

In the afternoon, as Larry and I are tucking her in bed with Tchaikovsky's "Swan Lake" on her tiny audio player, which she holds in her hand, she reports: "I feel so limp, with no strength." As she speaks, her hands tremble as they move toward her face. "If a rapist came now I couldn't do anything to resist. But if one comes, I hope he is young!"

The doorbell rings again. Opening the door, I see a now familiar man, returning, three long white boxes at his feet. He holds a bouquet in each hand, arms outstretched. He asks me: "What is happening?" I tell him my Mother is dying. I see tears in his eyes. I feel simply and warmly embraced by his presence. I receive the shape his body is making as his left hand extends toward me, giving me the translucent white lilies. He is somehow joining the circle appearing around Mother as she dies.

In the evening, surrounded by flowers that perhaps she can no longer see, but maybe can smell, I am aware that there is barely room on her bureau for our late Father's photograph. Mother tells me that this morning she saw an "image" of her own Mother in the back of the room, standing next to her Mother's bureau, where there is a plate of grapes, cheese, and crackers sitting on a doily. She falls asleep. I hem the shroud.

Though we had needed her only once, our nurse has been replaced due to scheduling issues. The new one has just arrived, and I leave Mother alone with her so that they can become acquainted. When I return to the room she is trying to persuade Mother to drink water! She is the only hospice person who does not support Mother's process. We know what to do: we dial Brenda at 930 as told, and we never see this woman again.

I brush Mother's hair, massage her hands, stroke her brow, change her clothing. These gestures feel like water pouring from me, so essential, so much what I need to be doing. I had promised her I would not hover so I am trying but my need to be with her is immeasurable. Now I can't be out of her room for more than five minutes at a time. Here I am now, from moment to moment. There is nowhere else to be. May my presence be enough.

As this journey accelerates, I am aware of choosing to not ask Mother questions about her inner experience. She has been so clear all along of not wanting any emotionality from her loved ones. More intimate questions could well invite her grief in leaving us, her worry about us, or actually intrude, even violate her concentration. Intuitively, I feel that she is focusing in her own way very specifically on what she is doing, her will silently, vividly, dominant. She speaks to me when she chooses. "We will meet again, I know we will."

After finishing the hem of the second side of the shroud, I crawl into the big bed. As I fall asleep, I see a vision. The grim reaper, our cultural symbol for the arrival of death, appears. I have never seen him before. His hand is just bones, his fingers look like talons. I reach up and gently pull the edge of his hood to the left, away from his face. Now I clearly see Mother's face. I see and I know. This process of transition has nothing to do with her being taken away by a dark force. Her face is filled with light.

This is her own natural, timely death just as natural and timely as her birth. In this moment I see her becoming without weight, and realize how deeply I long for a seamless exit from her body when it is time.

Together we wander toward and into the night, the kind I can remember when I was the one, as a child, in need of constant care from her. When she is awake, I read her poetry that she loves. I try to keep her mouth moist every ten minutes or so. She sleeps again. When she awakens, she reports a dream: "We are packing everything. Jan is taking things one by one and placing them from here to over there."

Philip arrives and I see him lean over Mother, embracing her. I see her recognize him and wrap her arms around him. How would I possibly do this without him? Dr. Sherman, who has been coming every other day, arrives and we all gather around her bed. Standing now at the head of her hospital bed, he says with such warmth: "Posy, you are very close." She responds, looking up at him, shining: "I am so happy." She lifts her arms wide to her side and blows us all kisses. She speaks to us: "I feel so loved."

The Last Three Days

Sunday comes and we all acknowledge an awareness of a transition. The beeswax candles burn, large and glowing with flame, all night, all day, one on the bureau in her room, one just outside her door, another in the kitchen, and one in the living room. Mother is less and less conscious.

Sunday evening she becomes increasingly agitated, and we can't keep her safely in bed. She is sweetly determined to get up. By the middle of the night Larry insists that we call hospice, which we do. They send their night nurse, Kathy, immediately. Kathy takes charge and explains that Mother is entering terminal agitation, something 30 percent of dying people experience. She tries many different ways of calming Mother, who finally falls asleep. Kathy invites us all into the kitchen for a meeting. Unable to be away from Mother, I go back to her room to check on her.

Shocked, I find her lying on the floor, on her back, her bent elbows on the floor supporting her as she looks up at me with enormous eyes. She does not look at all frightened, angry, or defiant. Instead she looks like a child, a bit surprised, and maybe cheerful. I call to the others and they rush in. Kathy adeptly directs us to slip a blanket under her, creating a hammock with which she can be lifted back into bed. I watch Philip and Larry's wife, Ruthie, do this so lovingly. I see Larry step back toward the door, looking as stunned and grief-stricken as I feel. I have scooted back on the floor toward the foot of Mother's big bed. I can only witness from a still place.

Kathy calls for another nurse to sit with Mother through the rest of the night so that we can sleep. The other nurse arrives and I beg her to wake me the instant anything changes, and then I lie down in the big bed. I witness the nurse who sits in a chair at the foot of the bed to make sure she is really awake and see her immediately fall asleep. I get up and sit with Mother, my Mother whom I now no longer recognize. Blinking toward imagining this is true, I notice there is only one side left of the shroud to hem. I sew each tiny stitch, not knowing.

Later Heather, from hospice, comes again and gives Mother a bath in bed and changes the sheets. In the late afternoon, I climb into the hospital bed, holding my Mother in my arms. Lying there with her, as though it is the first and last time, I see small droplets of light falling from a specific source above our heads, like a shower of tears made of light, not water. Raining, it is raining light, clear light, soothing me.

With the touch of her soft spine along the front of my torso, I hear myself telling Mother I am ready, whenever she is, for her to die, because her great love is within me, within all of us blessed by her life. Here is an infinite silence and I wonder where I am. I realize I can no longer find our Mother. I don't know where she is.

It is now early Tuesday morning and Philip takes his turn sitting with Mother while I try to sleep. Suddenly I awaken and join him. He goes to Larry and Ruthie's room and tells them to come. We witness, not knowing, as she takes her last breath—2:10 a.m., December 6, 2006—an eight-day journey complete, a life complete.

Ruthie and I wash her body with white cloths and gardenia-scented water, a candle burning at her feet. We dress her in her blue suit that she wore when she moved out of my body and so seamlessly into the bright light. Larry, Ruthie, Philip and I slowly unfold the shimmering turquoise fabric, beginning at her feet, until it reaches her chin. We pause. Can I actually make this last gesture of separation from my Mother's physical body? Her face is now covered, all of her is under the shroud and we follow Larry in chanting: *Shema Yisrael Adonai Eloheinu Adonai Echad.*

The great Indian poet, Tagore, makes this offering:

When I was born and saw the light
I was no stranger in this world
Something inscrutable shapeless, and without words
Appeared in the form of my mother.

So when I die, the same unknown will appear again
As ever known to me,
And because I love this life
*I will love death as well.**

*"First Light" from *On the Shores of Eternity: Poems from Tagore on Immortality and Beyond* by Deepak Chopra, M.D., copyright © 1999 by Deepak Chopra, M.D. Used by permission of Harmony Books, an imprint of Random House, a division of Penguin Random House LLC. All rights reserved.

Suffering

A Personal Inquiry

It is precisely suffering
one's own everyone's
that calls from the center
of those who commit
to a mystical practice.

Some say pain happens but suffering is a choice. Some say all of our experience in this world, including suffering, is an illusion. Some say G-d causes suffering as punishment. Others say G-d rescues people who suffer, even prevents suffering. There is a G-d in the world who saves people from their suffering through his own crucifixion. Others explain that we have caused our own suffering.

There is suffering seen and not seen, heard and not heard all the time everywhere, everywhere. Suffering caused by nature, by fellow humans, by invisible and mysterious forces. Suffering exists for each one coming and going, one by one, the one coming, the one going. Each one turns or does not turn into the suffering, grows or does not grow, recovers or does not recover. Completely subjective, comparison is meaningless.

Here on Retreat Cove, blessed by so much love and beauty around me, I live between the sea and the boulder. Two forces accompany me: gratitude and suffering. Like quiet water moving, my gratitude is clear and infinite. Like a stone, suffering is dense and heavy, without light. Dense and heavy, she cannot walk. I can. Without light, he cannot see. I can. And those, they cannot hear. I can hear. We are safe. They are not. How is it that I receive such blessings when others suffer the absence of them? I did not choose, deserve, accomplish, or earn these blessings.

For years, I have witnessed inside me the back of an elderly Asian man. I do not know him in my outer world. He is always sitting on the edge of an unadorned, single bed made with crisp white sheets, no blanket, the fingertips of his left hand reaching up, just touching the top edge of a tall bureau across from him. Dressed in a white night shirt, he is preparing to stand up. He is utterly alone, isolated and despairing.

In response, I hear Shantideva's prayer:

> *May I be a protector to those without protection,*
> *A leader for those who journey,*
> *And a boat, a bridge, a passage*
> *For those desiring the further shore.*
>
> *May the pain of every living creature*
> *Be completely cleared away.*
>
> *May I be the doctor and the medicine*
> *And may I be the nurse*
> *For all sick beings in the world*
> *Until everyone is healed.*

A paradox: It has taken me a long time to learn that when that woman's body is being stoned, it is not me that is being tortured. That man's starvation is not my own hunger. And simultaneously I directly know us humans to be the same. I know each flame in each heart as one vital flare of the great light in our universe. I know each soul as Divine. Since we are indeed the same, then her tortured body, his starvation, are actually my own. Both can be true. Two perspectives, and the tension between them—firmly bound within my experience of myself—have directed much of the way I have moved through the world.

I recognize my continuing need to be near. I can hold suffering with an infinitely compassionate embrace, recognition, know it at this time in our world as part of being human, part of loving, of growing, of, yes, transformation. And I commit once again toward turning in to my personal inquiry, repeatedly birthed by a longing. Is it to find a place within me where the dark side—the agony and torment of being human—can be safely held, ennobled, allowed to be?

It is the exact moment or extended moments of suffering, the immediate hit of it, not what precedes or follows, that relentlessly challenges me, demands my full attention. Since it is an inevitable part of being human at this time in the evolution of our species, I would so like to be able to accept it. But what is there to accept about human suffering . . . even if for the privileged ones of us it can seed transformative experience?

Physical or emotional pain invites, incites, triggers, or announces the arrival of suffering. Suddenly we are severed, anxious, hurled or undone, burned, depressed, crushed, broken or terrified, untethered, dropped, shredded. Or slowly and quietly, over time passing—minutes, days, or years—we are grieving, starving, falling, lost, sinking, aching, drowning.

In the moment of suffering, the utter force of it fills the space so that awareness of anything other than the suffering is obliterated. Here we can know a separation from our source. It is in these moments, when we most need that very particular light of the numinous, that it may be inaccessible. When we are indeed disconnected from the Divine, we are as far from unitive consciousness, from our original light, as a human being can be. I can't accept this. I cannot stand it.

My head drops forward. My shoulders follow. My fingers and thumbs try reaching out. As this happens, my head lifts a bit and tilts to the right and then drops again. My torso curves over. My knees tremble and bend. I must go down. A gap, a short time lapse, not tracking, and now I am kneeling on the floor. I cannot stand up so I am kneeling, received by the earth. Kneeling now, a posture to be found in sacred spaces across the entire earth.

I am kneeling directly into an infinite nothingness, not dark, not light. Here in this nothingness, I know *I am* endless, infinite suffering. I am not frightened here. I am not with or without beauty. There is no loneliness here. I am a bare knowing of what is true. Being here requires all of me. I see:

> *Newly born*
> *sickly, red and wrinkled*
> *lying on my back*
> *and being sliced open*
> *my heart*
> *becomes especially exposed.*
>
> *Close up on my left*
> *a man's hands, huge in size*
> *lift out my infant heart*
> *lift it up*
> *as it is pierced.*
>
> *I see it*
> *my heart enlarging*
> *beyond adult life size*
> *weeping from every pore*
>
> *the human heart*
> *weeping from every pore.*

Placed in my hands, now exposed to the light of consciousness, this heart first journeys home to my body, with the fire in my back just behind it. The fire burns, then propels my heart as it travels between two ribs on my left side and out of my body, being lifted, becoming clear seeing, clear and unencumbered.

Directly experienced, clear seeing is not about acceptance, rescue, or banishment. Turning from the inside out, becoming

transparent, from below to above and down once again—arriving in
the heart—

here is clear seeing
a light
vibrating invisibly
longed for
and cherished
illuminating
that which is true

But compassion!

—that transparent bloom
poised, apparent
in the white
fire
of the soul—

How will it find us?

without the devastation
of suffering
boldly carving
the pathway

ADDENDUM

EARLY ESSAYS AND RESOURCES

The Study of
an Autistic Child

"The Study of an Autistic Child" (1968)* is a synopsis of Janet's 1968 master's thesis at the University of Pittsburgh Medical School in which she describes her research and work with children diagnosed with severe autism. This paper was presented at the Third Annual American Dance Therapy Association Conference along with a short film sequence that later became important footage in Janet's film Looking for Me. *In this essay, Janet references R. D. Laing's term "inter-experience,"[1] following his description of the essential phenomenon of two people seeing and experiencing each other, and asking what this means for the development of the self. Janet and her colleagues were attempting to introduce concepts of body language as central to healing within the fields of psychiatry/psychology/education, at a time when embodied or intuitive methodologies and ways of knowing were generally dismissed as unreliable and primitive forms of research. This essay shows Janet standing at the threshold of what will become her life's work.*

BONNIE MORRISSEY & PAULA SAGER

I am anxious to share with you both aspects of my work in dance therapy, the therapy itself and the efforts in research. Both areas for me are exploratory, especially the latter, as I have resisted for several years any

---

*"Study of an Autistic Child" was first published in *Therapy in Motion,* edited by Maureen Costonis (Urbana: University of Illinois Press, 1978).

opportunity to objectively evaluate my work, assuming that research in such a realm as dance therapy would automatically require compromise. Also, I was hesitant to demand of myself any "laboratory" discipline, as I knew it would involve a new kind of work in which intuitive leaping and shouting would be of absolutely no help at all.

I will speak briefly about my therapy first. I am impressed with the simplicity of Ronald Laing's statement: "The sense of identity requires the existence of another by whom one is known." But of course, the difficulty is—how to know another and how to let another know you. My premise, at this point, is, if the other is a severely disturbed child, my "me-ness" can only be effective in developing her identity if it is genuinely reflective of what she knows best—her tiny, perseverative, intensely physical world. Therefore, at this time, in my own evolution, I am deeply invested in providing an opportunity for a disturbed child to BE—to BE herself literally, with all her "bizarre" and "crazy" mannerisms and expressions. I begin there, by reflecting her world, primarily on a body level. I try to "speak" her language by moving with her, as she moves in space. In the beginning, there is much direct imitation, which means delayed response on my part. However, as she permits my presence, and as the trust develops, I find that the one-sidedness falls away and a more mutual dialogue begins to creep into being; we become synchronous.

In terms of research, I want to share first my personal need to better organize, to better communicate what's happening within a dance therapy experience. I want to move from an intuitive to a more reflective level in understanding my own work. Secondly, I feel that as a group of people, dance therapists need to begin to look at their work, even though it is, for many of us, a very personal kind of work, because it is heavily dependent on intuitive response. Practically, if we are going to survive as a group with something to offer, we need to communicate, first with each other and then with the mental health professions. We have no finished research, per se, and we need to begin, no matter how crude our initial efforts might be—but we need to begin without compromise.

Thus I began on a very small scale. I studied one patient, in a controlled situation. I studied simply what was happening within the dance therapy experience. I studied a child called Amy, age 3.9, diagnosed as autistic after an intensive diagnostic workup at Children's Hospital in Pittsburgh. Amy had had no schooling or therapy, and the parents had had no attention from any "helping" agency or clinic when the recommended dance therapy was begun.

I saw Amy in a large empty room, three times a week for thirty-minute sessions for an eight-week period. During this time neither Amy nor her parents saw any other therapist, counselor, or psychiatrist. Dr. William Condon, a man sensitively skilled in observing body movement, observed each session. Each session was audiotaped, and after each session he and I discussed what occurred, on tape. I also made personal notes after each session. A professional photographer was in the room for the first, ninth, sixteenth, and twenty-sixth sessions making TV tapes. He came once prior to each filming session and took stills. Films for analysis were made only the first and last sessions.

At the end of the two-month (research) period, I began to study the films. I used the natural history approach, which entailed only looking for approximately eighty hours until the natural patterns of the experience began to emerge. Analysis ultimately occurred on four different levels:

1. Study of closeness/distance patterns based on offer and touch sequences.
2. Study of dyssynchrony, synchrony, and symmetrical synchrony.
3. Study of autistic gestures.
4. Study of Amy's patterns of expressive communication.

The first level of analysis revealed the most striking parameter, that of closeness/distance. In the first session, Amy approached or allowed me to approach her, then made a highly stylized autistic gesture or series of these, permitted touch, or moved away into the space of the room. By the ninth session, her distancing revealed new aspects; more space and fewer gestures. For example, once, in this session, she ran back and forth the length of the room ten consecutive times, each time coming closer to me (I was stationary at one end) and finally touching me the tenth time. By the twenty-sixth session there was much touching, more mutually and spontaneously initiated, and much wanting to be held. When she was ambivalent about touching, at the moment of touch, she pulled back, did not circle, did not gesture, and did not leave. She paused, often looking at me and then tried again, usually the second time sustaining contact.

TABLE A.1

Session Number	Therapist Offers	Amy Permits	% Total Permit/ Total Offer
Session 1	39	19	48.7
Session 26	9	6	75.0
Session Number	Amy Offers	Amy Permits	% Total Permit/ Total Offer
Session 1	0	0	0
Session 26	9	6	75.0

Intensive study of this pattern revealed an increase in the number of touches tolerated by Amy (see table A.1); an increase in the average duration of touch sequences not only as session 1 and session 26 progressed but also between the two sessions (see table A.2):

TABLE A.2

Session Number	First Five Touch Seq.	Last Five Touch Seq.	Total Frame Touch Seq.	Total Frames of Touch
Session 1	241.6	838.2	552.6	11052
Session 26	400.0	3889.8	1794.8	21538

The second level of analysis, unlike the first type—which demanded counting, or a macro look—involved a micro study of the movement patterns. Dr. Condon has just presented some of his work in which synchrony and dyssynchrony were explained. Therefore, I will not discuss these phenomena in any detail at this time. However, I found it significant that Amy and I were synchronous (we initiated and sustained directionality of change of body parts at the same 1/24 of a second) always when touching, which supports Condon's theory that touch heightens synchrony. Amy became dyssynchronous, or moved arrhythmically in such a way so that I could not "tune-in" usually after touch sequences. When this happened, as she distanced herself physically and emotionally, she would become self-dyssynchronous almost always within an autistic gesture.

Symmetrical synchrony (which is my own label) occurred when there was a sharing of the same body parts, moving in the same direction, with the same point of change in direction. These were beautiful moments in which this heightened form of synchrony was not only felt within the experience but verified on the screen.

The third level of analysis involved a study of Amy's autistic gestures. An autistic gesture, unique to each child, is a highly individualized movement with a formal structure. It is repeated consistently, impossible to totally imitate, or reflect back. A study of several of these isolated gestures revealed a decrease in occurrence within the sessions (see table A.3).

TABLE A.3. FREQUENCY OF AUTISTIC GESTURES

Gesture	Session 1	Session 26
Teeth Banging	53	10
Leg Thrusting	49	1
Head Shaking	27	11
Hitting Back of Hand or Record	17	4

In the fourth level of analysis, developing patterns of expressive communication were studied. For purposes of consistent recording, I studied only overt gestures. Eye contact only existed in the beginning when Amy was physically distant from me. By the final session, eye contact was occurring consistently when we were extremely close physically (i.e., face to face). She finally was gesturing for me to pick her up frontward, with her arms extended toward me, and by scooting into me backward, she was taking hold of my hands and putting them on her ankles, suggesting I pick her up backward. When she wanted me to be up and holding her, she pulled me up when I was sitting. When I held her and she wanted to gallop, she bobbed up and down, pushed my hand with hers in a "steering" position, and often moved her lips and looked at me, as if she were imitating talking.

Finally, Amy's development within the total dance therapy experience of two months reminded me of the developmental stages of the first nine months of an infant's life. For example, she first began to explore my body just as the infant explores the mother's body, then she explored her own (not a new experience for her as it is for an infant developing at age-appropriate levels), and then began to imitate me. Perhaps, as trust developed, this child slowly and safely regressed (within the sessions) and then gradually began to grow through the stages of infancy, experiencing herself, for the first time, as one of two people relating.

In summary, as there was an increase in touch tolerance and touch duration, there was concomitantly a decrease in autistic gestures. I have chosen fifteen minutes of film material, edited out of sixty minutes of possible data, which I feel best explains what I've been talking about. There are five segments sequentially taken from the first session and six segments sequentially taken from the twenty-sixth session.

Integrity of Body
and Psyche
Some Notes on Work in Process

"Integrity of Body and Psyche" (1972)* was written in the early years of Janet's studio explorations and work with therapy clients. It is the first formal record of her tracking of a student's "authentic movement." This essay offers reflections of Janet's then-recent work with Mary Whitehouse, in which Mary calls herself an observer and works with symbolic material, calling it "fantasy." Janet's commitment to the development of consciousness both in herself and within the individuals she works with is a central theme in this essay. "Integrity of Body and Psyche" offers early glimpses of what will become the Discipline of Authentic Movement, in the appearance of the word discipline, and in the ways in which Janet discovers order and meaning in a developing process of embodiment, both similar to and different from the processes of psychotherapy and meditation.

BONNIE MORRISSEY & PAULA SAGER

---

*"Integrity of Body and Psyche" was first presented in 1972 at the 7th Annual Conference of the American Dance Therapy Association in Santa Monica, California. It was revised and published in the *Proceedings of the Seventh Annual American Dance Therapy Association Conference* (Columbia, Md.: ADTA, 1972) and was later published in *Eight Theoretical Approaches in Dance/Movement Therapy,* edited by P. Lewis Bernstein (Dubuque, Iowa: Kendall/Hunt, 1979), 51–70 and *Authentic Movement: Essays by Mary Starks Whitehouse, Janet Adler, and Joan Chodorow,* edited by Patrizia Pallaro (Philadelphia: Jessica Kingsley Publishers, 1999), 121–31.

For many years I worked with people, mostly children, who were swimming in the realm of the unconscious. With movement as the medium, I tried to give them a taste of the conscious world and a hint at the joy of the power of choice between these two worlds. Recently, I find myself working, still primarily through movement, with adults, men and women, who want very much to release their constrained consciousness and know more deeply the life within themselves. They seek freedom of commerce between the two worlds. And so my work changes, as a reflection, I'm sure, of my own personal growth. I grew from being a young woman primarily unconscious of my inner world to becoming a woman with a developing consciousness of myself and the way in which I grow. As my own consciousness evolves, I feel more ready to be with others as they journey into their unconscious lives and back to a clearer and fuller sense of themselves as conscious adults.

In the last few years I have been exploring a particular way of movement work, which I experienced with my teacher, Mary Whitehouse. As I integrate some of what I learned from Mary, I realize that the mover can make deep and transformative journeys that can be appropriately understood within a psychological framework.

As I worked with people in their search for connection between body and psyche, I have discovered some clear similarities between the process of movement therapy as I experience it now and the processes described in verbal psychotherapy. I am going to briefly and simply try to identify some emerging parallels within a progression of five stages of development. Although I describe them as distinct stages, in actual experience the boundaries are fluid.

I will be speaking about this particular kind of movement therapy and verbal psychotherapy for people who are not mentally ill—people just like us who are searching for a way to live well—to live better by learning how to allow themselves fuller access to the complexities of their individual development. I speak of a *process* called movement therapy, not a cure. My clients are each in his or her own way choosing to listen to and speak from their inner lives with care. Some of them are also students of dance/movement therapy, of psychology, of the arts.

The Search for Authentic Movement

In my work the first stage in movement therapy with an individual in a one-to-one setting is the client's search for authentic movement. Movement that is authentic, as Mary Whitehouse described it,[1] is movement that is natural to a particular person, not learned like ballet or calisthenics, not purposeful or intellectualized as "this is the way I should move" to be pleasing, to be powerful, to be beautiful or graceful. Authentic movement is an immediate expression of how the client feels at any given moment. The spontaneous urge to move or not to move is not checked, judged, criticized, or weighed by the conscious mind.

Gradually, as a client becomes comfortable with authentic movement and can recognize when she is experiencing it and when she is not, the true discipline of this sort of work emerges. She can move completely freely, with less inhibition, and yet she is conscious of what she is doing, as if she is watching herself move but not interfering, not even commenting. She is allowing herself access to her unconscious and, as her unconscious speaks through her movement, she can become conscious of what she is doing. This is what I learned in Mary's presence, through her approach of "Movement in depth." Freedom to stumble upon movement that is authentic, and then to slowly bring such experience in relationship to one's will is not unlike the natural development of a small child. Mary often, and beautifully, spoke of this important parallel.

In psychotherapy there is a similar beginning. The client tries to sort out and disentangle authentic from "adopted" feelings. He is also seeking an experience in which he can speak freely from his heart, without his mind judging and criticizing that which he says. It sometimes can be more difficult to find one's authentic nature through speaking, as it seems to me that the body lives much closer to the unconscious aspects of the mind than the conscious aspects. And it is the realm of the unconscious that I believe holds our most important and powerful secrets. Growing closer to oneself means knowing, and then owning, these secrets as they are freed from hiding and allowed to be integrated with one's conscious reality.

The Expression of Authentic Movement

Again, in my work, the second stage in movement therapy is open expression of authentic movement. Once it is discovered, time is needed to learn to trust, to live with, to enjoy and explore the new discovery. Clients in this stage always experience the freedom to move with great joy. Some of my richest experiences in my work with Mary were imbued with such freedom.

In psychotherapy the corollary would be freely and continuously talking of one's true feelings, an experience that is strikingly rare and precious. Often during this stage in both types of therapy, the individual learns that she has permission to move in any way that she wants or say anything she wants to say. An awareness of freedom develops as the underlying ground of trust—in herself and in her therapist—becomes firm and reliable.

The Recognition of an Emerging Repertoire

The third stage in movement therapy is recognition by the client and therapist of a slowly emerging repertoire: the same movement patterns continually reappear. The client finds herself moving again and again in the same ways. Authentic movement seems to have powerful and self-imposed limits, and such limits often come to the client as an unwelcome surprise. In psychotherapy a similar phenomenon begins to appear—the client speaks repeatedly of the same themes or the same person, of the same behavior patterns.

The Exploration of Themes: Focusing

The fourth stage begins the real work for most of my clients. In response to recognition of repetitive behavior, they begin to experiment with ways to focus on a specific theme, to get to know more about it, to go with it, to exaggerate it, to confront it. In psychotherapy, it seems to me, the very same thing occurs: the client begins to explore, dissect, and work with the recurring themes in his repertoire. It is at this stage in both movement therapy and psychotherapy that different therapists guide the client in remarkably different ways in an effort to help them come into fuller awareness of the problem and its modes of resolution.

The Experience of Resolution

The fifth stage is in the experience of resolution. My teacher John Weir speaks so very clearly when he says: "The only way out is in and through."[2] In the fourth stage the client is going in and through the feelings that need to be experienced. The fifth stage is the coming out, emerging with freed energy for continued growth. The deeper and more authentic the fourth stage, the more powerful and clear is the resolution. Thus the fifth stage embodies feelings such as relief, amazement, clarity, peace—all of the good and deserved aspects of self-love.

In movement therapy this stage is often more verbal than the previous ones. It is a time to collect, synthesize, organize, and digest the process in which unconscious material has been experienced in the body and subsequently made conscious. The experience of the resolution in psychotherapy is very similar to the same experience in movement therapy. In the fifth stage of psychotherapy the client also experiences clarity and relief as the pieces of his puzzle finally fit together and make sense as whole.

A Case Study: Heather

I have referred briefly to these similar stages of work and want now to describe the illustrative journey of a movement therapy client whom I shall call Heather. My interest here is in providing an example, drawn from my own experience as a movement therapist, of a client's progression through the stages described above. I am not attempting an exhaustive account of the therapeutic process. I will address only a few aspects of Heather's work.

In discussing a client's work it is difficult to speak consistently of the therapist's behavior and to speak certainly of the relationship between the client and the therapist. Therefore, before describing Heather's journey, I want to say something of my behavior as a therapist with people like Heather who are not mentally ill.

The typical pattern of a movement session is as follows. Like Mary once did with me, I begin by asking my client if she wants a "movement problem" or if she wants to move freely. If she wants a "problem" to help her get started (this is often the case in early sessions), I suggest a simple one that may lead to or stimulate an authentic movement. These "problems," usually related to the exploration of polarities, were a central aspect of Mary's work. For example, I say: "Move, with your eyes closed, from a standing position toward the floor. Let gravity pull you down. When you are down as far as you want to be, begin to move up. And when you are up as far as you want, begin to move down. Continue to explore the cycle between the earth and the sky in this way."

Often, a client gives me a clue, like "I feel depressed," and then asks for a "problem." I might then suggest finding a way to move in which her body can feel heavy and move downward. After the client moves, we talk together about her experience and sometimes about my experience as an observer. Mary always invited discussion with me after I moved.

As Mary was to me, I am primarily a guide to my client as she explores her feelings through movement. I suggest going with, staying with, exaggerating, waiting and, most importantly, I encourage her to trust where she is—to trust herself—and to force nothing. I find I increasingly trust the natural process of growth. Learning to give ourselves what we need, as much as we need, means satiation, and satiation means free energy for more growth. As I learned first in my work with autistic children, there is great power in regression to unfinished periods of development. Reliving, reexperiencing unconscious material frees the client to bring that material into consciousness, to talk about it in a way that makes sense to her. When it feels appropriate, I selectively share personal experiences with my client as I too am "in process" and therefore do not represent a "finished product" in the client's eyes. Also, I feel more real, more present, when I can be honestly responsive.

I will speak about a series of twenty-eight sessions that cover approximately a three-and-one-half month period, with an average of two one-hour sessions per week. Heather and I first spoke together because she wanted to become a movement therapist and therefore had many questions about preparation for such a profession. I talked about psychology and dance but I also mentioned the critical importance of her own inner work. I insisted that those of us who want to truly help another person realize himself or herself more fully must first begin to realize and awaken to our own psychodynamics.

Heather understood and wanted to begin working at once on her own personal growth in movement therapy. I learned that she was nineteen years old and lived at home in the New York area with her parents. She was an only child. Her parents owned and together operated a toy store. She was not seeing friends, not going to school, not taking dance classes (she had been a dance student for years), and she was sleeping and eating a great deal. She felt immobilized: she couldn't leave her parents' home but she hated staying.

At the start of work with a client I rarely have more information than that with which I began in Heather's case. I find that I trust the client and come to know her best, in the beginning especially, through her movement. There are times, however, as the work progresses, when I explicitly ask for material from the client's personal history.

Heather moved quickly through the first stage of experience, in which she discovered authentic movement with little difficulty. Her only distraction was danced movement, which she gave up completely by the third session. As she then moved into the second stage, into free exploration of her authentic movement, there was great fullness, variety, and enthusiasm in her work. When Heather moved, she was "all there," moving almost always from an unconscious source. This gift of accessible unconscious movement is rare; its cost can be a tenuous grip on self-management. In the beginning she had little or no memory for her movement and little concern for clarifying, organizing, or verbalizing her experience. Heather simply had an insatiable need to move and, once she discovered the freedom with which she worked, she moved consistently with a sense of herself as free and newly found.

In the third stage I experience the themes in a client's repertoire emerging on three different levels: specific body parts emerge as more or less available and energized, culturally symptomatic movements become apparent, and idiosyncratic movements become visible. Heather's hands are the best example of specific body parts invested with energy.

In the very first session her hands were obviously more tense than the rest of her body. She wrote in her journal: "What was interesting was the more I tried to relax them, the tenser they got." In the second session, when her hands were again exceptionally tense, I suggested she focus on them, let them go where they wanted to go, not try to make them relax. She was able to do this easily and soon her hands clasped tightly together, her entire body sank and her face looked very sad. At the end of the experience she spoke briefly of a feeling of sadness. By the fifth session, Heather's hands were clawing at herself and she became aware of anger welling up beneath the sadness.

Heather was repeatedly shrugging her shoulders back and pushing away from her torso with her hands and arms during the first five sessions. These gestures might culturally be read as "get off" or "go away." When exaggerated, that gesture pattern might commonly suggest claustrophobia. Indeed, her verbal response after experiencing this pattern during the sixth session was: "I've always been very claustrophobic."

Idiosyncratic movements are most powerfully expressive of the less conscious aspects of the personality. They seem to have no meaning to anyone else and appear unrelated to anyone else's movement patterns. Of its very nature, then, it is difficult to identify an idiosyncratic pattern as such until it is repeated so many times that it becomes clear. Even then, I seldom have the slightest idea what it means or where its source lies. These movement patterns or qualities truly reflect the uniqueness and the enormously complicated nature of the individual.

An idiosyncratic movement pattern developed in Heather's work while she was lying on her side. She lifted one leg straight up and then put it down, bent, foot flat on the floor in front of her other leg. She then pushed against the floor with her bent leg, pivoting her body around ninety degrees. As early as the fourth session this pattern evolved into consecutive quarter turns until she was into a tantrum. It was very brief and very frightening to her. She wrote in her journal: "It's amazing how my body had remembered that motion where my mind had forgotten about it." After this experience she told me that she had temper tantrums frequently during latency between the ages of nine and twelve. This characteristic leg lifting and pushing reappeared in fragments consistently throughout the sessions until she experienced a resolution that I will describe in some detail later.

A second example of Heather's idiosyncratic movements was unusually slow movement. She appeared to be moving in slow motion. This quality of movement began to emerge around the eighth session and gradually became predominant in her work. I will also describe more of this later.

I have mentioned some of the themes: specific body parts, movement patterns, and qualities of movement of which Heather and I gradually became aware. I will now briefly sketch the way she worked these themes and thus developed a richer understanding of herself.

As we focused on her hands in the early sessions, they increasingly embodied feelings of anger. The feeling tone of the short tantrum was clearly anger. The more she lifted and pushed her leg, the more she stopped or changed this movement. She vaguely associated it with the tantrum but repeatedly stopped herself, rarely conscious of the stopping but very conscious of her fear. This is the kind of moment at which I urge my client to be aware of what she is doing—not stopping what she is doing but simply noticing. As Heather became conscious of the ways in which she was blocking her leg lifting and pushing movement, she experienced more and more frustration. I then suggested that she try to learn more about the movement by staying with it a little longer. As she did so her fear increased, as did the concomitant feeling of knowing she was getting closer to "something." Heather never chose to work on this pattern. It simply kept reappearing out of free movement. More and more time was spent in the sessions with this pattern and the variety of unconscious ways she blocked it.

During the thirteenth session she was violently stamping, covering the entire room. She appeared proud and, when she stopped, looking very satisfied, she said: "I stamped them out." She did not know to whom "them" referred. I asked her if she was finished and she decided she was not. She proceeded in pantomime to collect the remains of "them," burned them, smashed the ashes with a huge imaginary stone, and then suddenly noticed a tiny flower growing out of the ashes. This embodiment of a fantasy is a rich example of the power of imagery and its relationship to authentic movement. After the release of anger through the stamping, the fantasy extended the experience of aggression. When it seemed that "they" were totally and completely destroyed, new life freely grew from the ashes.

After the thirteenth session, when Heather's fantasy occurred, she began to talk openly of anger toward her parents, a feeling of which she could not remember being conscious before. There was also less self-directed anger in her movement after that session. The work with her hands, the gradual awareness of the leg lifting and pushing, and many other movement experiences in the first thirteen sessions seemed to be expressive of unconscious material related to feelings of anger. The expressive movement brought the feelings into consciousness, which, in turn, allowed Heather to examine them, own them, and accept them.

Heather felt less tense, relieved, with a clearer sense of herself and her situation at home. And then, slowly, during the following weeks, she became depressed. During the nineteenth session she reported feeling a little better. Then suddenly, in the midst of free movement, her leg went up and down in the obvious pattern of beginning the quarter turn push and, this time, unlike the very first brief tantrum, she did not stop. She was fully into a wild tantrum, her entire body deeply engaged in the expression of rage. The instant the tantrum concluded, much to my surprise, Heather became immobilized. She "could not move." Her breathing quickened. She looked pale. In a few minutes she sat up and spoke of a "film" that covered her the instant the tantrum felt finished.

And so came the resolution of one theme—she went into and through the rage—and, at the same time, came the beginning of a new theme. As we talked, it became clear that Heather had experienced the tantrums as a child as a fight against the "film." She said she felt claustrophobic and unhappy during much of her childhood. Some force was keeping her from being the "real Heather." The tantrum had been a successful way of keeping the film—the force—from overwhelming her. Perhaps because of the full expression of her anger toward her parents, her energy was now freed to address directly the threat of the film. The film, represented by a slow motion in Heather's movements, was the new "enemy."

Again, becoming familiar with this made it less of an unknown and, therefore, less frightening, so that confrontation was gradually possible. After the twentieth session she wrote in her journal:

> I had an image of greasy, grey film coming from the kitchen of our house. Before I could get to it, it engulfed me, coming very quickly toward me in swirls. I wanted to move but couldn't. It was so powerful, more powerful than my own will. At one point, one of the swirls turned into a face, looked at me and laughed, as if to say: "You idiot, move."

After the twenty-first session she wrote:

> I got the image again and still couldn't move. My body didn't mind because I didn't seem to panic. All my concentration was going towards the film. I started getting really dizzy. I seem to get dizzy when I get near to something.

During the twenty-second session the film seemed to her to be pulling her apart by encircling her legs and arms. She wrote again after the twenty-third session:

> For the first time the film made a clearing (I didn't make it, the film did on its own accord). It made a tunnel but at the end of the tunnel a person was standing there in red, calling me to go through the tunnel. I couldn't move.

By the twenty-fourth session Heather was experiencing extreme frustration and exhaustion. She was trying anything to get more information about the film, wanting so much to be freed of it. She tried cutting it, but it bounced back. She tried becoming the film and realized: "I was my own prison." This realization was an important turning point in Heather's owning and taking responsibility for her own experience. She had to encounter the film repeatedly, letting her unconscious emerge in her own time, before she could understand or fully accommodate the feeling and the roots of her immobilization.

During the last two weeks of this stage of her work, the film surrounded her frequently outside the movement sessions as well as dominating the sessions themselves. "All my feelings and movements are death-like," she wrote in her journal. On occasion, in the sessions, she would fall over and not catch herself responsibly. I told her that I would not catch her, that she had to catch herself. She then moved as if she had understood: she was responsible for her own work.

Feelings of fear increased as she remained in the immobilized state for longer and longer periods of time. Finally, during the twenty-seventh session, she lay "death-like" with rapid breathing, pale face, and tremendous fear for perhaps five minutes. When she sat up, she said she felt like a huge block of cement was falling on her. I encouraged her to lie down again and to go with that fantasy. She did, and the odyssey that followed, taking her through life and death passages, was indeed extraordinary, full of vivid imagery reflecting her struggle at that moment with the life and death issue of the "real Heather." She ended, in the personage of a bird, by climbing out of a horrible dark prison, out into the sky and the sunshine, growing new feathers as she climbed.

I think Heather had experienced what always had been most threatening and frightening to her: no self, no "real Heather." In reaching for her own identity as separate from her parents, her work brought her to the inevitable but very frightening choice to live as herself and let aspects of her experience of the patterns within her begin to die or to let her "real self" die and live only the reflection of her experience of her parents.

Conclusion

Heather worked through to resolution two closely related themes. Her movement released anger at a body level. Through consciousness of her frustration and fear, and acceptance of her anger, she was able to relive fully the tantrum that her body knew so well from childhood. The second theme had to do with fear of immobilization, which at first was expressed through the experience of the film enclosing her. Again, as consciousness and ownership developed in relation to the film, she was able to allow herself the feelings of immobilization and, finally, to let those feelings possess her. She then experienced a kind of death. Aspects of the internalized parents died, an archetypal occurrence in the experience of adolescence. And, as always, the psychic experience of death allowed a rebirth. More of the "real Heather" was available for living. Heather returned the next session announcing that she had applied to college. She said she felt much better. She soon moved out of her parents' house into a dormitory and fully into the experience of college.

Heather followed several problems through to resolution, two of which I have described in detail. The first stage of her work concerned her discovery of authentic movement. In the second stage she hungrily enjoyed expression of herself through the free movement. Conscious awareness of the meaning of the movement was irrelevant for her at that stage. In the third stage we watched specific themes emerge—through her hands as specific body parts highly invested with energy, through her culturally described claustrophobic movements and her slow-motion movement. The bulk of these notes is concerned with how these idiosyncratic patterns were trusted and followed. Heather was able to confront each of them and thus experience the joy of resolving these problems with clarity and intelligence in the fifth stage.

Heather continues to work with me in movement therapy and has circled back at times on some of the themes, but the struggle is less intense and often of a slightly different nature. Her work continues to be rich with imagery. New themes appear and old themes slowly disappear as she grows toward a deeper consciousness of herself.

Janet Adler
and the Discipline
of Authentic Movement
Additional Resources

Janet Adler's Writing

Books

Arching Backward: The Mystical Initiation of a Contemporary Woman.
   Inner Traditions, 1995.
Offering from the Conscious Body: The Discipline of Authentic Movement.
   Inner Traditions, 2002. This book was also translated into several
   languages, including Chinese, French, Italian, German, and Polish.

Dissertation

"Arching Backward and a Cross-Cultural Study of Mysticism as
   the Context for a Phenomenological Study" (1992). This can be
   accessed online through the ProQuest website at https://www
   .proquest.com/docview/304049516.

Films and Videos

Looking for Me (1968), expressivemedia.org
Still Looking (1998), expressivemedia.org

Somatics Festival 2019 Website

An archival website celebrating the work of Janet Adler, Bonnie Bainbridge Cohen, and Nancy Stark Smith, somatics2019.com.

Discipline of Authentic Movement Website

Janet Adler's professional biography, information about the Circles of Four program, and additional information and resources about the Discipline of Authentic Movement, disciplineofauthenticmovement.com.

Archives

The Janet Adler Collection of written works, books, papers, films, photographs, and interviews is permanently housed and made available through the Jerome Robbins Dance Division at the New York Public Library for the Performing Arts, nypl.org.

ACKNOWLEDGMENTS

The Discipline of Authentic Movement develops because of each person, one by one, committing toward what is true—in the presence of an inner and outer witness—until a wholeness is directly known within a collective body. This book feels like a collective body, formed as each one of us, in collaboration with Janet, brought into words our own longings, passions, questions, and concerns. We have trusted that our individual voices would emerge and intertwine into something whole and new, only because of the other. We hope this book, which was also envisioned early on as a boat, will sail into the world and offer something of value.

This process has required specific, necessary, and precious support from the following people and organizations:

We are grateful to Jeff Genung for his encouragement and for the generous grant from Contemplative Life that supported our early research and meetings with Janet. Thank you.

Early readers kindly offered their time and attention to thoroughly read the manuscript and answer questions we asked of them. The fullness of their responses has been invaluable in clarifying and enriching our efforts. Big thank yous to Joshua Boettiger, Annie Geissinger, Susan Marie Powers, Mandoline Whittlesey, Donald Rothberg, and Yu-Ling Hu.

Thank you, Rosalyn Driscoll, for your finely-rendered pencil drawings, from when you sat and drew as Janet's silent witness while she moved in the studio space in Northampton, Massachusetts. We have chosen twelve of more than one hundred of these drawings to complement the text. And thank you, Paul Boettiger, for recognizing and choosing one of these drawings to center your creation of the elegant cover design for the book.

In our lengthy process of creating this book, we have been consistently and thankfully aware of the grounding support from faculty, learners, and graduates within Circles of Four, the postgraduate-level program in which students become teachers of the Discipline of Authentic Movement. We offer our gratitude to each of you teaching, studying, and practicing within this collective body of like-minded souls as you faithfully support this offering with such warmth, wisdom, and trust.

We are indebted to Patrizia Pallaro and her work as editor of two volumes of essays, the first books to focus solely on Authentic Movement. Her abundant contributions to this wider field are replete with scholarly, respectful, and inclusive historical material. We are grateful to Julia Gombos for the seeds of thought and collaboration regarding Janet's legacy and to Nina Kungarova for filming one of our conversations with Janet.

We truly appreciate everyone who helped us with all of the necessary and practical challenges of the publishing world, the computer world, and the world of text. Thank you, Stephanie Turner, Joan Webb, Alison Granucci, Lindsay Williams, Amaryah Orenstein, Miles Shebar, Jen Stackhouse, and Judy Cardanha.

Our work with Inner Traditions has been seamless and invigorating. We have happily depended on the expertise in each department with which we have been engaged. Thank you, Ehud Sperling, Jon Graham, John Hays, Jeanie Levitan, Patricia Rydle, Aaron Davis, Erica Robinson, Jennie Marx, Virginia Scott Bowman, Eliza Homick, and our wonderfully receptive and very helpful project editor, Meghan MacLean.

We are grateful for every person at Inner Traditions who has assisted in bringing this manuscript to publication.

Our gratitude goes out to Sheila Bellefleur, Leslie Fry, Travis Morrissey, Marilyn Clements, Jeremy Sager, and Philip Buller for your nearness, your patience, and your continuing engagement in witnessing this writing project since its inception in 2018.

NOTES

Introduction by Bonnie Morrissey

1. Whitehouse, "An Approach to the Center: An Interview with Mary Whitehouse," 23 and "C. G. Jung and Dance Therapy," 81–82.
2. Buber, *I and Thou.*

Introduction by Paula Sager

1. Adler, *Looking for Me* (film), spoken narration.
2. Weir, "The Personal Growth Laboratory."
3. Janet Adler, personal communication, January 2021.
4. Whitehouse, "C. G. Jung and Dance Therapy," 90.
5. Adler, personal communication, January 2021.
6. Adler, *Arching Backward,* xiii.

Introduction to Chapter One

1. Adler, from her spoken introduction to the screening of her film, *Looking for Me,* at the Somatics Festival 2019.
2. Whitehouse, "C. G. Jung and Dance Therapy," 90.
3. Adler, personal communication, January 20, 2022.
4. Watson, *A Philosophy of Emptiness,* 14.

Presence:
From Autism to the Discipline of Authentic Movement

1. Laban, *A Life for Dance,* 90, 89, 91, 94.
2. Wigman, *The Language of Dance,* 16, 8, 11, 39, 18; *The Mary Wigman Book,* 52.
3. Duncan, *My Life,* 75, 76, 85.
4. Graham, *Blood Memory,* 4, 5, 16, 8, 260, 256, 251, 118, 144.
5. Graham, *Blood Memory,* 187.
6. Adler, *Offering from the Conscious Body,* 197.
7. Adler, *Offering from the Conscious Body,* 238, 239.

Introduction to Chapter Two

1. Adler, "Arching Backward and a Cross-Cultural Study of Mysticism as the Context for a Phenomenological Study." The Union Institute, 1992, part 2, 11.
2. Adler, "Arching Backward and a Cross-Cultural Study," part 2, 11.
3. Adler, "Arching Backward and a Cross-Cultural Study," part 2, 9.
4. Adler, *Arching Backward,* xiii.
5. Adler, *Arching Backward,* xvii.
6. Adler, *Arching Backward,* xvi.
7. Adler, *Arching Backward,* xiii.
8. Adler, "Arching Backward and a Cross-Cultural Study," part 2, 10.

Introduction to Chapter Three

1. Whitehouse, "Reflections on a Metamorphosis," 60.
2. Whitehouse, "C. G. Jung and Dance Therapy," 90.
3. Whitehouse, "C. G. Jung and Dance Therapy," 81.
4. Adler, "Arching Backward and a Cross-Cultural Study," part 1, 219.

Who Is the Witness?

1. Wilber, *The Atman Project.*
2. Whitehouse, "Physical Movement and Personality."
3. Wilber, *The Atman Project.*
4. Chodorow, "To Move and Be Moved," 39.
5. Chaiklin, *Marian Chace.*
6. Whitehouse, "The Tao of the Body"; Whitehouse, "Physical Movement and Personality."
7. Jung, "Psychology of the Transference," 243.

Introduction to Chapter Four

1. Adler, personal communication, July, 2007.
2. Adler, "Arching Backward and a Cross-Cultural Study," part 1, 222.
3. Adler, *Offering from the Conscious Body,* xvii.

Body and Soul

1. Scholem, *Major Trends in Jewish Mysticism,* 350.
2. Satprem, *Sri Aurobindo,* 333.
3. Satprem, *Sri Aurobindo,* 371–372.
4. Satprem, *Sri Aurobindo,* 102.
5. Satprem, *Sri Aurobindo,* 127.
6. Satprem, *Mind of the Cells,* 60.
7. Satprem, *Sri Aurobindo,* 208.
8. Buber, *Hasidism and Modern Man.*
9. Satprem, *Sri Aurobindo,* 281.
10. Satprem, *Sri Aurobindo,* 72.

11. Suzuki, *An Introduction to Zen Buddhism,* 10.
12. Unno, *Emptiness and Reality in Mahayana Buddhism,* 12.
13. Satprem, *Sri Aurobindo,* 94.
14. Scholem, *Major Trends in Jewish Mysticism.*
15. Satprem, *Sri Aurobindo,* 174.
16. Scholem, *Major Trends in Jewish Mysticism,* 10.
17. Grof, *Beyond the Brain.*
18. Wilber, *The Atman Project.*
19. Otto, *The Idea of the Holy.*
20. Myerhoff, *Peyote Hunt.*
21. Adler, "Who Is the Witness?"
22. Wilber, *The Atman Project.*
23. Scholem, *Major Trends in Jewish Mysticism,* 4.
24. Eliade, *Shamanism: Archaic Techniques of Ecstasy,* 8.
25. Halifax, *Shaman: The Wounded Healer,* 10.
26. Katz, *Boiling Energy,* 29.
27. Underhill, *Mysticism,* 83.
28. Merton, *Zen and the Birds of Appetite,* 26.
29. Merton, *Zen and the Birds of Appetite,* 36–37.
30. Merton, *Zen and the Birds of Appetite,* 37.
31. Suzuki, *An Introduction to Zen Buddhism,* 33.
32. James, *The Varieties of Religious Experience,* 64.
33. Epstein, *Kabbalah,* 36.
34. Merton, *Zen and the Birds of Appetite.*
35. Larsen, *The Shaman's Doorway,* 109.
36. Krishna, *Kundalini,* 131.
37. Neihardt, *Black Elk Speaks,* 43.
38. Larsen, *The Shaman's Doorway,* 108.
39. Corinthians 1:17.
40. Scholem, *Major Trends in Jewish Mysticism,* 14.
41. Petroff, *Medieval Women's Visionary Literature,* 42.
42. Petroff, *Medieval Women's Visionary Literature,* 43.
43. Merton, *Zen and the Birds of Appetite,* 46.
44. Merton, *Zen and the Birds of Appetite,* 37.
45. Bancroft, *Zen,* 7.
46. Hai, *The Zen Teaching,* 123.
47. Suzuki, *An Introduction to Zen Buddhism,* 33.
48. Unno, *Emptiness and Reality in Mahayana Buddhism,* 7.
49. Moyne and Barks, *Open Secret,* v.
50. Moyne and Barks, *Open Secret,* 41.
51. Moyne and Barks, *Open Secret,* 79.
52. Satprem, *Mind of the Cells,* 60.
53. Satprem, *Sri Aurobindo,* 240.
54. Satprem, *Mind of the Cells,* 163.
55. Blyth, *Zen and Zen Classics,* 28.

56. Epstein, *Kabbalah,* 84.
57. Katz, "The Conservative Character of Mystical Experience," 14–15.
58. Katz, *Boiling Energy,* 84.
59. Katz, *Boiling Energy,* 89.
60. Katz, *Boiling Energy,* 65.
61. Petroff, *Medieval Women's Visionary Literature,* 139.
62. Petroff, *Medieval Women's Visionary Literature,* 194.
63. Petroff, *Medieval Women's Visionary Literature,* 161.
64. Petroff, *Medieval Women's Visionary Literature,* 162.
65. Petroff, *Medieval Women's Visionary Literature,* 167.
66. Katz, *Boiling Energy,* 45.
67. Underhill, *Mysticism,* 60.
68. Underhill, *Mysticism.*
69. Petroff, *Medieval Women's Visionary Literature,* 259.
70. Krishna, *Kundalini,* 195.
71. Krishna, *Kundalini,* 86.
72. Conze et al., *Buddhist Texts,* 292.
73. Krishna, *Kundalini,* 97.
74. Epstein, *Kabbalah,* 97.
75. Krishna, *Kundalini,* 152.
76. Katz, *Boiling Energy,* 45.
77. Suzuki, *The Essentials of Zen Buddhism,* xvi.
78. Scholem, *Major Trends in Jewish Mysticism,* 52.
79. Satprem, *Sri Aurobindo,* 224.
80. Petroff, *Medieval Women's Visionary Literature,* 151.
81. Underhill, *Mysticism.*
82. Scholem, *Major Trends in Jewish Mysticism,* 16.
83. Scholem, *Major Trends in Jewish Mysticism.*
84. Underhill, *Mysticism,* 83.
85. Eliade, *Shamanism: Archaic Techniques of Ecstasy,* 109.
86. Eliade, *Shamanism: Archaic Techniques of Ecstasy,* 109.
87. Katz, *Boiling Energy,* 47.
88. Scholem, *Major Trends in Jewish Mysticism,* 16.
89. Petroff, *Medieval Women's Visionary Literature,* 41.
90. Petroff, *Medieval Women's Visionary Literature,* 139.
91. Underhill, *Mysticism.*
92. Epstein, *Kabbalah,* 143.
93. Petroff, *Consolation of the Blessed,* 51.
94. Underhill, *Mysticism,* 38.
95. Petroff, *Medieval Women's Visionary Literature,* 207.
96. Underhill, *Mysticism,* 214.
97. Underhill, *Mysticism,* 386.
98. Eliade, *Shamanism: Archaic Techniques of Ecstasy.*
99. Krishna, *Kundalini,* 237.
100. Eliade, *Rites and Symbols of Initiation,* 68.

101. Epstein, *Kabbalah.*
102. Petroff, *Consolation of the Blessed,* 60.
103. Underhill, *Mysticism,* 248.
104. Halifax, *Shaman,* 7.
105. Underhill, *Mysticism.*
106. Scholem, *Major Trends in Jewish Mysticism,* 44.
107. Yoshinori, *The Heart of Buddhism,* 16.
108. Eliade, *Rites and Symbols of Initiation,* 62.
109. Petroff, *Consolation of the Blessed.*
110. Underhill, *Mysticism,* 292.
111. Epstein, *Kabbalah,* 50.
112. Scholem, *Major Trends in Jewish Mysticism,* 135.
113. Merton, *Zen and the Birds of Appetite,* 114.
114. Blofeld, "Introduction," 31.
115. Satprem, *Sri Aurobindo,* 170.
116. Satprem, *Sri Aurobindo,* 171.
117. Wilber, *The Atman Project.*
118. Krishna, *Kundalini,* 237.
119. Abe, "Nisbiùanis Challenge to Western Philosophy," 9.
120. Campbell, *The Hero with a Thousand Faces,* 207.
121. Campbell, *The Hero with a Thousand Faces,* 218.
122. Bancroft, *Zen,* 96.
123. Adler, "Who Is the Witness?"
124. Gimello, "Mysticism in Its Contexts," 69.
125. Gimello, "Mysticism in Its Contexts," 81.
126. Epstein, *Kabbalah,* 118.
127. Ross, *The World of Zen,* 243.
128. Whitehouse, "Physical Movement and Personality."
129. Satprem, *Sri Aurobindo,* 281.
130. Satprem, *Sri Aurobindo,* 116.
131. Satprem, *Sri Aurobindo,* 270.
132. Satprem, *Sri Aurobindo,* 116.
133. Larsen, *The Shaman's Doorway,* 183.
134. Satprem, *Sri Aurobindo,* 71.
135. Suzuki, *The Awakening of Zen,* 36.
136. Merton, *Zen and the Birds of Appetite,* 52–53.
137. Merton, *Zen and the Birds of Appetite,* 7.
138. Satprem, *Sri Aurobindo,* 44.
139. Satprem, *Sri Aurobindo,* 49.
140. Hoff, *The Way to Life: At the Heart of the Tao Te Ching,* verse 34.
141. Wilber, *The Atman Project.*
142. Satprem, *Sri Aurobindo,* 348.
143. Krishna, *Kundalini,* 97.
144. Eliade, *Rites and Symbols of Initiation,* 134.
145. Satprem, *Sri Aurobindo,* 2.

146. Underhill, *Mysticism*.
147. Satprem, *Sri Aurobindo*, 243.
148. Satprem, *Sri Aurobindo*, 238.
149. Satprem, *Sri Aurobindo*, 185.
150. Satprem, *Sri Aurobindo*, 261–62.
151. Satprem, *Sri Aurobindo*, 289.
152. Satprem, *Sri Aurobindo*, 260.
153. Satprem, *Sri Aurobindo*, 198.
154. Satprem, *Sri Aurobindo*, 205.
155. Satprem, *Sri Aurobindo*, 284.
156. Satprem, *Sri Aurobindo*, 216.

The Collective Body

1. Russell, *The White Hole in Time*, 144–45.
2. Quinn, *Ishmael*, 89.
3. Quinn, *Ishmael*, 101.
4. Jung, *Memories, Dreams, Reflections*, 365.
5. Shore, "The Fractal Geometry of Experience."
6. Briggs, *Fractals, the Patterns of Chaos*.
7. Adler, "Who Is the Witness?"
8. John Weir, personal communication (1969).
9. Halifax, *The Fruitful Darkness*, 202.

Toward the Unknown

1. Martin, *The Modern Dance*, 59.
2. Haze with Stromsted, "An Interview with Janet Adler."

Introduction to Chapter Five

1. Adler, personal communication, December 30, 2021.

From Seeing to Knowing

1. Adler, "Who Is the Witness?"
2. Adler, *Offering from the Conscious Body*, xix.
3. van Loben Sels, *A Dream in the World*, 85.
4. van Loben Sels, *A Dream in the World*.
5. Deikman, *The Observing Self*.
6. Deikman, *The Observing Self*, 10.
7. Deikman, *The Observing Self*, 11.
8. Roy and Devi, *Pilgrims of the Stars*, 170.
9. Epstein, *Kabbalah*, 36.
10. Meister Eckhart, *Meister Eckhart*, 247.
11. Merton, *Zen and the Birds of Appetite*, 5.
12. Miller, "What Was Hidden?" 7.
13. de Nicholas, *St. John of the Cross*, 8.

14. de Nicholas, *St. John of the Cross,* 52.
15. Krishna, *Kundalini,* 179.
16. Vaughan, *Awakening Intuition,* 185.
17. Barrett and Aiken, *Philosophy in the Twentieth Century,* 303.
18. Barrett and Aiken, *Philosophy in the Twentieth Century,* 305.
19. Matt, "Varieties of Mystical Nothingness," 316.
20. van Loben Sels, *A Dream in the World,* 22.

Introduction to Chapter Six

1. Letter from Janet to Faculty of Circles of Four program, November 20, 2015.

Letters from Janet to a Learner

1. Excerpt of poem by Thomas Tranströrmer, *Vermeer,* is the epigraph in Watson, *A Philosophy of Emptiness.* All quotes from *Philosophy of Emptiness* are used with the kind permission of Reaktion Books LTD.
2. Watson, *A Philosophy of Emptiness,* 167.

The Study of an Autistic Child

1. Laing, R.D. *The Politics of Experience.* Routledge and Kegan Paul (1967), 2.

Integrity of Body and Psyche

1. Mary Whitehouse, personal communication (1970).
2. John Weir, personal communication (1969).

BIBLIOGRAPHY

Abe, M. "Nisbiùanis Challenge to Western Philosophy and Theology." Paper presented at the Annual Meeting of the American Academy of Religion, in Dallas, Texas, on December 19–22, 1983.

Adler, Janet. *Arching Backward: The Mystical Initiation of a Contemporary Woman.* Rochester, VT: Inner Traditions International, 1995.

———. "Arching Backward and a Cross-Cultural Study of Mysticism as the Context for a Phenomenological Study: Arching Backward." PhD diss., The Union Institute, 1992.

———. *Offering from the Conscious Body: The Discipline of Authentic Movement.* Rochester, VT: Inner Traditions, 2002.

———. "Questions: Teaching the Discipline." *A Moving Journal* 4, no. 3 (Fall/ Winter 1997): 10–11.

———. "Who Is the Witness? A Description of Authentic Movement." *Contact Quarterly* 12, no. 1 (Winter 1987): 20–29.

Bancroft, Anne. *Zen: Direct Pointing to Reality.* London: Thames & Hudson, 1979.

Barrett, William, and Henry Aiken. *Philosophy in the Twentieth Century: An Anthology.* Vol. 3. New York: Random House, 1962.

Blofeld, J. "Introduction." In *The Zen Teaching of Hui Hai on Sudden Illumination,* translated by John Blofeld. New York: Samuel Weiser, 1972.

Blyth, R. H. *Zen and Zen Classics.* Vol. 1. Tokyo, Japan: The Hokuseido Press, 1960.

Briggs, John. *Fractals, the Patterns of Chaos: A New Aesthetic of Art, Science and Nature.* New York: Simon & Schuster, 1992.

Buber, Martin. *Hasidism and Modern Man.* Atlantic Highlands, N.J.: Humanities Press International, 1958.

———. *I and Thou.* [Originally published in German as *Ich Und Du.* Leipzig, Germany: Im Imsel-Verlag, 1923.] First published in English in 1937. Multiple editions available.

Campbell, Joseph. *The Hero with a Thousand Faces.* Cleveland, Ohio: World Publishing, 1956.

Chaiklin, Harris (ed). *Marian Chace: Her Papers*. Columbia, Md.: American Dance Therapy Association, 1975.

Chodorow, Joan. "To Move and Be Moved." *Quadrant* 17, no. 2 (1984): 39–48.

Cleary, Thomas (trans). *Book of Serenity: One Hundred Zen Dialogues*. Boston: Shambhala, 2005.

Conze, Edward, L. B. Horner, David Snellgrove, and Arthur Waley. *Buddhist Texts Through the Ages*. Boston: Shambhala Publications, 1990.

Deikman, Arthur. *The Observing Self: Mysticism and Psychotherapy*. Boston: Beacon Press, 1982.

Duncan, Isadora. *My Life*. New York: Boni Liveright, 1927.

Eliade, Mircea. *Rites and Symbols of Initiation*. New York: Harper & Row, 1958.

———. *Shamanism: Archaic Techniques of Ecstasy*. Princeton, N.J.: Princeton University Press, 1964.

Epstein, Perle. *Kabbalah: The Way of the Jewish Mystic*. Boston: Shambhala, 1988.

Fry, Christopher. *Selected Plays*. Oxford and New York: Oxford University Press, 1977.

Gimello, R. M. "Mysticism in its Contexts." In Katz, *Mysticism and Religious Traditions*, 61–88.

Graham, Martha. *Blood Memory*. New York: Doubleday, 1991.

Grof, Stanislav. *Beyond the Brain: Birth, Death, and Transcendence in Psychotherapy*. Albany: State University of New York Press, 1985.

Halifax, Joan. *The Fruitful Darkness: Reconnecting with the Body of the Earth*. San Francisco: HarperSanFrancisco, 1993.

———. *Shaman: The Wounded Healer*. New York: Crossroad, 1982.

Haze, Neala, with Tina Stromsted. "An Interview with Janet Adler." In Pallaro, *Authentic Movement: Essays by Mary Starks Whitehouse, Janet Adler and Joan Chodorow*. London and Philadelphia: Jessica Kingsley Publishing Co., 1999.

Hendricks, Kathlyn. "What I Learned from Mary: Reflections on the Work of Mary Starks Whitehouse." *American Journal of Dance Therapy* 32 (2010).

Hoff, Benjamin. *The Way to Life: At the Heart of the Tao Te Ching*. Trumbull, Conn.: Weatherhill, 1981.

James, William. *The Varieties of Religious Experience*. New York: Penguin Books, 1982.

Johnson, Don Hanlon (ed). *Bone, Breath, and Gesture: Practices of Embodiment*. Berkeley, Calif.: North Atlantic Books, 1995.

Jung, Carl Gustav. *Memories, Dreams, Reflections*. New York: Random House, 1961.

———. "Psychology of the Transference." In *The Collected Works of C.G. Jung*, Vol. 16. London: Routledge & Kegan Paul, 1954.

Katz, Richard. *Boiling Energy: Community Healing Among the Kalahari Kung.* Cambridge, Mass.: Harvard University Press, 1982.

Katz, Steven T. "The Conservative Character of Mystical Experience." In Katz, *Mysticism and Religious Traditions,* 3–60.

Katz, Steven T., ed. *Mysticism and Religious Traditions.* Oxford: Oxford University Press, 1983.

Krishna, Gopi. *Kundalini: The Evolutionary Energy in Man (with Psychological Commentary by James Hillman).* Boulder, Colo.: Shambhala, 1971.

Laban, Rudolf. *A Life for Dance.* London: MacDonald and Evans Ltd, 1975.

Larsen, Stephen. *The Shaman's Doorway: Opening the Mythic Imagination to Contemporary Consciousness.* New York: Harper & Row, 1976.

van Loben Sels, Robin. *A Dream in the World: Poetics of Soul in Two Women, Modern and Medieval.* New York: Brunner-Routledge, 2003.

Martin, John. *The Modern Dance.* New York: Dance Horizons, 1933.

Matt, D. C. "Varieties of Mystical Nothingness: Jewish, Christian, and Buddhist Perspectives." *The Studia Philonica Annual, Studies in Hellenistic Judaism* 9, 316–31.

Meister Eckhart. *Meister Eckhart: A Modern Translation.* Trans. R. B. Blackney. New York: Harper & Row, 1941.

Merton, Thomas. *Zen and the Birds of Appetite.* New York: New Directions Publishing, 1968.

Miller, Patrick. "What Was Hidden? Looking Deeper into Christianity: An Interview with Richard Smoley." *The Sun* 333, September 2003, 4–13.

Moyne, John, and Coleman Barks. *Open Secret: Visions of Rumi.* Putney, Vt.: Threshold Books, 1984.

Myerhoff, Barbara. *Peyote Hunt.* Ithaca, N.Y.: Cornell University Press, 1974.

Neihardt, John Gneisenau. *Black Elk Speaks.* Lincoln: University of Nebraska Press, 1979.

de Nicholas, Antonio. *St. John of the Cross: Alchemist of the Soul.* New York: Paragon House, 1989.

Nishitani, Keiji. *Religion and Nothingness.* Berkeley, Calif: University of California Press, 1982.

Oliver, Mary. *The Leaf and the Cloud: A Poem.* 1st ed. Boston: Da Capo Press, 2000.

Otto, Rudolf. *The Idea of the Holy.* Oxford: Oxford University Press, 1923.

Pallaro, Patrizia, (ed). *Authentic Movement: Essays by Mary Starks Whitehouse, Janet Adler and Joan Chodorow.* London and Philadelphia: Jessica Kingsley Publishing Co., 1999.

Petroff, Elizabeth. *Consolation of the Blessed.* New York: Alta Gaia Society, 1979.

———. *Medieval Women's Visionary Literature.* New York: Oxford University Press, 1986.

Quinn, Daniel. *Ishmael.* New York: Bantam, 1992.

Ramsey, Mary. "A Dancing Spirit: An Interview with Edith Sullwold." *A Moving Journal,* 2, no. 3 (1995): 4–6, 12.

Ross, Nancy Wilson. *The World of Zen: An East-West Anthology.* New York: Vintage Books, 1960.

Roy, Dilip Kumar, and Indira Devi. *Pilgrims of the Stars.* New York: Macmillan, 1973.

Russell, Peter. *The White Hole in Time: Our Future Evolution and the Meaning of Now.* San Francisco: HarperSanFrancisco, 1992.

Satprem. *Mind of the Cells.* New York: Institute for Evolutionary Research, 1982.

———. *Sri Aurobindo: The Adventure of Consciousness.* New York: Institute for Evolutionary Research, 1984.

Scholem, Gershom. *Major Trends in Jewish Mysticism.* New York: Schocken Books, 1961.

Shore, Stephen. "The Fractal Geometry of Experience." *Annandale* 133 (1993): 1, 12–19.

Suzuki, D. T. *The Awakening of Zen.* Boulder, Colo.: Prajna Pres, 1980.

———. *The Essentials of Zen Buddhism.* New York: Dutton, 1962.

———. *An Introduction to Zen Buddhism.* New York: The Philosophical Library, 1949.

Tagore, Rabindranath. *On the Shores of Eternity: Poems from Tagore on Immortality and Beyond.* D. Chopra, trans. New York: Harmony Books, 1999.

Terman, S. A. *The Best Way to Say Good-bye: A Legal Peaceful Choice.* Carlsbad, Calif.: Life Transitions Publications, 2007.

Underhill, Evelyn. *Mysticism: A Study in the Nature and Development of Man's Spiritual Consciousness.* London: Methuen & Co, 1911.

Unno, T. "Emptiness and Reality in Mahayana Buddhism." Paper presented at the Symposium in Honor of Keiji Nishitani, April 25–28, 1984.

Vaughan, Frances E. *Awakening Intuition.* New York: Anchor Books, 1979.

Watson, Gay. *A Philosophy of Emptiness.* United Kingdom: Reaktion Books, 2014.

Weir, John. "The Personal Growth Laboratory." In *The Laboratory Method of Changing and Learning: Theory and Application,* edited by K. Benne, L. P. Bradford, J. R. Gibb, R. D. Lippitt, 293–325. Palo Alto, Calif.: Science and Behavior Books, 1975.

Whitehouse, Mary Starks. "C. G. Jung and Dance Therapy." In Pallaro, *Authentic Movement: Essays by Mary Starks Whitehouse, Janet Adler, and Joan Chodorow.* London and Philadelphia: Jessica Kingsley Publishing Co., 1999.

————. "Physical Movement and Personality." *Contact Quarterly* Winter 1987: 16–19. Lecture originally given for the Analytical Psychology Club of Los Angeles in 1965.

————. "The Tao of the Body." In Johnson, *Bone, Breath, and Gesture,* 241–51. Lecture originally given for the Analytical Psychology Club of Los Angeles in 1958.

————. "Teacher, Leader, Mediator." *A Moving Journal* 9, no. 1 (2002): 3–7.

Wigman, Mary. *The Language of Dance.* Middletown, Conn.: Wesleyan University Press, 1966.

————. *The Mary Wigman Book: Her Writings.* Edited and Translated by Walter Sorell. Middletown, Conn.: Wesleyan University Press, 1973.

Wilber, Ken. *The Atman Project: A Transpersonal View of Human Development.* Wheaton, Ill.: The Theosophical Publishing House, 1980.

Yoshinori, Takeuchi. *The Heart of Buddhism.* New York: Crossroad, 1983.

INDEX

body, the
    awareness, 77, 205
    collective body and, 153–54
    density encounter and, 215
    experience of, 13, 15
    impact of change in, 132
    mystical experience and, 124–29
    psyche connection, 331
    as teacher, 153
    transformation of, 130
    visionary stress on, 132
    visual images and, 203–4
"Body and Soul," 110, 111–12, 115–46
body dancing soul, 26
body ego structure, 90
Body-Mind Centering, 10

"Call, The," 160–63
Campbell, Joseph, 137
ceremony
    about, 186–87, 221–23
    experience of, 231–33
    field of awareness and, 226
    moving and witnessing in, 227–29
    organic evolution and, 223–27
    preparation for, 224–25
    speaking and listening in, 229–33
chanting, 58, 162, 316
children. See autistic children
Chodorow, Joan, 1, 145
Christian mystical experiences, 134
Circles of Four, 239–40, 264–65,
    292–93, 300
Cohen, Bonnie Bainbridge, 10
collective body
    Authentic Movement and, 151–54
    belonging and, 147–50

conscious development stories,
    154–63
conscious manifestation of, 186
defined, 11
development of, 117
direct experience of membership
    in, 150
evolution into, 145
individualism and, 150
safety and, 173
spirit, 150–51
"Collective Body, The," 111–12
collective consciousness, 239, 261
collective unconscious, 99
commitment, 261–62, 263
compassion, 31, 153, 167, 175, 199,
    212, 281–84, 302–3
concentration, 28, 29, 77, 102, 141
conscious embodied speech, 5, 13, 123
consciousness. See also embodied
    consciousness
    cellular transformation of, 40
    collective, 239, 261
    development of, 24
    holding, 143
    mover, 13, 29, 30, 268
    personal, 239, 261
    place in community and, 3–4
    practice with, 173
    witness, 12–13, 29, 30, 213
Contact Improvisation, 10
containers
    body as, 94–95
    crack in, 33
    Discipline of Authentic Movement,
        140, 145–46
    energy experience and, 174